THE SUBSTANCE OF FICTION

Premodern East Asia: New Horizons

PREMODERN EAST ASIA: NEW HORIZONS

This series is dedicated to books that focus on humanistic studies of East Asia before the mid-nineteenth century in fields including literature and cultural and social history, as well as studies of science and technology, the environment, visual cultures, performance, material culture, and gender. The series particularly welcomes works with field-changing and paradigm-shifting potential that adopt interdisciplinary and innovative approaches. Contributors to the series share the premise that creativity in method and rigor in research are preconditions for producing new knowledge that transcends modern disciplinary confines and the framework of the nation-state. In highlighting the complexity and dynamism of premodern societies, these books illuminate the relevance of East Asia to the contemporary world.

Becoming Guanyin: Artistic Devotion of Buddhist Women in Late Imperial China, Yuhang Li
Kinship Novels of Early Modern Korea: Between Genealogical Time and the Domestic Everyday,
    Ksenia Chizhova

The Substance of Fiction

Literary Objects in China, 1550–1775

Sophie Volpp

Columbia University Press　New York

This publication was made possible in part by an award from the James P. Geiss and Margaret Y. Hsu Foundation.

Columbia University Press
Publishers Since 1893
New York   Chichester, West Sussex
cup.columbia.edu
Copyright © 2022 Columbia University Press
All rights reserved

Library of Congress Cataloging-in-Publication Data
Names: Volpp, Sophie, 1963– author.
Title: The substance of fiction : literary objects in China, 1550–1775 / Sophie Volpp.
Description: New York : Columbia University Press, [2022] | Series: Premodern East Asia: new horizons | Includes bibliographical references and index.
Identifiers: LCCN 2021038662 (print) | LCCN 2021038663 (ebook) | ISBN 9780231199643 (hardback) | ISBN 9780231199650 (trade paperback) | ISBN 9780231553223 (ebook)
Subjects: LCSH: Chinese fiction—Ming dynasty, 1368–1644—History and criticism. | Chinese fiction—Qing dynasty, 1644–1912—History and criticism. | LCGFT: Literary criticism.
Classification: LCC PL2436 .V65 2022 (print) | LCC PL2436 (ebook) | DDC 895.13/4609—dc23
LC record available at https://lccn.loc.gov/2021038662
LC ebook record available at https://lccn.loc.gov/2021038663

Cover image: Enameled tray of the Kangxi Reign period. National Palace Museum, Taipei.

For Daniel and Julia

Contents

Acknowledgments   ix

INTRODUCTION
The Substance of Fiction   1

CHAPTER ONE
The Python Robe of *The Plum in the Golden Vase*   12

CHAPTER TWO
Ling Mengchu's Shell   38

CHAPTER THREE
Du Shiniang's Jewel Box   54

CHAPTER FOUR
Li Yu's Telescope   78

CHAPTER FIVE
The Plate-Glass Mirror in *The Story of the Stone*   109

CHAPTER SIX
Historicizing Recession via *The Story of the Stone*
and the Juanqinzhai   145

CONCLUSION
Literary Objects   169

Notes   175
Bibliography   219
Index   233

Acknowledgments

This book grew out of many conversations with colleagues at Berkeley and beyond; I am grateful to all the scholars who took the time to share their knowledge with me. I thank Patricia Berger, Andrew Jones, Chana Kronfeld, Susan Maslan, Nick Paige, Karin Sanders, Bob Sharf, Mario Telò, and Paula Varsano for reading various chapters, and Robert Ashmore, Mark Blum, Mark Csikszentmihalyi, Ling Hon Lam, and Michael Nylan for answering my questions. Many thanks to Weihong Bao for her writing company and for convening our "summer writing group," which extended far beyond a single summer. I thank Deniz Göktürk, Luba Golburt, and Anne Nesbet for suggestions both lighthearted and practical. My conversations with Dori Hale always led to new realizations. Liu Bo, Karl Britto, Judith Butler, Tim Hampton, Michael Lucey, Leslie Kurke, Nelly Oliensis, and Sandra Sjardono shared their wisdom in matters large and small.

I am grateful that several colleagues at institutions across the United States read the entire manuscript: Lynn Festa, Paize Keulemans, Dorothy Ko, Susan Naquin, Anna Shields, and Judith Zeitlin. I am particularly grateful to Shang Wei for his support of the research in chapter 6. My deepest thanks go to Judith Zeitlin, who somehow was there at every significant stage in the writing of this book.

Many historians of art and architecture answered my questions about boxes, telescopes, mirrors, and *tongjing hua* painting, among them

Nancy Berliner, Craig Clunas, Ellen Huang, Liu Chang, Wu Hung, and Ying Feier. Team-teaching a graduate seminar on *The Story of the Stone* with Patricia Berger was one of the most memorable experiences of my teaching life. Marco Musillo hosted me for several days in Florence, where we spent many hours in conversation about the wall painting that we playfully named "The Lady with the Clock." At the Palace Museum in Beijing, Zhang Shuxian and Yuan Hongqi were extraordinarily generous. I am grateful to Wang Shiwei of the Palace Museum for permission to use his images in chapter 6. Many thanks to my large family of aunts, uncles, and cousins for all the fun they provided on my research trips to Beijing, and especially to my aunt Yuan Jiu for her hospitality.

I worked on this book for many years, and in the final stages had occasion to remember every one of the research assistants who stood by my side. I would like to name those who pursued graduate study in Chinese literature: Naixi Feng, Hanyu Hou, Site Li, Tianyi Liu, Allyson Tang, and Jiaqian Zhu. Elysee Wilson-Egolf was my right arm for many years. Jane Yarnell gave me assistance at a critical moment. The questions and insights of many students enlivened my understanding of these texts over the years; in addition to those named above, I thank Keru Cai, Matteo Cavelier-Riccardi, Zijing Fan, Xiangjun Feng, Kris Kersey, William Ma, Hannibal Taubes, Michelle Wang, Xiaoyu Xia, and Shoufu Yin.

I am indebted to Dorothy Ko, the editor for the series in which this book appears, as well as to Christine Dunbar, Kathryn Jorge, Mary Bagg, and Christian Winting at Columbia University Press. The research for this book was supported by the American Philosophical Society, the American Council of Learned Societies, the Mellon Foundation, and the University of California, Berkeley.

So much of what brought me to this moment exists only in memory. I am thankful for those who remember with me: Leti, Kevin, and Serena Volpp; Matt Franklin; Tsing, Pat, and Elizabeth Yuan; Graciana Lapetina, Richard Perry, and Marjorie Volpp; Mike Bruhn, Nancy Kates, Kyu-hyun Kim, Karen Lam, Jenny Lin, Clemens Reichel, and Patrick Reichel.

In Daniel, I was blessed with a son of rare maturity, kindness, and consideration; and in Julia, with a daughter of extraordinary warmth, radiance, and courage. I love you both always and forever. This book is for you.

Introduction

The Substance of Fiction

This book was inspired by the questions of my students, who pressed me to conceptualize more concretely the fictional worlds we jointly entered. Reading Feng Menglong's 馮夢龍 (1574–1645) story "Jiang Xingge Reencounters His Pearl Shirt" (蔣興哥重會珍珠衫), they wanted to know why a vendor of pearls states that the silver she receives better have enough "crackle" in it (銀水要足紋的).[1] In researching the answers to such questions (and finding that the pattern of the crackle indicates the percentage of silver in the alloy), I discovered the pleasure of unearthing lost historical resonance. And I began to wonder, thinking of another character in a Feng Menglong story, whether we would better understand the metaphorical relation between Du Shiniang and her jewel box if we had a more detailed portrait of the material features of seventeenth-century boxes.

I have organized *The Substance of Fiction* around two questions. First, how might we read the vernacular fiction of the late Ming through the mid-Qing differently if we could recover the material histories of fictional objects—in other words, how can research regarding material culture illuminate literary texts? Second, what role do fictional objects as *literary* objects play, and how might their qualities as literary objects help us to understand how fictionality was conceptualized in the Ming and Qing? I argue that our readerly experience of the objects of vernacular fiction from the Ming and Qing is bifurcated. On the one hand, these fictional objects invite us to think of them as illustrative and to imagine historical analogues. On the other, they speak in quite complex ways to questions of fictionality. Once we delve into the material histories of fictional objects, we see that often they are represented inconsistently within a text. Such disruptions might be the result of either authorial carelessness or inadvertent textual interpolation that sutures new texts into an existing matrix. Some objects are viewed so differently by various characters that the representations become irreconcilable. Whatever the cause, discontinuous representation disconnects the literary object from potential historical analogues, letting us know that the fictional objects in fact have no analogues beyond the text. As subtly discordant portrayals create momentary bewilderment, the fictional object becomes more than the sum of its descriptive parts. Those interstitial moments of doubt allow readers to recognize the limits of readerly perception and, paradoxically, grant a sense of verisimilitude.

The study of Ming and Qing China has taken a material turn since the early 1990s, inspired in part with the publication in 1991 of the art historian Craig Clunas's *Superfluous Things: Material Culture and Social Status in Early Modern China*, which brought attention to the late-Ming discourse on connoisseurship.[2] In the decades that followed, the study of material culture became deeply developed in Ming and Qing studies in a variety of disciplines. Within literature, for example, Wai-yee Li's research on epistemic shift in the discourse on objects between the late Ming and early Qing, Judith Zeitlin's writing on dramatic objects, and the work of Kaijun Chen, S. E. Kile, and Kristina Kleutghen on technology and craft have invited us to look more closely at both the discourse on objects and the material artifacts themselves.[3]

For many years, novels such as the anonymous late sixteenth-century *The Plum in the Golden Vase* (*Jin Ping Mei* 金瓶梅) and Cao Xueqin's 曹雪芹 (1715?–1763) mid-eighteenth-century *The Story of the Stone* (*Honglou meng* 紅樓夢) were read as romans-à-clef (literally, "novels with a key") in the belief that the codes of equivalence between their characters and historical figures might be recovered.[4] In recent decades, the conception of the "key" has shifted from historical figures to historical objects. In China, numerous scholarly monographs regarding the depiction of architecture, gardens, food and drink, medicine, and clothing in the major novels of the Ming and Qing have been written in a vein of belletristic writing that matches the objects named in literature to historical artifacts (*mingwu xue* 名物學).[5] This mode of inquiry originated with the famed Republican writer Shen Congwen's research regarding the antique teacups described in chapter 41 of *The Story of the Stone*.[6] In its current incarnation, this scholarship mines historical resources, such as the records of the imperial workshops and archaeological reports, to find analogues to the literary objects of vernacular fiction. With a novel as central to the tradition as *The Story of the Stone*, the detail in this vein of scholarship is extreme: one scholar has found included on a historical list of tribute gifts the ancestor of a suckling pig oafishly consumed by the minor character Xue Pan.[7]

In this book, I focus on the novels and short fiction of the late Ming through mid-Qing that scholars in China and the United States most frequently mine for information about material culture. Scholars turn to vernacular fiction (rather than drama, poetry, or classical fiction) as a repository of information regarding the sensorial repertoire of the material world. Even though scholars of Chinese fiction have emphasized that "vernacular" fiction is a misnomer—that is, not truly written in the vernacular—the belief that it is written in the language of daily use grounds the widespread assumption that it illustrates everyday life.[8] Many historians and art historians rely on vernacular fiction to provide illustrative examples of historical practice. No novel is more quoted for this purpose than *The Story of the Stone*, the subject of my final two chapters.

To think of the objects of vernacular fiction as having such an intimate relation with the historical record, however, is to ignore their essential literariness. In a series of case studies, I show that exploring the historical resonances of literary objects can shift our understanding of the rhetorical strategies of the canonical novels and short stories of the Ming and Qing. Surprisingly, attention to historical context leads us to see that fictional objects are often portrayed inconsistently across the pages of a single text, leading to a momentary confusion that readers ignore in the belief that these objects must be self-same. Taken as a group, the case studies show how this readerly experience of misapprehension speaks to the distinctive conception of fictionality in late-imperial China.

Much of the most stunning research at the intersection of literature and material culture in European and American literature in past years has taken the recovery of lost historical significance as a point of departure in recovering repressed logics. In *The Ideas in Things: Fugitive Meaning in the Victorian Novel*, for example, Elaine Freedgood shows us that *Jane Eyre* both inscribes and represses the knowledge of the sociological and ecological devastation that the British desire for mahogany caused in Madeira and Jamaica.[9] In contrast, I ask that we aspire to the recovery of repressed *illogic*. In part because the fictional objects of the late Ming and Qing are not represented consistently, they cannot be viewed simply as illustrations of historical objects. We might think here of the plate-glass mirror in *The Story of the Stone*, which in chapters 17, 26, and 51 is described as being set in a floor-length, freestanding screen frame at the entrance to Baoyu's private chambers, but in chapter 41 is set into a partition between walls and functions as a secret door. Literary objects, like characters, are textual effects created not by consistent depiction but by the readers' repeated encounters of disjunctive depictions that must be resolved through imaginative supplementation.[10] Just as important, the larger concerns with misperception and misapprehension in these texts are reinforced as the reader becomes confused by contradictory presentations of the fictional object.

The fictional objects I examine in this book call attention to the texts' strategic highlighting of the fallibility of readerly perception. In so doing, they foster the sense that there is a world interior to the text that readers cannot fully perceive. Like fictional characters, fictional objects are produced out of an imaginative conflation of contradictory depictions that readers, consciously or unconsciously, permit to exist in tandem. As readers of literary texts, we absorb both nascent and overt inconsistencies in the depiction of objects without attempting to resolve them. The literary object, then, has a haziness to its edges. For most readers, providing the imaginative supplementation that permits incongruity to persist is a naturalized aspect of reading.

It is precisely because literary objects as textual effects are condensations of incongruous representations that we cannot take the objects of vernacular fiction to be illustrations of historical antecedents. Our efforts to tie fictional objects such as Du Shiniang's box or Baoyu's mirror to historical objects constrains them. To ask a fictional object to conform to the shape of a specific historical analogue is to tie it to a Procrustean bed. The fictional object inevitably exceeds the space of any historical predecessor.

Over the following chapters, I consider a robe, a shell and a box, a telescope, a plate-glass mirror, and a trompe l'oeil painting. I chose those objects for two reasons: first, in each case a secondary literature with which one can engage in dialogue already exists; second, the novels and short stories in which they appear are commonly taught in undergraduate courses on Chinese literature. I begin with the novel *The Plum in the Golden Vase*, the first domestic novel in the Chinese tradition, which has frequently been consulted for evidence regarding furnishings, clothing, stage practices, and even the price of rice. The three short stories that I discuss—Ling Mengchu's 凌濛初 (1580–1644) "A Man Whose Fortune Has Turned Coincidentally Happens Across Oranges from Dongting" (轉運漢巧遇洞庭紅), Feng Menglong's "Du Shiniang Sinks the Jewel Box in Anger" (杜十娘怒沈百寶箱) and Li Yu's 李漁 (1611–1680) "A Tower for the Summer Heat" (夏宜樓)—have attracted the greater part of the writing on vernacular short fiction and material culture. I close with two chapters examining *The Story of the Stone*, the late-imperial literary text to which art historians and historians have most often turned for illustrative examples.

As we progress in a roughly chronological fashion from the late sixteenth to the mid-eighteenth century, the texts claim an increasingly complex role for objects as signs of fictionality. In *The Plum in the Golden Vase*, we can gloss over the inconsistent and incongruous depictions reminding us that the text is fictional. In Feng Menglong's "Du Shiniang Sinks the Jewel Box in Anger," readers misperceive (along with the characters), and these mistaken understandings of both the jewel box and Du Shiniang herself become the central theme of the text. Li Yu teases readers in his "A Tower for the Summer Heat" as to the nature of the telescope, alternately figuring the telescope as a fantastical object with oracular powers and as a mere device. By the time we arrive at *The Story of the Stone*, we can intuit that the text is training us to see that we misperceive doubly, first in our moments of misapprehension, and consequently in not realizing the productive possibilities of confusion, but instead settling for shallow explanations that are not true to experiences of the lived world. *The Story of the Stone* repeatedly shows us characters before the plate-glass mirror who all too quickly dismiss their own confusion. These scenes of misperception are instructive, training us to become self-reflective regarding the productive possibilities of misapprehension.

I start with *The Plum in the Golden Vase* in part because the novel's interest in objects as they circulate and knit characters into a web of transaction is characteristic of Chinese short fiction from the early and middle period. The author is far more interested in depicting the circulation of multiple objects than in describing singular objects as though they had the heft of central characters. In keeping with this rhetorical emphasis on multiplicity, the novel focuses on the misbegotten distribution of objects as they are pawned, purloined, and forged. As the dispersal of people and possessions at the end of the novel might suggest, the emphasis on the relentless circulation of persons and things is in part a means of leading the reader to an understanding of the ephemerality of the forms of this world.

In the latter part of chapter 1, I recover the historical resonances of the python robe (*mang pao* 蟒袍), a type of court robe that readers encounter in many of the major works of Qing fiction and drama but no longer understand to be rife with meaning. The historical sources not only show us why the unauthorized weaving and circulation of the python robe were so fraught, but also help us understand why the appearance of the python robe in texts such as *The Peach Blossom Fan* (*Taohua shan* 桃花扇), *The Scholars* (*Rulin waishi* 儒林外史), and *The Story of the Stone* signals the illicit assumption of power and an imminent fall from favor. The python robe also helps us think about the relation between fictional objects and fictionality. Its depiction in *The Plum in the Golden Vase* is both historically inaccurate and internally incongruent, creating moments of misperception that as readers we overlook and naturalize. It is important to note, however, that although this lack of internal consistency becomes more and more pronounced in the later texts that I consider, in *The Plum in the Golden Vase* this inconsistency is treated very lightly; consistency was simply not valued by its author. Whether or not the inconsistency is thematized, it functions to create the conflation of contradictory depictions that we will come to see is characteristic of the fictional object.

In chapter 2 I discuss the first story of Ling Mengchu's collection *Slapping the Table in Amazement* (*Chuke pai'an jingqi* 初刻拍案驚奇, 1627), titled "A Man Whose Fortune Has Turned Coincidentally Happens Across Oranges from Dongting." Ling Mengchu's story treats a series of objects, most crucially a wondrous reptilian shell. A voyage to foreign lands furnishes a premise for thinking about objects as sources of hidden value. The story takes an ethnographic encounter as an occasion to cultivate the readers' awareness of moments when perception falls short. Objects control the circumstances under which they appear and have mysterious ways of escaping the valuations conventionally assigned to them. Their elusiveness gives them a value beyond their capacity to be exchanged.

A comparison of Ling Mengchu's vernacular story and his classical source texts shows that in fact he has introduced hidden ellipses into the vernacular story. At times he omits information given in the story's classical sources, limiting what the reader is told. The potential for readerly misunderstanding signaled in the ethnographic encounter with the fictional object becomes linked to the sense that readers do not have full access to the events taking place "inside" the text. The text positions itself as literary by suggesting that it contains a world the reader can only partially apprehend.

Chapter 3 concerns Feng Menglong's most famous story, "Du Shiniang Sinks the Jewel Box in Anger," which appeared in his 1624 collection *Stories to Caution the World* (*Jingshi tongyan* 警世通言). Within Ming and Qing vernacular fiction, "Du Shiniang" defines the trope of a central character distinguished by relation to a particular object. Fifteenth- and sixteenth-century Chinese fiction is typically rather uninterested in developing the interior life of its characters. Unusually, the jewel box becomes the emblem of Du Shiniang, the courtesan who is the story's protagonist, and the opacity of the box becomes a metaphor for her own inscrutability. The title of Feng Menglong's story suggests the metaphorical relation between Du Shiniang and the box, which develops as each is figured as a space of mysterious potential. Ultimately, however, the story draws on the material properties of the box to explore the insufficiency of the metaphorical mapping between courtesan and box.

In my last three chapters I consider new technologies—the telescope, the plate-glass mirror, and the trompe l'oeil techniques of Italian *quadratura*, a style of illusionistic mural painting that pairs painted architectural features with actual ones. Understanding these objects in terms of material culture helps to prevent us from reinscribing our own assumptions about what it might have been like to encounter those technologies for the first time. The telescope, plate-glass mirror, and perspectival painting are deceptively legible to modern readers, who tend to think of them from the point of view of visual culture; by contrast, considering them from the point of view of material culture allows us to consider the means by which these novel objects of Western import were subsumed into Chinese topoi of long standing.

I chose these objects in part because the novelty of their technologies calls attention to new techniques of narration. In chapter 4, I examine Li Yu's short story "A Tower for the Summer Heat," in which the "single-eyed" lens of a curious device, a telescope, inspires experiment regarding the representation of thought. Most modern readers will view the defining quality of the telescope as its capacity for magnification. But if we take a moment to consider the telescope's material housing, we become attuned to a feature that was unprecedented for seventeenth-century readers, its monocularism. Li Yu takes the monocular lens as a pretext to drop traditional omniscient narration in favor of representing a single character's more restricted point of view.

Li Yu's portrayal of the telescope alternates between a charismatic object with the transporting powers historically attributed to the bronze mirror, and a technical instrument whose powers of magnification are in fact quite limited. This alternation is in part an artifact of Li Yu's unmarked citation of a discourse on lenses titled *History of Lenses* (*Jingshi* 鏡史) written by a young lens maker in Suzhou, Sun Yunqiu 孫雲球 (1650?–after 1681). The demystification of the telescope is not permanent; Li Yu repeatedly reinvests in the illusion of the telescope's powers as if rehearsing the reader in a process of successive entrance into illusion and disinvestment from it. In the hands of Li Yu's sanguine narrator, this switching between illusion and disillusion takes a very different form than it does in *The Story of the Stone*. But it can be seen as preparation for my thinking in chapters 5 and 6 regarding the main charge that *The Story of the Stone* issues to its readers: to simultaneously invest and disinvest in the sensual world it describes, without privileging one over the other.

If we envision late Ming and Qing vernacular fiction from the distinctive vantage point of material culture, we will see that a concern regarding the instability of phenomenal form is central. In chapter 5, I examine a well-known set of scenes in *The Story of the Stone* concerning a plate-glass mirror in the chambers of its protagonist, Jia Baoyu. As in chapter 4, new technologies make possible fresh perspectives; plate glass disrupts established modes of spatial perception. Here I engage with the mirror from the point of view of material culture as much as visual culture, asking what difference it might have made that the plate-glass mirror in eighteenth-century China was conventionally set in a double-sided wooden frame meant for a standing screen. The double-sidedness permitted by the material housing of the screen frame is crucial in that it ensures that the mirror cannot be conceptualized in terms of a reinforcement of the sense of an "I." Rather, the mirror allows those who encounter it to overcome a singular and subjective perspective. This is used with striking effect in a poem by the Qianlong emperor in which his plate-glass windows act as mirrors. His observation of the reflections in the windows allows him to inhabit space in a new way, freeing him from a corporeal viewing position and granting him a suddenly panoramic perspective. That undergirds his claim to the self-reflection and impartial insight associated with good governance, for which the polished bronze mirror was a traditional figure. Qianlong thus interprets technological advances newly imported from western Europe in terms that are local and of long duration.

The plate-glass mirror in Baoyu's chambers suggests a way of envisioning representation that undercuts assumptions regarding the stability of the referent and enables us to reconsider the trope of the mirror as book. Contrary to what we as readers have come to expect, the mirror does not encode reflection in the sense of resemblance or similitude, but instead illuminates the insubstantiality of that which it reflects. The plate-glass mirror of *The Story of the Stone* thus ruptures structures of reference rather than providing them. In effect, it reverses the terms of verisimilitude, suggesting that the reading of fiction makes us aware that quotidian experience itself is illusory.

I ask in chapter 6 whether literary texts can provide historians and art historians with strategies to read historical texts and material artifacts. Here I am not thinking about the kind of information that vernacular fiction can give us about historical practices, but rather, about reading material culture with the habits of mind that vernacular fiction cultivates in its readers. As the historian Dorothy Ko and the art historian Jonathan Hay have shown us, Ming and Qing decorative objects are as complex to read as literary texts.[11] How can the fiction of the period help us interpret artifacts with the channels of thought that literature carves in us?

In chapter 6 I examine a painting of a girl standing in a doorframe, executed in the Forbidden City during the early 1770s by Chinese students of *quadratura*. I read this painting in conjunction with a scene from *The Story of the Stone* in which Grannie Liu, a rustic old woman from the countryside, sees a painting of a girl whom she takes to be real. My intention in revisiting the well-known pairing of this painting and scene is to show that when the painting is read in terms of *The Story of the Stone*'s own remarks about perspectivalism, and in light of the novel's concern with the relation between language and material form, we understand the painting anew.

Rather than imagining that monofocal perspectivalism produces the trompe l'oeil of the painting, and focusing on the illusion of volume in shape and form, we see that Bolognese polyfocalism, which uses multiple vanishing points, was employed to create the appearance of *recessed* space as viewers walk past. Eighteenth-century Chinese accounts of the encounter with Italian *quadratura* in Beijing show that, for Chinese viewers, perspectivalism was understood in terms of the fluid materialization of recessed space, for it was recessed space that invited viewers to enter the painted wall. Here again, a European technology is interpreted in terms of a long-standing Chinese trope. Scholars have viewed the panoramic trompe l'oeil paintings affixed to the walls and ceilings of the Qianlong emperor's palaces as having been meant literally to fool the eye. In fact, when we consider these paintings in the context of fictional and anecdotal accounts of the painted wall, it becomes clear that, rather than simply fooling the eye, they reference the notion of misperception in order to encourage a meditative insight. The architectural placement of these paintings reinforces this view. Often placed near spaces dedicated for the emperor's meditation, they reminded viewers of the illusory quality of phenomenal form.

We cannot entirely resist the vision of vernacular fiction as illustrative of historical reference, nor should we reprimand ourselves for indulging in it. Rather than simply reinforcing the notion that fiction captures historical circumstance, I offer an alternative: the fictional objects I consider here suggest that we misapprehend if we believe in the integrity of the world as it appears to us. It is not simply the textual object's approximation to a historical object that makes it seem real. The confusion created by the occasionally contradictory depiction of a fictional object in fact enlivens that object. In this sense, these fictional objects ask us to be aware of the fallibility of perception rather than use them as a transparent lens to the past. The text creates a tension between the belief that the fictional object derives from a historical object on the one hand, and the fictional object's peculiar status as a locus of misperception on the other. It is this tension that ultimately convinces readers of the fictional object's verisimilitude.

CHAPTER ONE

The Python Robe of *The Plum in the Golden Vase*

The Plum in the Golden Vase, the first Chinese novel to describe in detail the minute transactions that make up quotidian life, focuses an unprecedented degree of attention on furnishings, food, and clothing.[1] For decades, scholars have mined this novel for corroborative detail regarding the cost, use, and placement of furniture and other material objects.[2] As Naifei Ding has observed, however, the rich accumulation of detail regarding the world of objects in *The Plum in the Golden Vase* does not subtend an early "realism."[3] It speaks instead to a fascination with the linguistic evocation of objects. The lush descriptions serve the Buddhist teleology that furnishes the arc of the plot; they seduce readers with the forms of the material world (*se* 色) in order to reveal at novel's end the ephemeral nature of all phenomena and the ultimate futility of the impulse to possess.

The plot of *The Plum in the Golden Vase* is notoriously nonlinear. As a sequel that expands five of the one hundred chapters of *The Water Margin* (*Shuihu zhuan* 水滸傳), *The Plum in the Golden Vase* answers a counterfactual question: What might have resulted if the heroic Wu Song had not murdered the merchant Ximen Qing after Ximen seduced his brother's wife? Ximen's voracious sexual appetite drives the plot: within the first nineteen chapters, he acquires three wives in addition to his original three. Succeeding chapters concern his affairs with servants, dalliances with courtesans, and illicit liaisons with elite women. As his sexual fortunes increase, his career prospers. In chapter 79, four-fifths of the way through the novel, Ximen Qing dies of sexual exhaustion. The remaining chapters concern the dissolution of his family and the dispersal of his wealth and possessions.

Just past the midpoint of the novel, in chapter 56, one of Ximen's cronies, Chang Shijie 常時節, asks Ximen for a loan. Ximen's friend Ying Bojue 應伯爵 encourages him to lend the money by appealing to his hopes for his infant son, stating that among the ancients, those who thought little of circulating their wealth freely saw their descendants come to glory. Ximen replies, "Things of that sort like to move and do not enjoy staying still [兀那東西是好動不喜靜的], so how could I be willing simply to bury them somewhere? These are things that naturally should be used; if one person piles them up; others will feel the lack. For this reason it is a grievous sin to accumulate wealth and precious objects."[4] He continues:

> When heaps of jade and accumulated gold begin to be cherished,
> Who realizes that wealth and precious objects are the root of calamity?
> One who loves a single coin as though it were his blood and marrow,
> Will be laughed at for his stupidity by magnanimous men.[5]
> The miser parts ways with family and friends;
> That one's body remains even after one's heart stops is certainly cause for grief.
> I suspect that he [the miser] also will not live forever,
> And will go to the netherworld empty-handed and alone.

> 積玉堆金始稱懷，誰知財寶禍根荄.
> 一文愛惜如膏血，仗義翻將笑作呆，
> 親友人人同陌路，存形心死定堪哀.
> 料他也有無常日，空手伶仃到夜臺.[6]

Here Ximen cites a poem ridiculing the miser, a stock figure in the fiction of this period; the poem contrasts the miser with men who are rewarded for recognizing that capital moves according to its own logic.[7] Ximen's fetishization of capital as "the sort of thing (東西) that likes to move" contrasts the animacy of silver with the lumpen passivity of the heaps of jade and gold the miser adores.⁸

Ximen speaks of capital in an unspecific way, prefacing the word *dongxi* ("thing") with the colloquial expression *wuna* ("that sort"). Even more significant, Ximen does not identify what "thing" refers to until quite late in the conversation (when it becomes clear that silver is "the sort of thing that likes to move and doesn't like being still"). The vernacular term Ximen uses here for *thing* inscribes a quality that suggests the fungibility of objects being exchanged.⁹ As the object that "likes to move" and "does not enjoy staying still" acquires mobility, it also seems to acquire volition; it gains animacy via circulation. The sense that silver has volition is reinforced by the arbitrariness of its destinations.

The novel itself reads like an exposition of Ximen's claim that things "like to move." *The Plum in the Golden Vase* tends to focus on objects and characters at the moment they enter circulation in order to be redistributed. The novel highlights both people and things as they pass into the commodity sphere, as if this were a precondition for them to be depicted at all. For example, the opening chapters are structured around Ximen's acquisition of his last three wives, Pan Jinlian 潘金蓮, Meng Yulou 孟玉樓, and Li Ping'er 李瓶兒 (and in the case of the latter two, of their valuables) in such a way as to train our attention on the act of acquisition rather than its consequences. The affair of Ximen Qing and Pan Jinlian is interrupted when he meets and marries Meng Yulou, but instead of depicting Meng Yulou's entrance to the household, the narrative immediately turns back to the completion of Ximen's marriage to Pan Jinlian, and then to the courtship of Li Ping'er and the acquisition of her possessions.

The close attention the novel pays to getting and spending could be construed as the natural consequence of its emphasis on the quotidian. But *The Plum in the Golden Vase* is less concerned with showing that the representation of objects in movement is necessary to the depiction of everyday life than it is with portraying everyday life as though it were centered on the acquisition and loss of objects. Meng Yulou's Nanjing alcove bed (*Nanjing babu chuang* 南京拔步床) is never shown in use; we never see anyone sleeping in it. The bed is mentioned on only three occasions: when Meng Yulou brings it to the Ximen household as part of her dowry; when it rather shockingly leaves the household shortly thereafter in the dowry of Ximen Qing's only daughter; and when Pan

Jinlian's servant Chunmei 春梅, who by the end of the novel becomes wealthier than Ximen Qing's widow Wu Yueniang 吳月娘, inquires as to its whereabouts in hopes of purchasing it.

The focus on exchange empties the object of any intrinsic qualities that might be invested in it by human use; the spectrum of possibilities with regard to its assigned value becomes restricted to the value the object accrues in circulation.[10] It is something of a feat in a novel of this magnitude, featuring eight hundred characters over the course of its hundred chapters, that objects are never depicted as beloved possessions. Whereas in *The Story of the Stone*—a novel strongly influenced by *The Plum in the Golden Vase*—objects are worn, torn, and mended, becoming deeply associated with specific characters, the relentless movement of objects in *The Plum in the Golden Vase* precludes their entering into a deep relation with individual characters.

THE LIST: MAPPING, MULTIPLICITY, AND THE UNEVOCATIVE OBJECT

The Plum in the Golden Vase contains voluminous descriptions of objects whose relation to the thematic concerns of the text could best be considered tangential or contiguous. Verisimilitude seems to result from the rough-and-tumble jostling of diverse objects in indiscriminate lists instead of from a faithful depiction of specific things. The circulation of objects, which amplifies the sense of multiplicity, is not simply a theme that speaks to the novel's interest in economic transaction, but also a means by which the narrative projects a sense of verisimilitude. The circulation of objects creates a multiplier effect that contributes to the construction of verisimilitude via the sense of the multiple.

The novel is far more concerned with giving a sense of the topography of circulation than with investigating the singular and evocative object in stasis. Rather than endowing specific objects with singular properties, *The Plum in the Golden Vase* makes meaning by enlisting multiplicity. The novel seldom depicts objects with the singularity that renders the object (or "the thing") significant in contemporary criticism. Perhaps for this reason, objects rarely function as emblems of specific characters, and seldom acquire a metaphorical resonance. Instead, descriptive passages underscore the significance of the material world and also highlight the insignificance of individual objects, which typically are devoid of identifying characteristics.

The profusion of objects in *The Plum in the Golden Vase* is organized in lists—lists of gifts, of recipients of gifts, of guests at the head table of a banquet, and of dishes presented at a banquet. These lists distribute our attention evenly over many objects rather than focus it on a singular, evocative object. In chapter 52, for instance, we learn the foods that were served at an impromptu feast hosted by Ximen Qing:

> [There were] two large platters of roast pork, two platters of roast duck, two platters of newly pan-fried fresh shad, four saucers of rose-flavored pastries, two saucers of boiled chicken and bamboo shoots, and two saucers of boiled squab. These were followed by four saucers of chitterlings, blood pudding, pork tripe, fermented sausage, and the like.
>
> 兩大盤燒豬肉, 兩盤燒鴨子, 兩盤新煎鮮鰣魚, 四碟玫瑰點心, 兩碟白燒笋雞, 兩碟燉爛鴿子雛兒, 然後又是四碟臟子, 血皮, 豬肚, 釀腸之類.[11]

The distributed attention of such lists has an equalizing effect; the reader has no sense of whether the roast pork is more important than the boiled squab. The rhetoric of the list highlights multiplicity rather than demonstrating hierarchy.

This divided quality of attention extends to the description of the materials used to make the objects. For example, the Dongpo 東坡 chairs in Ximen's study appear in the wake of a long train of attributive nouns: "low Dongpo chairs made of Yunnanese agateware, lacquer, gilt nails, and wickerwork rattan seats" (雲南瑪瑙漆減金釘籐絲甸矮矮東坡椅兒).[12] The lists of objects or lists of materials used to make the objects are difficult for the reader to parse, precisely because it is not clear whether any term is more significant than another. Without an organizing principle to suggest the connections between items on the list, the series of nouns used as adjectives becomes less digestible, and the pace of reading subsequently slows. In the context of the novel's interest in stressing the social aspiration of the parvenu Ximen's interior decor, the awkwardness of this series of lengthy and excessively precise modifiers underscores the fact that the chairs have been acquired not to be used but to be displayed.[13]

The paratactical juxtaposition suggests that the objects have no relationship other than being bought and placed.

Clothing in *The Plum in the Golden Vase* is particularly unevocative, especially when depicted as an item of exchange. The descriptions of the characters' clothes often draw attention to sumptuary violation, indicating that the items were improperly acquired.[14] The capacity for clothing to have figural resonance is typically left unexplored. In a scene from chapter 8, the femme fatale Pan Jinlian sits naked, except for a silk shift, as her unfortunate stepdaughter Ying'er 迎兒 draws her a steaming bath. As Pan Jinlian waits, she warms a tray of meat dumplings for Ximen Qing's birthday celebration, to be eaten when Ximen returns:

> At that time the summer solstice had already passed and the weather was extremely hot. The house was so uncomfortable the woman could hardly bear it and ordered Ying'er to heat some water and prepare the tub so she could take a bath. She also put a tray of meat dumplings into the steamer so she would have something to offer him if Ximen Qing happened to show up. Wearing nothing but a short shift of thin floss silk, she sat on a low stool longing in vain for Ximen Qing to come.
>
> 那時正值三伏天道, 十分炎熱. 婦人在房中害熱, 分付迎兒熱下水, 伺候澡盆, 要洗澡. 又做了一籠夸餡肉角兒, 等西門慶來吃. 身上只著薄繡短衫, 坐在小杌上, 盼不見西門慶來到.[15]

Pan Jinlian's flesh in the thin shift evokes the meat within the pale skins of the dumplings, lending an additional steaminess to the scene as she readies herself to enter the bath. But the narrative does not pursue any further correspondence between the meat of the dumplings and the flesh beneath Pan Jinlian's shift. A few pages later, the narrative again toys with a potentially bawdy morphological reference as it describes a double-headed hairpin among the gifts of clothing that Pan Jinlian has prepared for Ximen's birthday:

> There were: a pair of jet satin shoes; a pair of scent bags with the drawnwork inscription:

> In secret tryst a lover's vow,
> I'll follow you where'er you go;

a pair of russet satin kneepads, the borders of which were decorated with a motif of pines, bamboos, and plum blossoms, the "three cold-weather friends"; a sand-green waistband of Lu-chou pongee, decorated with the motifs of auspicious clouds and the symbolic representations of the "eight treasures," lined with watered-silk, fastened with purple cords, and enclosing a pocket filled with aromatic lysimachia and rose petals; and a hairpin in the shape of a double-headed lotus blossom, engraved with a pentasyllabic quatrain that read:

> I have a lotus blossom with two heads;
> To help keep your topknot in place.
> As they grow from the same stem on your head,
> So may we never abandon each other.

一雙玄色段子鞋, 一雙挑線密約深盟隨君. 膝下香草邊闌松竹梅花, 歲寒三友. 醬色段子護膝, 一條紗綠潞紬, 永祥雲嵌八寶, 水光絹裡兒, 紫線帶兒. 裡面裝着排草梅桂花兜肚. 一根並頭蓮辨簪兒, 簪兒上鈒着五言四句詩一首云: "奴有並頭蓮, 贈與君關髻. 凡事同頭上, 切勿輕相棄."[16]

Once again, the suggestive quality of the hairpin is quickly dropped. The potential for figuration gives way to seriation. The structure of the list resists the notion that any single item of clothing could be independently evocative. The inscription on the scent bags, for example, is reduplicated, so that the writing seems more decorative than expressive. None of the clothing, beginning with the shoes for Ximen's feet and the hairpin for Ximen's head, is important in and of itself. Each item is significant only as it enumerates a part of Ximen's body. Put otherwise, the *place* of inscription is as important as *what* is inscribed—neither the color of the kneepads, nor the motif embroidered on them, are as important as the place the kneepads occupy in the list of gifts.

This focus on seriation extends to the description of Ximen's study. After gaining official position, the semiliterate Ximen Qing constructs a "study" in the literati fashion, which he dedicates not to the reading of the classics or of poetry but to the storage of gifts. Here, the emphasis on the list foregrounds the role of gifts in facilitating the relations among officials. When his crony Ying Bojue first enters the study, his attention is immediately drawn to the letter case holding lists of gifts that Ximen has exchanged with his new colleagues:

> After some time had passed, Ying Bojue wandered into the inner study, where he found standing on the floor a black lacquer summer bedstead with incised gold ornamentation and a decorative marble panel, and fitted with bed curtains of blue silk. To either side of this there were painted lacquer bookcases adorned with gold tracery, which were filled with presentation gifts of privately printed books with brocade wrappers and bolts of fabric. There was also a desk, piled high with writing implements and books. . . . A letter case was also visible containing Ximen Qing's social correspondence, calling cards, and lists of people with whom Mid-Autumn Festival gifts had been exchanged.
>
> 良久, 伯爵走到裏邊書房內. 裏面地平上安着一張大理石黑漆縷金凉床. 掛着青紗帳幔. 兩邊綵漆描金書廚, 盛的都是送禮的書帕尺頭. 几席文具. 書籍堆滿. . . . 書篋內都是往來書柬拜帖, 並送中秋禮物帳簿.[17]

For Ying Bojue, those lists of gifts are by far the most interesting reading in Ximen's study, granting as they do a privileged insight into Ximen's new social contacts. The pace of reading slows as we encounter each name that Ying Bojue silently reads:

> Picking up the first list, Ying Bojue opened and perused it. He found inscribed there the names of His Honor Cai Jing, His Excellency Cai Yu, Defender-in-Chief Zhu Mian, Defender-in-Chief Tong Guan, His Honor Privy Councilor Cai the Fourth, His Honor Commandant Cai the Fifth, as well as the names of the four principal officers from both the local district and prefectural yamens. The second list contained the names of Commandant Zhou Xiu, Judicial Commissioner Xia Yanling, Military Director-in-Chief Jing Zhong, Militia Commander Zhang Guan, and the two Eunuch Directors Liu and Xue. The items indicated were bolts of satin brocade, preserved

pork, goose, and other gifts appropriate for major occasions, each gradated differentially according to the status of the recipient.

應伯爵取過一本. 揭開觀開, 上面寫着: 蔡老爺, 蔡大爺, 朱太尉, 童太尉, 中書蔡四老爹, 都尉蔡五老爹, 并本處知縣, 知府四宅. 第二本是周守備, 夏提刑, 荊都監, 張團練, 并劉, 薛二內相. 都是金段尺頭, 豬酒金餅, 鰣魚海鮮, 雞鵝大禮, 各有輕重不同.[18]

As the pace of the text slows, we inadvertently linger over the spectacle of Ximen's jocular sidekick Ying Bojue silently reading the names of officials with whom Ximen has exchanged gifts at the Mid-Autumn Festival. The novel's engagement with various forms of voyeurism—overhearing, peeping, and spying—takes a fresh turn as Ying furtively reads the list that furnishes evidence of Ximen's rapid social ascent. Ying Bojue's silent perusal of Ximen Qing's social correspondence suggests a capacity to ruminate and reflect that has heretofore not surfaced. Readers intuit that the lists of names present valuable information for Ying, even though the text does not describe his thoughts. Only because Ying Bojue remains uncharacteristically silent for an extended time as he stands before the objects do we sense his interior mental life, created via a process of deflection.

The network of gifts, not the sociality of literary pursuits, has earned Ximen his place in officialdom. The books, printed to be presented as gifts, share space on the bookshelves with the conventional all-purpose gift, fabric. Although books might be thought of fundamentally as objects that suggest interiority, in this instance books are devoid of that association. A literal translation of the line that reads "a desk, piled high with writing implements and books" in the list of gifts quoted above underscores this point: the shelves of the bookcases "contain fabric wrappers for sending books as gifts, bolts of fabric, several sets of writing implements, and piles of books." In other words, there are no books or writing implements to be used by Ximen; those in his study are gifts awaiting circulation.

THE REDISTRIBUTION OF GIFTS: A PRESERVED SHAD

The value of gifts in *The Plum in the Golden Vase* is determined in large part by their provenance. In chapter 34, Eunuch Director Liu gives

Ximen some preserved shad to thank him for intervening in a court case on his younger brother's behalf. The brother, having built a home with timber taken from the Imperial Lumber Depot, was in danger of having to appear before the Imperial Ministry of Justice. Liu had actually offered Ximen a hundred taels to stop the case from going forward, but Ximen refused to take the money. When Ximen has the case dismissed, Eunuch Director Liu sends over a slaughtered pig, a jug of homemade lotus blossom wine, two packages of preserved shad, and two bolts of satin brocade. Ximen states explicitly that there was no need for money; this exchange was more refined.[19] Ximen then criticizes his colleague Xia Yanling 夏延齡, who has taken a bribe of one hundred taels of silver on the case, and yet is still threatening to write a memorial about the case in hopes of receiving further bribes.[20] Given Ximen's own accumulation of wealth, there is no point in accepting another one hundred taels; what interests him now are goods that are difficult to procure.

The innocent shad is thus tangled in a complex web with the imperial lumber stolen by Eunuch Director Liu's brother. Gifts in Ximen's world cannot help but be seen as bribes. We read of goods entrusted to Ximen's pawnshop being appropriated by his wives; of wagers lost that speak to the arbitrariness of fate; of shoes, flagons, and bracelets gone missing. In other words, the narrative focuses on objects that have lost their place, illuminating the role of such objects in instantiating a misbegotten sociality. As objects in *The Plum in the Golden Vase* are misplaced, pawned, swindled, and stolen, they are diverted from their intended destinations and are consumed in ways that deviate from the norm.

As the narrative reveals how gifts pave Ximen's path into officialdom and facilitate his relations with his new colleagues, it emphasizes the special role of the recycled or recirculated gift in affirming social networks.[21] If the original donor is higher in status than subsequent recipients, his status infuses the gift and dignifies all those touched by subsequent transactions. Thus when an object is regifted, it earns something like "interest," added value that accrues simply because it has passed through another set of hands. For example, take the shad given to Ximen Qing by Eunuch Director Liu later in the chapter. Ximen recirculates two of the shad, sending them to Ying Bojue. Thanking him for the gift, Ying adds that he in turn sent some of the shad on to his brother and his daughter:

> I still haven't thanked you, Brother, for the two fine shad that you were kind enough to send me the other day. I gave one of them to my elder brother and said to my wife, with regard to the other, "Cut it in two with a cleaver, and send a piece to our daughter. As for what's left over, chop it into thin slices, marinate it in the red mash it came in, mix in a little sesame seed oil, and store it in a porcelain jar, so that, early or late, when we're having a meal, or if a guest should show up, we can steam a saucerful for our delectation, thereby not failing in our appreciation of Brother's lavish generosity."

> 我還沒謝的哥, 昨日蒙哥送了那兩尾好鰣魚與我, 送了一尾與家兄去; 剩下一尾, 對房下說拏刀兒劈開, 送了一段與小女; 餘者打成窄窄的塊兒, 拏他原舊紅糟兒培着, 再攪些香油, 安放在一個磁罐內, 留着我一早一晚吃飯兒. 或遇有個人客兒來, 蒸恁一碟兒上去, 也不枉辜負了哥的盛情.[22]

This regifting of the shad comes as close to an example of the normative circulation of things as we will find in *The Plum in the Golden Vase*.[23] In thanking Ximen, Ying Bojue tells him how he redistributed the gift, establishing Ximen as the patron of a subsidiary portion of the network. Indeed, by asking his wife to preserve it in a ceramic crock and add more ingredients, mixing the shad with sesame oil as well as the fermented mash it came in, Ying both extends the life of the gift and increases its volume so that it can be further regifted. To recycle a gift in this manner accords it greater honor than to consume it oneself and incorporates one's network of family and friends into the genealogy of the gift. Because things in *The Plum in the Golden Vase* have neither interiority nor intrinsic qualities, they are well suited to being recirculated. As the shad is redistributed, it acquires a provenance, so that the shad's value becomes a function of the hands through which it has passed.

THE PYTHON ROBE

Among the multitude of objects that populate this novel, we might expect clothing to have a supplemental relation to interiority, such that the part might signify the whole.[24] The python robe (*mang pao* 蟒袍 or *mang yi* 蟒衣), a type of robe awarded by the Ming emperors to favored officials in recognition of loyalty and service to the state, is a case in point. The English term "python," however, is not an accurate translation for the mythical *mang* 蟒, as the *mang* resembled a dragon more than a snake. The *mang* derived its importance in part from its resemblance to the dragon depicted on imperial robes, as is apparent in figure 1.1. The python robe was prescribed apparel for certain officials when the emperor presided over sacrifices.

FIGURE 1.1 Leng Jian, *The Python Robe Worn by Civil Official of the 7th Rank*, ink and color on silk, Qianlong reign period. *Source*: Victoria and Albert Museum.

The Python Robe of The Plum in the Golden Vase 23

Woven under the auspices of the imperial Weaving and Dyeing Bureau of Jiangnan (*neizhi ranju* 內織染局), python robes were produced as presentation gifts that the Ming and Qing emperors bestowed upon favored officials as well as rulers of other principalities.[25] Embedded in the robe given by the emperor to a subject was imperial recognition of service.[26] Indeed, the synecdochal relationship between robe and imperial recognition was so strong that those who possessed python robes were typically buried in them, since the robes signified their close relation to the emperor.[27] The novel's depiction of the python robe, however, focuses on its illicit transfer and unauthorized use. The circulation of the python robe, in theory highly restricted, becomes deracinated.

This concern regarding indiscriminate circulation of the python robe appears repeatedly in Ming and Qing fiction and drama. In Kong Shang-ren's 1698 drama *The Peach Blossom Fan* the villainous Ruan Dacheng ascends the stage in a python robe.[28] In the great confiscation of *The Story of the Stone*, eight rolls of fabric bearing the python insignia (*mang duan* 蟒段) are among the possessions the imperial Embroidered Guards seize from the Jia family, presumably a sign of the Jia family's overreaching.[29] In chapter 34 of the novel *The Scholars*, a Hanlin scholar surnamed Gao inappropriately wears a python robe to a private party.[30] In chapter 18 of *Marriage Destinies to Awaken the World* (*Xingshi yinyuan zhuan* 醒世姻緣傳), the libertine Chao Yuan 晁源 invites an artist to paint a portrait of his father wearing a python robe.[31] The artist is reluctant to attempt the painting, and he asks whether the father, given his low rank, truly could have received a python robe (in chapter 42, however, it becomes clear that the painter complied).

The genealogy of the python robe's distribution and circulation was the most salient aspect of the robe to authors of the fifteenth and sixteenth centuries. When we examine the many statutes and anecdotes regarding the python robe in historical sources such as the *History of the Ming* (*Ming shi* 明史), *Collected Statutes of the Ming Dynasty* (*Da Ming huidian* 大明會典), and *Veritable Histories of the Ming Emperors* (*Ming shilu* 明實錄), it becomes clear that one of the primary concerns of those sources is the misdirected redistribution of the robe after the emperor bestows it upon an official. The proper flow of circulation was from emperor to officials of high rank, but as we see both in

The Plum in the Golden Vase and in the historical sources, eunuchs controlled the production of the robes and had a strong hand in their redistribution.

THE GIFT OF A PYTHON ROBE

The gifting and regifting of python robes in chapters 25 and 71 of *The Plum and the Golden Vase* is particularly significant in that python robes, produced in the imperial workshops to be used as imperial presentation gifts, were explicitly prohibited from being recirculated.[32] Punishment for giving a python robe received from the emperor to someone else was a hundred strokes of the rod (*zhang* 杖) and loss of office.[33] The Ming emperors presented python robes to members of the Grand Secretariat (*neige* 內閣) and officials of the first through third rank, as well as to their relatives.[34] Python robes were also bestowed upon prominent Daoist patriarchs and imperial physicians, leaders of tributary countries, and local chieftains.[35] The earliest mention in the *Ming History* of the python robe being used as a presentation gift is in 1417, when the sultans of the eastern and western Sulu were given gold-threaded python robes in return for gold and precious stones they sent as tribute.[36] Official histories as well as notation books (*biji* 筆記) record numerous instances of officials, aristocrats, and foreign leaders requesting python robes. In the Jingtai reign period (1428–1457), for example, ambassadors from Java requested to be given python robes and received them.[37] In some instances, such requests were rejected, suggesting that there was an element of negotiation to the bestowal of the robes.

In that python robes could be neither exchanged nor regifted, they were "inalienable possessions" of the sort that Annette Weiner has described.[38] The provenance of the robe was meant to distinguish the bearer, but were someone other than the recipient of imperial favor to don the robe, the disjunction between original recipient and bearer would be underscored. Hence the many anecdotes in unofficial histories about the brazen behavior of those who sport the python robe unauthorized. Ximen Qing's acquisition of a python robe must be seen in this light. As an inalienable object, the python robe ought to be the *opposite* of what Ximen Qing calls "things of that sort" that "like to move." In

The Plum in the Golden Vase, however, the novel's portrayal of the relentless exchange of objects suggests a strong concern that objects that should be preserved from entering circulation are sacrificed to it. Precisely because the robe was an enclaved object, the violation of the prohibition on regifting was particularly meaningful. In essence, it flattered the recipient by suggesting that the relation between donor and recipient was so exceptional that it warranted such a breach of protocol.[39]

In chapter 25, Ximen includes four python robes in a set of birthday gifts that he assembles for the Grand Preceptor Cai Jing 蔡京 (1047–1126), the most powerful minister in Emperor Huizong's 徽宗 court (r. 1100–1126). The robes please Cai Jing so much that as a result not only Ximen but also his sworn brother Wu Dian'en 吳典恩, who delivers the gifts, will gain official position. Ximen has acquired the four python robes through irregular channels. Two of them were procured in Hangzhou, where the robes were produced by weavers contracted by the imperial workshops; these two have clearly been sourced in a deal on the black market. Ximen's favorite concubine, Li Ping'er, gives him the other two, which she inherited from her husband's uncle, the Eunuch Director Hua.

Li Ping'er, upon hearing that Ximen needs two more python robes, states casually:

> "On the second floor of my place over there, I've got a number of python robes that haven't been made up yet. Let me go take a look." Before long, Ximen joined her, and they went up to the second floor of her belvedere to have a look. She pulled out four items, two bolts of jet abaca linen, and two python robes of light scarlet silk with variegated insignia and brocade borders, ten times better in quality and design than the ones from Hangzhou. Ximen Qing was as pleased as could be.
>
> 李瓶兒道：「我那邊樓上，還有幾件沒裁的蟒，等我瞧去。」不一時，西門慶與他同往上樓去尋，揀出四件來. 兩件大紅紗，兩疋玄色焦布，俱是金織邊五彩蟒衣，比杭州織來的花樣身分更強十倍。把西門慶喜歡要不的。[40]

The presence of the python robes in Li Ping'er's apartments reinforces the novel's earlier suggestion that Li Ping'er had an inappropriately close relationship with her foster father-in-law, the Eunuch Director Hua. The robes in Li Ping'er's trunks were not worn by the Eunuch Director himself, but were still uncut, kept ready for redistribution. This suggests that the robes were not presented by the emperor, but rather acquired illicitly, perhaps from a eunuch supervising an aspect of the production process in the Weaving and Dyeing Bureau of the imperial workshops.[41] The imperial workshops did not produce python robes so much as contract for their production with local weavers in Hangzhou and Suzhou, and eunuchs oversaw every aspect of their production. In this regard it is noteworthy that every illicit transaction involving a python robe in *The Plum in the Golden Vase* involves a eunuch.

As we try to imagine why the robes in Li Ping'er's possession should have been more finely executed than those obtained in Hangzhou, several possibilities emerge. Nanjing and Suzhou produced work of a higher quality than Hangzhou; Hangzhou became prominent as a site of silk weaving only during the Qing dynasty. Also, by the mid-Ming the system of the Yuan (1276–1367) and early Ming whereby textiles for court use were produced by registered artisans had begun to break down. In 1425 the Imperial Weaving and Dyeing Bureau enlisted over 1,700 weavers and dyers (*guanji* 官機).[42] By the 1540s, only 680 artisans were affiliated.[43] Local officials became responsible for producing the silk that the Weaving and Dyeing Bureau could not provide.[44] The gap was filled by weavers outside the bureau (*minji* 民機), who were recruited at peak times, in particular just before the New Year.[45] *The Veritable Records of the Xizong Reign* (*Ming Xizong shilu* 明熹宗實錄) documents, for example, that in 1579 it was so hard to find sufficient numbers of weavers registered as artisans that additional local weavers had to be recruited.[46] Such temporary weavers wove silk to imperial specifications on their own looms, and were free to use their own looms the rest of the year.[47] This created opportunity both for unauthorized reproduction of imperial patterns and for unclaimed robes to find their way to the market.

Ximen's illegal purchase of the robes in Hangzhou underscores the recurring concern in historical sources about the inability of the state to police the boundaries of the realm of imperial production. From the mid-fifteenth to the sixteenth century, a number of edicts prohibited unauthorized weaving of python robes. In the year 1447, according to Shen

Defu 沈德符 (1578–1642), an imperial edict sent to the officials of the Department of Works forbade the weaving of robes with python, flying-fish (feiyu 飛魚), and horned-bull (douniu 鬥牛) insignia outside the imperial workshops, stating that those who wove such robes would be beheaded and their families conscripted and sent to the border regions. Those who wore privately woven python robes would receive heavy punishment.[48] In 1504, the Hongzhi 弘治 emperor (r. 1487–1505) noted during a conversation with the Grand Secretary Liu Jian 劉健 (1433–1526) that unauthorized private weaving (si zhi 私織) of python robes was illegal.[49] Liu Jian observed that officers who had been presented with python robes should not be permitted to have them rewoven even if they grew tattered with long use, lest the python insignia be altered in the process to resemble the five-clawed dragon, the imperial insignia.[50]

The government's inability to prevent the altering of the python robe, particularly given its similarity to the dragon robe, was a perennial concern.[51] Shen Defu cites a memorial written in the first year of the Hongzhi reign period (1488) by a censor named Bian Yong 邊鏞 (d. 1501) affiliated with the Board of Rites. "These days the python patterns on robes all assume the shape of a dragon," lamented the censor.[52] He continued: "Python robes were never part of the system of dress for officials. The python has no horns or feet, but palace eunuchs (nei guan 內官) these days often ask for python insignia that resembles the dragon; this is not part of the system of official dress."[53] He added that, having checked the oldest extant dictionary, *Approaching Elegance* (*Erya* 爾雅), he found that the python is a type of snake, not a type of dragon. "The python has no horns or feet," the censor repeated, "whereas the dragon has both."[54] Clearly he was concerned that it might be a simple step to add a fifth claw to the four claws of the python unless additional distinguishing characteristics were considered.

Eunuch Director Hua's pile of uncut robes suggests an accumulation with intent to redistribute, which in the *Ming History* and in informal writings of the Ming is frequently linked to the aspirations of eunuchs in usurping imperial power. A notable example is Liu Jin 劉瑾 (d. 1510), the most powerful eunuch of the Zhengde 正德 reign (1506–1522) and the leader of the notorious Eight Tigers (bahu 八虎), a group of eight eunuchs especially close to the emperor. After Liu's arrest in 1510, the emperor went in person to Liu's residence to inspect his confiscated possessions.[55]

He found a dragon robe (*gunlong pao* 袞龍袍) and an imperial crown of a sort called "a cap that reaches the heavens" (*pingtian guan* 平天冠), as well as 470 python robes and 4,162 jade belts.[56] The dragon robe and crown were taken as proof of seditious intent.[57] Liu's possession of hundreds of python robes and thousands of jade belts usurped imperial prerogative; the *Ming History* in fact criticizes Liu for inappropriately bestowing the python robe upon his favorites.[58]

After the downfall of the powerful eunuch Wei Zhongxian 魏忠賢 (1568–1627), the eunuch Liu Ruoyu 劉若愚 (1584–1642?), imprisoned as his presumed ally, sought to distinguish himself from Wei Zhongxian by describing the latter's abuses in a memoir written from prison. According to Liu Ruoyu, under Wei Zhongxian even palace eunuchs and palace women wore python robes to attend the emperor, and new types of python robes proliferated for use on specific holidays.[59] Over the New Year, eunuchs wore python robes decorated with roundels featuring gourds (*hulujing buzi* 葫蘆景補子). At the lantern festival that crowned the New Year celebrations on the fifteenth day of the first month, they wore python robes whose roundels were decorated with lantern scenes,[60] and on the Double Ninth (the ninth day of the ninth month), they wore python robes whose roundels were embroidered with chrysanthemums.[61] According to Liu, the abuse of sumptuary law was such that it had become fashionable to use the python pattern in rain gear. If the weather was inclement on days when eunuchs were in attendance on the emperor, they wore red rain gear with multicolored square roundels bearing the python insignia.[62] Under Wei Zhongxian, Liu continues, even those with offices no higher than provincial military commander (*tidu* 提督) wore the python robe, and they did so in Wei Zhongxian's name.[63]

Details of Affairs Recorded in the Ming History (*Ming shi jishi benmo* 明史紀事本末), a collection of topical historical accounts that informed the *Ming shi*, describes the defeat in 1511 of government forces under Li Jin 李瑾 (d. 1489) in Shandong by the rebel Zhao Sui 趙鐩 (d. 1512). The rebels captured not only weapons and armor, but also Li Jin's python robe: "The bandit [Zhao] Sui put on the python robe and roamed through the streets showing it off. Passing through Tai'an, he composed a poem, daring everyone to capture him. The poem circulated everywhere."[64] The unauthorized donning of the python robe signaled the usurpation of power as few other kinds of sumptuary violation could.

EUNUCH HE'S GIFT OF A FLYING-FISH ROBE TO XIMEN QING

In chapter 71, Ximen Qing receives a flying-fish robe (*feiyu* 飛魚) when he journeys to the capital to express thanks to the emperor for his promotion in the Office of Public Works. He receives the robe from the powerful Eunuch Director He 何, who wishes to make his acquaintance because his nephew is to take up a post in Ximen's office.

The trip to the capital shows Ximen in a fresh light: suddenly he is no longer the source of largesse, but anxiously aspires to be the recipient of it. He is unsure as to what is expected of him at court, and he meets with uncertainty the mingled threats and cajoling of his patron Zhai Qian 翟謙, the majordomo of Grand Preceptor Cai Jing. As the invitation to Eunuch He's home is couched somewhat mysteriously, Ximen is quite confused upon his arrival. He is ushered into a resplendent hall where several places are laid for a banquet and flowers in gilded vases adorn the tables. Eunuch He appears in a green velvet python robe with a bejeweled girdle. When Ximen asks for whom the lavish banquet has been prepared, Eunuch He presses Ximen to sit in the seat of honor.

The eunuch suggests that he remove his outer robe, but Ximen protests that he is wearing nothing suitable underneath. The eunuch then tells his servants to fetch one of his own robes for Ximen, a green velvet flying-fish robe (飛魚綠絨氅衣). When Ximen protests, saying, "That is part of your official regalia, venerable sir. How could your pupil presume to wear it?" (老公公職事之服, 學生何以穿得), the eunuch replies:

> Go ahead and put it on, Your Honor. What is there to be afraid of? The other day the Lord of Ten Thousand Years bestowed a python robe on me, so I will no longer be wearing it. In fact, I will donate it to Your Honor to wear over your other clothes.
>
> 大人只顧穿, 怕怎的。昨日萬歲賜了我蟒衣,我也不穿他了, 就送了大人遮衣服兒罷。[65]

Even emperors engaged in violations of sumptuary protocol when giving gifts to their favorites. Wang Shizhen 王士禎 (1634–1711) observes that the Jiajing emperor gave Yan Song 嚴嵩 (1480–1567) robes made in Nanjing with roundels in the crane and *qilin* patterns that were of a shade of yellow called *shan huang* 閃黃, noting that this hue was reserved for imperial use.⁶⁶ As the banquet scene in chapter 71 reveals, the emperor had violated sumptuary protocol with his gift of the python robe to Eunuch He; the flying-fish pattern, one grade below the python robe, was the only kind of robe that eunuchs were allowed to wear. In the conversation of 1504 between the Hongzhi emperor and Grand Secretary Liu Jian mentioned above, both men had also expressed the need to reiterate the proscriptions regarding the clothing styles permitted to eunuchs, noting that the horned-bull and python robes were forbidden.⁶⁷ Whereas the python robe was meant to be worn by officials of the first rank, the flying-fish robe, which differed in that the flying fish had scales and a tail but not claws, was meant to be worn by officials of the second rank; the horned-bull robe was designated for officials of the third rank.

The hierarchy of the python and flying-fish robes at this time is apparent in a memorial that tells how the Jiajing emperor grew angry upon seeing a minister (*shangshu* 尚書) of the Board of War named Zhang Zan 張瓚 (1473–1542) wearing what the emperor took to be a python robe. The emperor asked how an official of the second rank (*erpin* 二品) could wear a python robe. A member of the Grand Secretariat (*gechen* 閣臣) named Xia Yan 夏言 (1482–1548) reassured the emperor, "Zan is wearing a flying-fish robe that the emperor gave him; it merely resembles a python robe" (瓚所服, 乃欽賜飛魚服, 鮮明類蟒耳). To which the emperor replied, "How can a flying-fish pattern bear two horns? This is severely prohibited" (飛魚何組兩角?其嚴禁之).⁶⁸

When Eunuch He first suggests that Ximen wear the robe, he tells Ximen to spread it over his shoulders like a cloak to "cover his clothes" (*zhe yifu* 遮衣服). The Chongzhen commentator notes, "The single bland phrase expresses the rottenness of his relation to his emperor" (淡淡一語寫出名分之爛).⁶⁹ Two chapters later, Ying Bojue is amazed to find Ximen lounging in the robe at home:

> Under the lamplight, Ying Bojue observed that, over his white satin tunic, Ximen Qing was wearing a green velvet variegated flying-fish version of a python robe, the coiled image on which was:

Showing its claws and brandishing its fangs, the horns on its head projecting formidably; flaunting its whiskers and shaking its mane, its golds and greens setting each other off.[70]

It gave him quite a start, and he asked, "Brother, where did that garment of yours come from?"

Ximen Qing responded by standing up and saying, "Take a good look at it, all of you, and then guess where it came from."

"How could we hope to guess correctly?" said Ying Bojue.

"It was given to me by Eunuch Director He Xin in the Eastern Capital," said Ximen Qing. "I was having a drink at his place and was feeling cold, so he brought out this garment and gave it to me to put on. This is the flying-fish version of the python robe. Since the emperor had recently bestowed a regular python robe and a jade girdle on him, he had no longer planned to wear this one, so he gave it to me, which was a considerable favor."

伯爵燈下看見西門慶白綾袄子上,罩着青段五彩飛魚蟒衣,張爪舞牙,頭角崢嶸,揚須鼓鬚,金碧掩映,蟠在身上,諕了一跳. 問: "哥, 這衣服是那裡的?" 西門慶便立起身來, 笑道: "你每瞧瞧, 猜是那裡的?" 伯爵道: "俺每如何猜得着?" 西門慶道: "此是東京何太監送我的. 我在他家吃酒, 因害冷, 他拿出這件衣服與我披. 這是飛魚, 朝廷另賜了他蟒龍玉帶, 他不穿這件, 就相送了. 此是一個大分上."[71]

Ying Bojue is frightened when he sees Ximen, who is merely a military officer of the fifth rank, lounging at home in his new robe. It is worth lingering a moment on the description of Ximen's robe. Readers of the Chinese text may notice a discrepancy in the robe's depiction that is smoothed over in the translation. In chapter 73, the robe is of indigo satin (青段), whereas in chapter 71, it is of green velvet (綠絨). It is worth calling attention to the inconsistency not because the text invests it with significance, but precisely because it does not.

Although in most sources, the flying fish robe is opposed to the python robe, in some, the flying fish robe is treated as a sub-category of the python robe. The translator David Tod Roy here adopts the latter understanding, translating Ximen's simple statement "This is a flying-fish robe" (這是飛魚) as "This is the flying-fish version of a python robe." Here David Roy is making sense of the earlier depiction in this passage of Ximen Qing's robe as a "flying fish-python robe" (飛魚蟒). It is possible, however, to read these earlier lines to suggest that Ying Bojue is startled to see, under the light of the lamp, that Ximen is wearing "a flying fish, or perhaps even a python robe" (rather than a "flying fish-python robe"). In other words, Ying Bojue cannot quite make out the design, but sees enough to know that Ximen is wearing the robe of a high-ranking official, whether a flying fish robe or a python robe. Ying Bojue is clearly frightened by Ximen's boldness in doing so. We could then understand Ximen's explanation, "This is a flying-fish robe" as Ximen's protest that he is only wearing a flying-fish robe and has not been so bold or transgressive as to wear a python robe.

The *Great Ming Code* (*Da Ming lü* 大明律) stated that unauthorized wearing of a python robe, flying-fish robe, or horned-bull robe would be treated under the law as severely as the unauthorized wearing of the imperial dragon or phoenix robe.[72] These gradations date at least to the sixteenth year of the Jiajing reign (1537), when the Board of Rites memorialized that only ministers of the first, second, or third rank would be allowed to wear the python, flying-fish, or horned-bull patterns, respectively.[73] Yan Shifan 嚴世蕃 (1513–1565), the rapacious son of Yan Song, rode in his carriage wearing a python robe without imperial authorization; this was cited as evidence of his lack of loyalty (*bu cheng zhi xin* 不誠之心) when he was sentenced to death.[74]

In this scene Ying Bojue seems frightened by the flying fish itself, which is animated, literally opening its mouth to display its teeth and playfully swiping its claws. The startled attention that Ying bestows upon the robe enlivens it. The robe's menacing aspect suggests that Ximen is engaged in an activity more dangerous than he himself knows. Far from conferring power, the mismatch between the robe and Ximen's low rank makes it immediately apparent that Ximen's aspirations are illegitimate. The robe seems more powerful than Ximen, who is ultimately diminished by it.

Ying Bojue quickly recovers from the shock of seeing Ximen in the robe, and accounts for the dissonance between Ximen's present status and the robe by stating that the robe is an augur of Ximen's future promotion.

Ying Bojue, expressing himself in exaggerated terms, said, "Such an ornately decorated garment must, at the very least, be worth a good deal of money. This is a propitious omen for you, Brother. In the future, when you are promoted to the position of commander-in-chief, you need not worry about wearing a regular python robe and a jade girdle yourself, not to mention a flying-fish robe, for your rank will entitle you to more than that."[75]

伯爵方極口誇獎: "這花衣服, 少說也值幾個錢兒. 此是哥的先兆, 到明日高轉, 做到都督上, 愁玉帶蟒衣？何況飛魚, 穿過界兒去了!"[76]

Ying Bojue states with his typical sycophancy that Ximen will receive a python robe next.

Both Eunuch He's description of the robe and Ximen Qing's reply to Ying Bojue focus on the genealogy of the object's acquisition. As Mary Douglas has noted, the distribution of goods regulated by sumptuary protocol fosters a patron-client relationship.[77] In *The Plum in the Golden Vase*, such patron-client relationships are fostered not only within the enclaved realm of imperial patronage, but also by the diversion of goods from that realm. In wearing the robe, Ximen displays the close relationship that the gift of this robe has forged between him and Eunuch He. A kind of sociality is embedded in the bestowed robe that is alien to its original purpose. As Ximen Qing wears the robe casually at home, the novel caricatures his social aspirations and cultural illiteracy. The episode also illustrates the way in which, as the robe circulates illegitimately, it becomes alienated from its symbolic meanings. The robe bears witness to the genealogy of its redistribution; it is dignified both by its imperial pedigree and by the fact that it has been regifted to Ximen by the Eunuch Director He.

CONCLUSION

The scenes from *The Plum in the Golden Vase* regarding the python robe become newly legible when placed in the context of concerns expressed in the official and unofficial histories of the late Ming. Ximen Qing's purchase of python robes in Hangzhou recalls the problem of unauthorized production by weavers outside the Imperial Weaving and Dyeing Bureau; Eunuch He's gift of the robe to Ximen Qing recalls Eunuch Liu Jin's bestowal of the python robe on his favorites and its indictment in the *Ming shi*. Ximen wears the robe as he entertains his guests, echoing the flaunting of the python robe by the rebel Zhao Sui as he rode through the streets. The trajectories of the python robe bear witness to the unseemly aspirations of all those involved in its inappropriate circulation.

The python robe encapsulates the choices before us as we think of the primary trends in the criticism of *The Plum in the Golden Vase*. If we view the novel as a Confucian text, we will view the misappropriation of the python robe in terms of a critique of the violation of Confucian norms. Andrew Plaks has argued that the Ximen household is a negative example of the principles for the management of family and state as outlined in the Confucian classic *The Great Learning* (*Da xue* 大學).[78] In such a reading, the influence of the seventeenth-century commentator Zhang Zhupo is still felt: Zhang remarked that "the description of Eunuch He giving a flying-fish robe reveals the extreme lack of respect for propriety in a declining age" (寫和太監送飛魚衣, 真是末世無禮之極).[79]

As we trace the fortunes of the python robe, the novel's concern with the inversion of normative hierarchies is evident.[80] But even though *The Plum in the Golden Vase* registers concern regarding sumptuary violation, it also takes pleasure in it. The astonishing visual of Ximen Qing in a python robe brings pleasure in an unexpected juxtaposition—the merchant outfitted in an imperially granted garment—that is characteristic of the novel's use of citation from heterogeneous sources. Shang Wei has observed that this aesthetic of disjunction is characteristic of the riddles and drinking games of the period, which create a comic effect by placing a line from a classical text, such as one of the Confucian *Four Books*, next to a line from a vernacular text.[81] In this view, the eunuch's gift of the python robe to Ximen becomes like a wayward citation. The robe functions in the same mode as a deracinated line from a classical text. When Ximen wears the robe given him by Eunuch He, the contrast between the values presumably embodied in the python robe (service to the state and loyalty to the sovereign) and the crassness of the merchant produce the sort of comic juxtaposition characteristic of the rhymes of drinking games. The solemnity of the robe contrasts with Ximen's own lack of gravitas.[82] Such a disjunction inhabits the tradition of provocative and witty juxtapositions of citations from classical texts and popular forms that is characteristic of *The Plum in the Golden Vase*'s own textual practice.

We could say that because *The Plum in the Golden Vase* is so intensely citational, it is relieved of the responsibility of providing a terminus for interpretation.[83] As Chaoyang Liao has written, the traditional commentarial practice of reading images to discern themes in *The Plum in the Golden Vase* does not contribute to an understanding of how the novel makes sense, because the novel's own logic is not exclusionary but all-inclusive.[84] An effort to illuminate the cultural histories of the objects that dot the pages of *The Plum in the Golden Vase* presents an analogous problem to examining its practices of citation: no interpretive framework can encompass such profusion. When we consider the entire field of objects that populate the novel, the notion that the cultural histories of an object can allow us to read a text in a new light dissolves as our entire field of vision is saturated by tangential information. The endless potential for contiguity, as one object gives way to the next in lists such as those above, means that no single object can frame the text. The heterogeneous texts that *The Plum in the Golden Vase* cites point in multiple directions, unraveling the possibility of a unifying interpretation; so too do the material histories of the heterogeneous objects that populate it. In this sense, my attempt to restore the particular historical associations of the python robe runs counter to the novel's own efforts to rid objects of particularity in order to better ready them for redistribution.

The principles of seriation and juxtaposition that characterize the depiction of objects in *The Plum in the Golden Vase* lead to incongruity. This is not a deliberate strategy but an effect. As we recall, in chapter 73 the robe is of indigo satin, whereas in chapter 71 it is of green velvet. The text neither explores the inconsistency nor considers it meaningful. Authors of the late Ming did not value coherence in the long form of a hundred-chapter novel, and subtle discrepancies appear even in the vernacular short story. As readers of Ming and Qing fiction, we are trained not to dwell on such moments, but rather to sustain them without resolution or to resolve them imaginatively without remark. As we turn in the next two chapters to the stories of Ling Mengchu and Feng Menglong, published some thirty years after *The Plum in the Vase* first began to circulate, we will see that such unnoticed moments of illogic are central to the representation of fictional objects, and help anchor the late-imperial conception of fictionality.

CHAPTER TWO

Ling Mengchu's Shell

Among Chinese literary genres, the vernacular story (*huaben* 話本) is likely the genre we would least associate with opacity. Notoriously garrulous, unabashedly interested in the prosaic, the vernacular story seems to tell too much. Terms such as "concealed" (*yin* 隱), "secret" (*mi* 密), and "interior" (*nei* 內) are more likely to refer to the physical location of objects in the vernacular short story than to be thought of as an apt description of its aesthetic. Indeed, we rarely link the words "vernacular" and "aesthetic," in part because we believe that vernacular fiction lays itself bare, that it contains few of the productive ellipses of the classical tale. Yet even as the loquaciousness of the vernacular seems to suggest an aesthetic of "what you see is what you get," many of these stories find ways to let us know that what you see is *not* what you get, that perception in fact falls short of full knowing or possession. The hidden aesthetic question in the vernacular tale, then, is the relation between exposition and enigma.

Ling Mengchu's "A Man Whose Fortune Has Turned Coincidentally Happens Across Oranges from Dongting" features a fabular reptilian shell that hides luminous pearls in its crevices, pearls that remain unseen until a Persian trader buys the shell and reveals them to the naïve Chinese merchant who found the shell and fell for its charms. The tale's protagonist is an educated young man whose given name is Wen Shi 文實 and literary name Ruoxu 若虛; he tries his hand at business, attempting to sell fans on which he has inscribed plagiarized calligraphy and paintings by famous artists. He is implicitly punished for his venality when the counterfeited fans mold in the humidity of Beijing. It is only when he no longer attempts to think strategically that he gains wealth beyond conception. The story depicts a long sea voyage to foreign lands, and the ethnographic encounter with other cultures furnishes a premise for thinking about contrasting systems of valuation. The story's deeper concern, however, is to diminish the importance of mercantile valuation itself by describing an ineluctable affinity between character and object that suggests implicit and unarticulated forms of valuation. This ineluctable affinity makes visible an opacity in both character and object. The useless shell is an enigma, but it has a singularity that allows Wen to feel that he alone recognizes its potential.

Wen's given and literary names recall terms used in Chinese literary criticism to designate the historical circumstances described in a text (*shi* 實) and the imaginative envisioning of those circumstances (*xu* 虛). The character 文 (*wen*) refers to pattern, writing, or literature. The interplay of these terms in the story comments on a fundamental question: How does vernacular fiction create verisimilitude? The story plays games with hidden ellipses, in which bits of information that had been available in the story's classical precedent are withheld in the vernacular version unbeknownst to its readers. These hidden ellipses contribute to the story's creation of a sense of verisimilitude. The text then toys with the literary terms *xu* and *shi* to develop a line of thinking regarding the relation of historical circumstance to literary text. Ultimately, the tale shows that historical circumstance is not antecedent to the literary text—the notion that there is a historical world external to the literary text is a fiction that the literary text itself creates.

LING MENGCHU'S PROLOGUE TALE: THE ANIMACY OF SILVER

Most critics who discuss Ling Mengchu's tale have omitted mention of the prologue story, but it is worth beginning with the prologue because it addresses the question of hidden value in terms so concrete as to be almost cartoonish. Set in the Song dynasty, the prologue seemingly presents the thinking of an older, simpler time with regard to the relation between materiality and value. It tells us that capital literally has a life of its own, that it cannot be controlled by human actions and decisions. These are conclusions that Wen, the protagonist of the main tale, will reach in the course of his adventures in overseas trade. Because the very animacy of capital allows it to escape the confines of human strategies, it exceeds the valuations of any particular system. The discovery that valuation is a cultural fiction strengthens, rather than weakens, the notion that capital is animate.

In the prologue tale, silver is fetishized as a sensuous object that has a mercurial presence and controls its own fate. The prologue tale features a miser, Jin Weihou 金維厚, a professional middleman (經紀行中人) who is a precursor to the Persian middleman we will encounter in the main tale. He conceives a strategy to achieve wealth to pass on to his sons: he reserves the bits of silver of good quality that come his way and melts them into large ingots, tying red thread around the "waist" of each one. The ingots are kept by his pillow, where he fondles and plays with them before falling asleep each night. By his seventieth birthday he has accumulated eight ingots, tied in four pairs of two. He tells his sons he intends to present them with these ingots, which, he states proudly, have been kept by his pillow, never once used or even touched (永不動用的).[1]

That night Jin goes to bed a bit tipsy, and in his drunkenness gazes at the ingots gleaming by his pillow, caressing them as he chuckles to himself. He is half-asleep when he hears the sound of footsteps by his bed. When he lifts the bed curtain, he sees eight stalwart men (*da han* 大漢) by his bedside wearing white robes, their waists tied with red sashes. The former ingots bow and advance, telling him that they were given human shape thanks to his excessive love.

Now, however, their allotted time with him has reached its end; they have no karmic affinity with his sons. They state that they will "seek refuge with a man surnamed Wang in a certain village of a certain province" (往某縣某村王姓某者投托) and promise that if their karmic affinity with him is not exhausted, they will meet again.[2] Jin wakes to find that this was all a dream—and yet the ingots are gone. Tremendously distressed, he travels to the home of the man surnamed Wang whom the ingots had mentioned, where indeed he finds them. Although Jin bemoans his loss, he states that he feels no resentment because clearly his dream shows fate at work. He asks that he be allowed "only to look at the ingots one more time, to end this old man's affair of the heart" (但只求取出一看, 也完了老漢心事).³

As a professional middleman, the aptly surnamed Jin (whose last name could be translated as "gold" or "money") inhabits a world in which objects are abstracted and fungible. Yet the ingots have an auratic particularity that is evident in their personification. Jin's relation to his eight ingots is clearly eroticized, even homoerotic; as the ingots themselves tell him, his loving caresses have given them human form.⁴ Oddly, given that their defining characteristic as material objects is Jin's effort to cast uniform silver ingots, they seem the sort of object that should least elicit this qualitative fascination. The materiality of the ingots should be subsumed into abstraction, but there is a residue that resists.

The ingots, then, encapsulate a contradiction: they bodily incarnate a form of capital whose standardization has been hard won (as Jin's efforts to save the best bits of silver he receives in the context of his everyday commercial exchanges suggest).⁵ Yet as they take human form and speak of their own fates, they seem to recall a potentially animate world of things reminiscent of precapitalist exchange.⁶ Here capital, the ur-incarnation of the commodity fetish, has become a fetish in the eighteenth-century European sense of the word: the ingots are material objects personified. The story of the ingots graphically illustrates how an earlier notion of fetishism might adhere within commodity fetishism and even enable it.⁷

The ingots, as the anthropomorphized incarnation of value, have the ability to hide themselves. This capacity gives them a value beyond their silver content. It is not that value is obscured only to be detected by the discerning observer, but rather that value incarnate has a mercurial presence—it appears and disappears of its own volition. Otherwise put, because the ingots can make themselves disappear, they control the possessor's relation to them; this is what grants them animacy.

Prior to Jin's caresses, the ingots had the characteristic properties of the commodity fetish: their material specificity was of little interest, their fungibility being their relevant feature. As the ultimate object of transaction, the silver was presumed to have no volition. The anthropomorphized ingots have desire and purpose, know themselves to have their own fates (*ming* 命), and are absolutely clear that humans do not control the conditions of their exchange. They disappear when Jin attempts to pass them on; they were his only if he did not use them. They control the conditions under which their valuation becomes possible. Resisting circulation on any terms but their own, they refuse to be reduced to an abstraction, to be dulled or diminished by becoming capital.

Because it takes place during the Song dynasty, the prologue story initially appears to propose an older way of thinking about capital than we will find in the main tale, which takes place in the Chenghua 成化 reign period of the Ming (1465–1487). But the productive contradiction in which elusiveness gives capital a value beyond its capacity to be exchanged suggests that this notion has achieved significance and gained currency in part because of the symbolic pressures exerted by money and the mercantile system during the seventeenth century.[8] Rather than describing a vanished mode of thought, the prologue story proposes a way of thinking about things that adheres even within the relentless world of commodity exchange.[9] The prologue story, then, seems a parable in which the conceptualization of the ingots in terms of their exchange is trumped by an insistence that they have something ineffable controlling valuation itself. They have volition as well as relationships with specific characters. Like the shell that we will encounter shortly, they can only be found or happened upon; their will surpasses the will of the humans who would possess them.

THE FANS AND THE ORANGES: SPECIE VALUE AND SUBSTANCE VALUE

The main story furthers the concern incipient in the prologue, set several hundred years earlier, regarding the unintelligibility of objects in a mercantile culture. As the pairing of the protagonist's given name Wen Shi 文實 and literary name Ruoxu 若虛 might suggest, he is a failed literatus who has tried his luck as a tutor in residence to gentry families only to be disdained for his shallow learning. Rather than merely making much of the way in which Wen's literary learning actually lacks substance, the text uses the play on words inherent in his paired given and literary names to introduce the notion that *wen* 文 (writing or marking) that seems *shi* 實 (substantive, concrete, factual) may become *ruo xu* 若虛 (as if insubstantive, indeterminate, imagined) in the context of commercial exchange. The story plays with various perspectives regarding the combination of *xu* and *shi*. It is not just that the insubstantial seems substantive (*xu ruo shi* 虛若實) but that the substantive seems insubstantial (*shi ruo xu* 實若虛), so that which is insubstantial but seemingly substantive (*xu ruo shi* 虛若實) appears substantive but seemingly insubstantial (*shi ruo xu* 實若虛). As these reversals might suggest, the terms *xu* and *shi* are linked in such a way as to create an elaborate shell game in which value seems self-evident, but then, through a sleight of hand, disappears.

The terms *shi* and *xu* have significances in late-imperial literary criticism that will allow us to link such concerns regarding the elusive intelligibility of the thing to conceptions of fictional verisimilitude. In Chinese poetics, *shi* designates couplets that describe a historical scene; this usage predates the usage in fiction. *Xu*, by contrast, is used to describe the space of subjective coloring with feeling or opinion. In critical writings on Chinese fiction and drama, the terms *xu* and *shi* have quite specific meanings. The terms speak to the degree to which the narrative is based on historical events: *shi* refers to the historical events that undergird the story, whereas *xu* refers to the imaginative component.[10] The terms also may refer to the directness of presentation; elements that are directly presented are described as *shi*, whereas elements that are indirectly presented are characterized as *xu*.[11] *Xu*, because it connotes insubstantiality and emptiness, embodies the principle of constant mutation, and so seems to embody a wider range of meanings than *shi*.[12] It is precisely because the significance of *shi* seems readily available that *xu* gains importance as an indefinable quality. But although the significance of *shi* seems transparent, it is likewise capacious; perhaps only because it signals solidity, actuality, and concreteness does it appear more readily grasped. Both *xu* and *shi* are terms that resist encapsulation; *xu* in particular is a term that almost exaggerates its own capaciousness.

The notion that fiction and drama ideally are formed from an admixture of *xu* and *shi* was developed around the time that Ling Mengchu wrote this story. The notion that each quality should contain the other became an ideal, as encapsulated by Li Rihua's 李日華 (1565–1635) phrase "render the *xu* more *shi*, and the *shi* more *xu*" (虛者實之, 實者虛之).[13] Jin Shengtan's 金聖嘆 (1610?–1661) commentary on *The Water Margin*, published in 1644, used the phrase "*shi* within *xu*, and *xu* within *shi*" (虛中有實, 實中有虛) as a form of praise.[14] As is the case with other dyads in traditional Chinese thought, such as the pairing of *you* 有 (being) and *wu* 無 (nothingness), *xu* and *shi* were thought to be generated from each other, so that *shi* took form in the extremes of *xu*. In the words of Ye Xie 葉燮 (1627–1703), "as *xu* and *shi* mutually take shape, presence and absence are mutually established" (虛實相成, 有無互立).[15] Ling Mengchu's story uses the playful juxtaposition of *shi* and *xu* in Wen's given and literary names to show us that the substantive and insubstantial not only contain each other but are immanent in each other.

Wen, who is an incorrigible failure in business, hears that fans from his native Suzhou sell well in Beijing. He hits upon the idea of having well-known artists inscribe calligraphy on some fans of high quality. A few strokes of the brush from celebrities such as Wen Zhenheng 文震亨 (1585–1645) and Shen Zhou 沈周 (1427–1509) instantly make his fans many times more valuable. Wen then takes fans of middling value and plagiarizes the calligraphy. But in the unusual humidity of Beijing that year, the fans decorated with calligraphy and painting—both the originals and the counterfeits—are damaged by mold. By a strange coincidence, the only fans not ruined by the humidity are the ones he left blank because they were originally so cheaply made. He sells these blank fans, but the proceeds only enable him to pay for his return trip home. He has made no profit and lost his capital to boot.

The embellishments inscribed on the fans focus our attention on the value added by the famed calligraphers and the plagiarism of their work, so that we remain somewhat indifferent to interrogating the valuation of the blank fans; in contrast to the excitingly unpredictable valuation of the inscribed fans, the value of the uninscribed fans seems straightforward. The unembellished fans thus furnish a kind of false bottom. This dynamic will become more marked in the next episode, in which Wen embarks on an overseas voyage with a group of merchant friends.

After his business failures, Wen is cured of the notion that he might make a profit. He has no capital, just a bit of silver that his friend Zhang Shihuo 張識貨 (literally, "Zhang who knows merchandise") has lent him. Directly before he boards ship, he sees some oranges from Lake Dongting for sale, and hits upon the idea of buying some of this fruit, famous for its fragrance, to treat his companions on board. When he brings the oranges on board the ship, however, his shipmates exclaim sarcastically, "Mr. Wen's precious merchandise has arrived" (文先生寶

貨來也).¹⁶ He hangs his head in shame and leaves the oranges buried in their baskets until the boat arrives at its destination. When the ship docks at a foreign country named Jiling 吉零, Wen's shipmates depart to sell their wares, and he is left alone.¹⁷ He takes out the oranges to check for mold, and a crowd of natives assembles, attracted by the brilliance of the fruit, which they have never before seen. A man in the crowd ventures to ask the price. Wen cannot understand the language of this country, but a sailor raises one finger as a joke: one coin per orange. Wen has no idea how much the coins he receives are worth, nor has he any way of weighing the oranges. He has no way of estimating or calculating during these transactions at all. He simply accepts the cheapest coinage of the country, which is silver marked with pictures of seaweed, one coin per orange.

As he begins to run out of oranges, Wen raises the price, pretending that he would rather keep the remainder for himself. A customer claims that he will buy all the remaining oranges to present in tribute to the Khan, and offers him a different sort of coinage, silver marked with trees. Wen refuses, saying he wants only the kind he received before. The stranger then offers a coin with dragon and phoenix markings. When Wen refuses again, the stranger laughs sardonically, saying that these coins are worth many times the coins with depictions of seaweed. Wen sticks to his guns: for each orange, he wants three of the coins embossed with seaweed.

When the transaction is finished, he weighs the silver. By accepting the least valuable coins, he has gained a much greater weight in silver than he would have had he paid attention to the markings on the coins. Since the markings on the coins are meaningless to the Chinese, he traded as though there were no such thing as specie value, accepting only the substance value of the silver.¹⁸ Despite his attempt to strategize and bargain—he did, after all, raise the price when the oranges become scarcer—he refused to treat silver as currency. His failed attempt to create capital in the episode of the fans seems to have shocked him from the mercantile age back to an era reminiscent of the story's prologue.

The markings on the coins distinguish specie value from substance value. To borrow the terms of the story—the markings, as if insubstantial (*ruoxu*) to Wen, have the effect of making the substance value of silver appear to be truly substantive. Like the blank fans, the silver furnishes a false bottom. It seems to have a concrete value outside a particular place and time. However, when we are told that the people of Jiling do not pay for cloth with silver but only with other goods, it becomes clear that the valuation of silver is culturally specific. Even the value of silver, then, is a cultural fiction; it too is as if insubstantial, *ruoxu*. In this regard, the text rejects the notion that materiality precedes signification; the unmarked silver does not have value in and of itself.

As Patrick Hanan has observed, Ling Mengchu's stories tell us that it is useless to try to control one's destiny.[19] In this story, that concern takes shape precisely because *wen* (writing, inscription) that seems *shi* (substantive) becomes *ruoxu* (as though insubstantial) once it enters a new geographical context. The relativity of value is what makes strategizing unprofitable; there is no way of appreciating the degree to which value is relative because the units of valuation are inaccessible. Thus an encounter with another culture exposes the very claim that specie value is substantive (*shi*), and in fact shows it to be insubstantial (*ruoxu*). The play between Wen Shi's own given name, Shi, and literary name, Ruoxu, speaks to the inability to control one's fate.

THE SHELL: THE HIDDENNESS OF VALUE

The story's interest in exploring the significance of ethnographic encounter in revealing hidden sources of value reaches an apogee in its final episode, in which Wen Ruoxu finds an enormous shell on a deserted island and drags it on board ship to keep as a souvenir. Unbeknownst to him and the other Chinese merchants, hidden in its recesses are two dozen rare pearls with a marvelous capacity to emit light. Once the ship docks in Fujian, a Persian merchant comes to evaluate the merchandise of Wen's companions. He happens to see the shell and purchases it from Wen for 50,000 taels, a sum that means a lifetime of ease for Wen but a trivial amount for the Persian, who says that in his home country each one of the pearls is worth that price. Wen is ultimately rewarded with an incalculable windfall for his affection for this object with no obvious use, in what is clearly a reproach to mercantile values. As in the episode of the oranges, Wen is mocked by the other merchants for bringing such laughable merchandise on board, but then is rewarded for his lack of calculation as he encounters the alternative system of valuation or proprietary knowledge of another culture.

Wen seems to happen upon the shell as a reward for truly understanding that things have their own destinies, that humans do not control their trajectories. Sitting alone on the highest point of a desert island, mournfully meditating his fate, it occurs to him that "even though I am fortunate to have over a thousand silver coins in my purse, how do I know if it is in their fates to be mine or not?" (雖然僥幸倖有得千來個銀錢在囊內, 知他命裏是我的?不是我的?).[20] Wen's thoughts recall the sentiments of the prologue. The episode of the fans has taught him what the miser Jin did not realize: capital has a predestined fate (*ming* 命) of its own. Just as Wen is lamenting that he has no control over his fate or that of the silver, he spies the empty shell—his prize for realizing that life is not a game of skill but of chance.

The shell has no clear use, and this is central to Wen's affection for it. Wen's liking for the shell reactivates his shipmates' jibes about his inability to evaluate merchandise. As he drags it on board, the crowd of merchants laughingly speculate on the possible uses of the shell, whether in divination or for making elixirs. Wen states, "It doesn't matter whether it's useful or not; it's just unusual and I didn't have to spend any of my capital on it, so I will take it home" (不要管有用沒用, 只是希罕, 又不費本錢, 便帶了回去).[21] Wen then washes the shell out and makes it into a suitcase, keeping his valuables in it. His shipmates joke, "What a great strategy! What a great strategy! Mr. Wen is quite clever after all" (好算計! 好算計! 文先生到底是個聰明人). Their use of the term "strategy" reveals the narrow band of understanding within the mercantile mentality. The island on which the shell is found looks as though it has never been inhabited, and this ensures that the shell has no cultural context, making it possible for the shell's significance and value to be completely opaque. The island is explicitly described as a space that is not "solid ground" (*shidi* 實地), invoking the dyadic relation between *xu* and *shi* to suggest that the island is a vacant space of potential.

Once Wen's ship docks in Fujian, the shell enters an economy in which the trade in rarities stretches all the way to the Middle East. Within the context of this global trade, the shell's significance is easily legible.

Wen Shi had an affection for the shell itself; for the Persian, the shell is mere casing, packaging for the pearls. As the shell enters the hands of the Persian and is captured by this network, it is no longer described as a thing, but as precious merchandise (*baohuo* 寶貨) and then as a precious instrument (*baoju* 寶具). With each shift, the shell's rarity is more precisely indicated, but the narrative does not describe its concrete features.[22] The shell itself is an enigma, its mysterious quality stemming from its uselessness, which renders it unintelligible.

The Persian's capacity for recognition exceeds that of any Chinese. He can see through matter to find value, and he values financial transactions over all bonds of human relation, in stark contrast to the Chinese. Ling Mengchu draws here upon a stock figure of the Persian merchant, who has a superior capacity to detect hidden stores of value and so fleeces the unsuspecting Chinese. The depiction of the Persian in Ling Mengchu's story may be indebted to the depiction of Persian traders in the Song-dynasty collection *Extensive Records of the Taiping Era* (*Taiping guang ji* 太平廣記). One tale, originally drawn from the collection *A Broad Account of the Strange* (*Guang yi ji* 廣異記), describes a Persian traveling in China who spotted a square stone outside someone's door. He lingered about for some days before the owner of the residence asked him why he was loitering there. The Persian said:

> "I'd like to use the stone as a washing stone to wash clothes." He offered 2,000 cash for it. The owner was quite happy to get the cash and gave him the stone. The Persian took the stone, and when he had left the region, cut it open and took out a gem one inch in diameter. He used a knife to cut a slit in his armpit, hid the gem inside, and then returned to his home country.

> 我欲石擣帛. 因以錢二千求買. 主人得錢甚悅, 以石與之. 胡載石出, 對眾剖得徑寸珠一枚. 以刀破臂腋, 藏其內, 便還本國.[23]

The parallels with Ling Mengchu's story are clear: the Persian has an uncanny ability to spy concealed value, seeing through matter to find gems where the Chinese do not perceive them. He then extracts the gems to take to his native country and leaves the casing of the washing stone behind.

The narrator of Ling Mengchu's story assumes an ethnographic tone in describing the Persian, observing that the Persian has an eccentric last name: his surname is Ma with a jade radical, as in "agate" (*manao* 瑪瑙). Chinese Muslims often had the surname Ma 馬, the same character without the jade radical. The jade radical hidden in the pronunciation of the Persian's name is a pun that one cannot hear. It is detectable only to the observer of the written word, who discovers hidden gemstones in the Persian's name. As a professional middleman, the Persian incarnates a purely mercantile sensibility, and in that sense seems uninfluenced by the potential animacy of things. In this, he is the opposite of the poor Jin Weihou, the middleman of an earlier time who fell in love with his ingots and lost them when he believed he could control their fates.

The Persian's quickness to cast the shell aside once he has extracted the pearls stands in stark contrast to Wen's affection for it. For Wen, the shell has no value as an item of exchange, but instead has a singularity that allows him to have a specific but unspecifiable relation with it. The element of happenstance in Wen's finding the shell, the ineluctable quality of his affection for it, all point to a quality of relation that is in excess of strategic thinking, and therefore opaque. His shipmates cannot comprehend him; they do not understand his affection for the shell, and repeatedly misperceive his intentions. These moments make visible an opacity in Wen that readers might not otherwise see.

Ultimately, the tale relates this episode of the shell to the question of the historical referents of vernacular fiction. If we return to the significance of *xu* and *shi* in seventeenth-century fictional and dramatic criticism, the world of historical events, which presumably exists beyond the text, is the *shi* to the *xu* of the literary. As we have seen in this tale of false bottoms, however, that which is considered substantive often proves to be a cultural fiction. The latter part of the tale examines the relation between writing and its referents, ultimately suggesting that the fictional text is not so much an approximation of the "historical" as that "the historical" is a fiction created by the literary text.

THE CONTRACT

The signing of the contract regarding the transfer of the shell from Wen to the Persian offers a momentary fissure that allows us to pursue this question further. The contract is copied into the text with an exactitude that is customary with regard to the depiction of contracts in vernacular fiction of this period:

Big Zhang pointed to one of the men who had come with them and said, "This traveler, Zhu Zhongying, has good calligraphy," and ceded paper and brush to him. Zhu ground the ink till it was thick. He spread out the paper, raised his brush and wrote:

> A contract established by Zhang Chengyun and his friends: At present there is a traveler from Suzhou named Wen Shi, who has brought a large dragon drum shell from abroad; he presents it to the store of the Persian Ma Baoha, who is willing to offer 50,000 taels of silver; once the agreement is completed, one party will hand over the goods, the other the silver, and neither will renege on the contract. If either party does so, the penalty will be the amount plus 10%. The contract is the proof.

The two copies were the same; on the back of the paper the year, month, and date were inscribed, and beneath this Zhang Chengyun's name was written, followed by the names of the ten travelers who had accompanied them. Zhu Zhongying, because he had drafted the agreement, wrote his name last. Before the date, where there was a blank line, he placed the two contracts side by side, and wrote a single line across the seam with the words "contractual agreement," placing the names of the seller Wen Shi and the buyer Ma Baoha beneath.

張大指着同來一人道："此位客人褚中穎, 寫得好," 把紙筆讓與他. 褚客磨得墨濃, 展好紙, 提起筆來寫道:
　　立合同議單張乘運等, 今有蘇州客人文實, 海外帶來大龜殼一個, 投至波斯瑪寶哈店, 願出銀五萬兩買成. 議定立契之後, 一家交貨, 一家交銀, 各無翻悔. 有翻悔者, 罰契上加一. 合同為照.
　　一樣兩紙, 後邊寫了年月日, 下寫張乘運為頭, 一連把在坐客人十來個寫去. 褚中穎因自己執筆, 寫了落末, 年月前邊, 空行中間, 將兩紙湊着, 寫了騎縫一行, 兩邊各半, 乃是 "合同議約" 四字, 下寫 "客人文實, 主人瑪寶哈."24

As the story describes the writing of the contract, the temporality of reading shifts, so that the pace of reading approximates the pace of transcription. The text transcribes the words of the contract exactly as they are written down. We no longer have the sense of an approximation; the aesthetic has shifted from *ruoxu* (若虛) to *shi* (實). The use of Wen's given name, Wen Shi, in the contract is striking in that, up to this point, he has been identified primarily as Ruoxu. It reminds us that the written language (*wen* 文) of the contract presumes itself to be *shi* (historically factual) and must make explicit that it is not indeed *ruo xu* (as if insubstantial).

There is a fissure in the texture of the text after the replication of the words of the contract. As the contract was being written, the words of the literary text had followed Zhu Zhongying's brush. With the next words, "The two copies were the same," there is a rupture; suddenly the words in the world within the text have multiplied beyond the words on the page, so that another contract has been generated in the space of four characters. In this instant, we become aware of the impossible demand on the text. The false bottom of the fictional—the equivalent of the blank fans or the substance value of silver—is the presumption that it describes a world that exists in a fuller, more realized state beyond the boundaries of the fictional text. In fact, this fiction exists *within* rather than *beyond* the tale, hidden in its recesses like the pearls in the shell. The substantive quality of the real is a fiction created by the literary.

It becomes clear that the language of the contract is not in itself *shi* when the Persian brings out silver to seal the deal. Silver here is the standard that backs language, rendering language *shi*. "Now that they saw the dazzling white silver coming to serve as a deposit, they knew for the first time that it [the deal] was for real" (*fang zhi shi shi* 方知是實). We recall the dichotomy between substance value and specie value in the coins of Jiling and also remember that in fact the inscription of specie value made substance value seem substantive. In this instance, the language of the contract serves a function similar to the inscription of specie value. It allows silver to *act* as a standard.

The presumed transparency and accessibility of what is *shi* renders what is *xu* mysterious and evocative. As our attention is arrested by hidden recesses, information has been elided in a manner that has escaped notice. The use of the term "a certain" (*mou* 某) in the prologue provided an instance in which the literary text created a sense of a mysterious "real" that exists within the confines of the narrative and is inaccessible to its readers.[25] In the prologue, the ingots told the miser Jin that they were moving to "seek refuge with a man surnamed Wang in a certain village of a certain province" (往某縣某村王姓某投托). Notably, the address was not disclosed to the readers but only to Jin, the proof that Jin has received the address being that he eventually visits the ingots. The address is in fact stated in the classical tale or anecdote on which Ling Mengchu based the vernacular prologue; Ling Mengchu removed this detail in his vernacular adaptation, substituting the term "a certain," a detail easily passed over. Here we can see how the conventions of vernacular fiction are used to create the sense that a lived world that we cannot fully perceive exists in the interstices of the text. The source text for Ling Mengchu's prologue had been published only seventeen years before in Zhou Hui's 周暉 (b. 1546) *Nanjing Trivia* (*Jinling suoshi* 金陵瑣事). The distinctions between the classical and vernacular texts thus speak not to the values of different periods but to the choices Ling Mengchu made as he adapted the classical source text for the vernacular story.

CONCLUSION

As I noted earlier, vernacular fiction is usually thought to have a different relation to verisimilitude than does the classical tale, in that the vernacular is more explicit and less evocative. Ling Mengchu's tale shows us that the aesthetic of the vernacular story is predicated on a hidden tension between loquaciousness and ellipsis. The combination of Wen Ruoxu's personal name and style name suggests as much. This story repeatedly opposes writing or design (*wen*) that has become "as if empty" (*ruo xu*) to the substantive (*shi*)—cases in point being the contrast between the plagiarized calligraphy and the blank fans, and between the embossed images on the coins and the silver that gives them substance value. Yet as we have seen, this was just a bit of sleight of hand that contributed to the apparently substantive nature of what was coded as *shi*. This, ultimately, may be the story's comment on the relation of the literary to its referents, that through a similar dynamic fiction becomes verisimilar. The literary is not deemed deficient by being entirely unable to encapsulate the quotidian; instead, the substantive quality of the quotidian is a fiction created by the literary itself.

Ling Mengchu masterfully employs hidden, rather than evident, ellipses. We expect the vernacular version of the prologue tale to tell us more than the classical version, but actually it tells us less. The use of the character *mou* (某) to fill an ellipsis is a naturalized convention in the vernacular that becomes interesting in the context of our concern regarding the limits of verisimilitude. When a date ought to appear on a fictional bill of divorce or contract, the convention in vernacular fiction is to insert the character *mou* (某), so that the text reads "a certain year, a certain month, a certain date" (某年某月某日). Or alternatively, as in the case of the contract for the Persian's purchase of the tortoise shell, the text simply reads, "on the back of the paper the year, month and date were inscribed" (後邊寫了年月日). In these instances, the narrative telegraphs the fact that it is a literary text. As Ling Mengchu's vernacular story omits specific information given in the classical anecdote that is its source, it creates a hidden ellipsis that emphasizes the alignment of the vernacular version with the fictional as opposed to the historical.

Through such means, the fictional text creates the sense that there is a limit to what the readers of the narrative, rather than the characters, can be told, so that the true "real" remains inside the story, in the world of the characters, and the approximation is left on the page for the reader. The miser Jin knows the address to which the ingots remove themselves; the reader does not. At these moments, the literary text is telling us that it is not a failed approximation of historical circumstance. Rather, the text suggests that the action has moved beyond the field of vision afforded by the literary text. This creates the sense that perception falls short of possession, that the reality interior to the text can only be partially apprehended. It is by this inscription of a falling short that vernacular fiction creates verisimilitude.

CHAPTER THREE

Du Shiniang's Jewel Box

Like Ling Mengchu's tale about a shell that contains untold wealth in the form of unseen pearls, Feng Menglong's story "Du Shiniang Sinks the Jewel Box in Anger" concerns a casket that conceals silver, pearls, and gems of value beyond imagination. Originally published in Feng Menglong's 1624 collection *Stories to Caution the World*, "Du Shiniang" is an oft-anthologized text that has had contemporary afterlives in regional opera as well as film. It tells the familiar saga of a courtesan whose devotion to her literati lover is underscored by his haplessness and witlessness. Du's lover Li Jia 李甲, a perennial student at the imperial academy, impoverishes himself by romancing her in the pleasure quarters, and is no longer welcomed by the madam of the brothel once he is destitute. Du prepares to buy herself out of prostitution and plans for their joint future as a married couple. But Li Jia, desperate for money, sells her to a salt merchant named Sun Fu 孫富 for 1,000 taels of silver, not knowing that the valuables she has stored with an eye to their joint future are worth far more. Du Shiniang jumps to a watery death after revealing the jewels stored in her signal possession, a mysterious box.

The scholar Shen Guangren has rightly argued that Du Shiniang would simply be another courtesan were it not for the box, that the equivalence between courtesan and box suggested by the title of Feng Menglong's story is what renders Du Shiniang so memorable.[1] Du Shiniang's box is an emblem of her force of character, its unfathomable depths pointing to Du Shiniang's own. I would add, however, that an unresolved quality to the metaphorical mapping between courtesan and box is what gives the figural equivalence its particular force. In this chapter I ask how the material features of the box might shape this metaphorical mapping or, in other words, how the formal properties of the box might contribute to the structure of the narrative (see figure 3.1).

The elliptical quality of the description of the box originates in a biography that was the classical source for Feng Menglong's tale, Song Maocheng's 宋懋澄 (1569–after 1620) "The Faithless Lover" (*Fuqing nong zhuan* 負情儂傳). "The Faithless Lover" was published in 1612, only twelve

FIGURE 3.1 Dressing case, polychrome inlaid lacquer on a wooden core, Qing dynasty. *Source*: Victoria and Albert Museum.

years before Feng Menglong published "Du Shiniang Sinks the Jewel Box in Anger," and is included in the section titled "Biographies" (*zhuan* 傳) in Song Maocheng's collected writings, the *Jiuyue ji* 九籥集.[2] It is a biography not of the courtesan Du Shiniang but of the man who betrays her, the faithless lover of the title. The box plays an insignificant role. Feng Menglong's revision, however, gave the courtesan and the jewel box a shared central position.[3] Feng also paired "Du Shiniang" with the preceding story in *Stories to Caution the World*, "Zhao Chun'er Restores Prosperity to the Cao Farmstead" (趙春兒重旺曹家莊), which similarly concerns a courtesan who hides her savings in an innocent-looking receptacle, a porcelain jar, in order to secure a future with her literati lover. The pairing offers readers clues as to how to interpret the enigmatic courtesan and her box.

In Feng Menglong's revision, Du Shiniang's box is a locus of hidden value, its depths only partially manifested when the courtesan reveals the gems and precious stones within its recesses. A plethora of terms describe the box. One character refers to the box as a dressing case or make-up stand (*zhuang tai* 妝臺); the narrator describes it as a box for writing implements traced with gold (*miaojin wenju* 描金文具). The inconsistency of these terms suggests that the materiality of the box partially eludes us. We can look to the various clues the text furnishes regarding the shape, size, and form of the box to better understand how the box can function as a figure for Du Shiniang, but ultimately the power of the analogy lies in the inconsistency of the metaphorical mapping between courtesan and box, which renders Du Shiniang an enigma.

OPACITY

"Du Shiniang Sinks the Jewel Box in Anger" has become famous in the modern era in part because it meets the contemporary expectation for a protagonist with a presumed psychic depth. Contrary to what we might expect, however, this psychic depth is not delineated in the text via the expression of thought or feeling. In the hierarchy of characters, the more the narrator discloses of a character's thought process, the shallower the character seems. The sense that Du Shiniang has knowledge that she chooses not to disclose is critical to the construction of an interior life that appears to exist beyond what surfaces on the page.

Psychic depth, then, is not suggested by the representation of thought. When Du Shiniang continues to see Li Jia even after he has spent all his money in the brothel, the madam, at her wit's end, tells Shiniang that Li Jia must either cease to see her or redeem her from prostitution. Du Shiniang masterminds her own release from the brothel, first negotiating with the madam, then lending Li Jia 150 taels with which to obtain the remainder of the funds needed to redeem her. She bargains the madam down from 1,000 taels to 300 and gains a ten-day period in which to find the funds—all features of the vernacular tale that were not present in the classical version. But even though Du Shiniang's strategies place her in control of the plot, the narrative never discloses her thoughts.[4]

The vernacular story creates a garrulousness in the characters surrounding Du Shiniang that highlights her enigmatic quality. For example, the story includes a scene not found in "The Faithless Lover," in which Du Shiniang bargains with the madam of her brothel regarding the amount of time Li Jia will have to buy her out, winning an extension from three days to ten. During the scene in which Du Shiniang and the old woman bargain, readers are privy to the old woman's internal calculations, but we are not given a reciprocal access to Du Shiniang's thoughts. The narrator uses various means to explore what is going on in the old woman's mind, from the narration of subverbal states ("Knowing that it was impossible for the penniless Li Jia, who had pawned everything he owned, to come up with any money, the madam . . ." 媽媽曉得李甲囊無一錢,衣衫都典盡了,料他沒處設法) to direct quotation of thought as speech ("The madam thought to herself, 'That miserable wretch has nothing left now but his bare hands. Even if I allow him a hundred days, he won't be able to do anything'" 這窮漢一雙赤手, 便限他一百日, 他那裡來銀子).[5] In contrast, Du Shiniang's speech is narrated, but her thoughts are never described, even in oblique fashion. In a sense, this opacity is necessary to resist her commodification, to ensure that she does not seem to take part in the kind of calculation regarding her worth in which the other characters are engaged. Yet tragically, it also makes possible her commodification; her silence produces the misunderstandings that ultimately lead Li Jia to sell her to Sun Fu.

By rendering the figure of the courtesan opaque in this way, the narrative ups the ante regarding recognition of the courtesan's true qualities. "Du Shiniang" draws on the concern regarding recognition in the literature of connoisseurship to suggest that the one true owner of an object is not the one who recognizes its monetary value but the one who recognizes its charms and is willing to sacrifice to remain in relation with it.[6] Feng Menglong created a new character in the vernacular story not found in its classical source, that of Li Jia's friend Liu Yuchun 柳遇春. Liu Yuchun, from Li Jia's hometown, is also a student at the National University, and explores the pleasure quarters with Li Jia before Li Jia gives himself over completely to the relationship with Du Shiniang. Liu Yuchun is a sympathetic spectator who serves as a barometer of understanding. He is the only character to mention Du Shiniang's personal name, Mei 媺, a character so unusual that it is typically mistranscribed as "Wei," as Shuhui Yang notes.[7] "Shiniang" is not a name but rather means "Du the Tenth," which presumably indicates her place in the fictive hierarchy of kinship in the brothel.

When Li Jia is unable to raise the funds to redeem Du Shiniang, Liu Yuchun, moved by Du Shiniang's devotion, borrows the remaining 150 taels that Li Jia needs. Du Shiniang had given Li Jia a mattress of cotton wadding in which she has hidden her savings, telling him that hidden inside the mattress were 150 taels. The matching sums produced by Du Shiniang and Liu Yuchun underscore that it is Liu Yuchun, not Li Jia, who is Du Shiniang's true match. He is the first to have faith in her trustworthiness, and his recognition of her steadfastness underscores Li Jia's lack thereof.

The mysterious box of the title that becomes an emblem of Du Shiniang's inscrutability is first introduced as a parting gift from Du's neighboring courtesans in the pleasure quarters after she redeems herself from servitude. A servant hands Du Shiniang a box for writing implements traced with gold "locked so securely that there was no clue as to its contents. Shiniang neither opened it nor declined the gift, but busied herself in saying thanks" (封鎖甚固，正不知什麼東西在裡面。十娘也不開看，也不推辭，但殷勤作謝而已).[8] Thus the narrator underscores from the introduction of the box that its contents are a mystery to all but Du Shiniang. She keeps the box locked, only opening it when Li Jia finds himself without funds for the journey. At the moment the box is first opened, the narrative deflects the reader's attention from the box, first redirecting it to Li Jia and his shame at not being able to provide for the couple, and second, following his line of sight to a red purse that Du Shiniang takes out of the box and throws onto the table:

> Li was standing beside her, but he felt too ashamed to look into the box. All he saw was a red silk purse, which Shiniang took out. She threw the purse on the table and said, "Won't you open it and see what's inside?" When he picked it up, Li thought it was quite heavy. He opened it and found it was filled with pieces of silver amounting to fifty taels. Shiniang locked the box again without mentioning what else it contained. Instead, she said to him, "Thanks to the kindness of my sisters, we have not only enough money for this journey but also some to spare for our stay south of the river."

> 公子在傍自覺慚愧，也不敢窺覷箱中虛實。只見十娘在箱裡取出一個紅絹袋來，擲於桌上道："郎君可開看之。"公子提在手中，覺得沉重，啟而觀之，皆是白銀，計數整五十兩。十娘仍將箱子下鎖，亦不言箱中更有何物。但對公子道："承眾姊妹高情，不惟途路不乏，即他日浮寓吳越間，亦可稍佐吾夫妻山水之費矣。"⁹

Just as Li Jia's shame prevents him from seeing the contents of the box, the *description* of Li Jia's shame prevents us as readers from seeing the box. In deflecting our attention, it plants an enigma. This structure of relation, where the spectator's response is highlighted even as the contents of the box remain a mystery, grants the box an opacity that mirrors Du Shiniang's own. The unrecognized value of the jewel box speaks to that of the protagonist herself.

The opacity of Du Shiniang contrasts with the transparency of Sun Fu, the conniving son of a merchant family; his shockingly obvious plot to win Du Shiniang from Li Jia is explicated by the narrator at every step. Sun Fu's name itself suggests that his character is easily read; his personal name, which means "wealth," is unthinkably vulgar. Sun Fu, a hardened dissolute, determines to meet Du Shiniang after hearing her sing in her exquisite voice. He attempts to gain the attention of Li Jia by donning a leopard-fur cap and fox-fur cape and leaning against his window to chant two lines from the early Ming poet Gao Qi's "Nine Poems on the Plum Blossom."¹⁰ Sun Fu, like Li Jia, has purchased a position at the imperial university; unlike Li Jia, he is descended from a long line of salt merchants. This is the kind of detail that is reassuringly familiar to readers of late Ming fiction, for whom the term "salt merchant" is equated with imposture. A descendant of salt merchants chanting lines from Gao Qi's poems on the plum blossom signals a kind of imposture of the most threadbare sort. Li Jia, on hearing the poem, believes that there must be a like-minded man on the next boat, and falls into Sun's trap.

Imposture, however, is not the primary concern of "Du Shiniang." Rather, the transparency of Sun Fu's imposture is a foil that underscores the opacity of Du Shiniang herself. Sun invites Li Jia to go ashore for a meal, and he soon takes advantage of Li Jia's concerns about funds for his journey. The narrator describes the facial expressions Sun Fu assumes as he lays a trap for Li Jia, offering to take Du Shiniang from him for 1,000 taels.[11] Sun Fu is more capable than Li Jia of reading character—he is able to read Li Jia himself quite easily—but his capacity for recognition is not coupled with faithfulness of intent.

If we were to rank the characters from most easily read to least, Sun Fu and the madam of the brothel would clearly top the list. The vulgarity of these minor characters is indicated not only by their thoughts but by the fact that their thoughts are described at all. For example, when Li Jia hands the madam the 300 taels with which to buy Du Shiniang out of prostitution, the expression on her face reveals the madam's intentions: "The madam, who had not expected him to produce any money, was dumbstruck. Her face hardened, and she looked as if she were going to back out of the deal" (鴇兒不料公子有銀, 嘿然變色, 似有悔意).[12] The facial expressions of vulgar characters are relatively transparent; the characters are minor precisely because they yield so readily to interpretation.

If, in "Du Shiniang Sinks the Jewel Box in Anger," transparency devalues, then opacity enhances value. To the degree that Du Shiniang's elliptical interiority is emblematized by the box, she transcends the shallowness of the other characters whose motives are as easily read as their faces. This may seem self-evident to modern readers, but it is a system of valuation more relevant to the classical tale than to vernacular fiction. Feng Menglong's vernacular revision of Song Maocheng's classical account, then, imports the hierarchy of values that contrasts the economy of classical prose with the loquaciousness of the vernacular, granting Du Shiniang an opacity born of the elegant reticence of the classical biography "The Faithless Lover."

"ZHAO CHUN'ER RESTORES PROSPERITY TO THE CAO FARMSTEAD"

In its original context, "Du Shiniang" is one of a pair of stories in Feng Menglong's anthology *Stories to Caution the World*. The story that directly precedes "Du Shiniang" in the anthology, "Zhao Chun'er Restores Prosperity to the Cao Farmstead," creates a set of expectations that would have given readers an idea as to how to read Du Shiniang's intentions despite the story's emphasis on her opacity. Both this story and Song Maocheng's "The Faithless Lover" provide interpretive contexts for "Du Shiniang" that have been lost as it has been repeatedly republished in anthologies of Ming vernacular stories and premodern Chinese literature.

"Zhao Chun'er" and "Du Shiniang" each concerns a courtesan who has fallen in love with the scion of a wealthy family who has squandered his inheritance in the pleasure quarters. In both stories, the courtesan, realizing that she cannot trust her young lover with the valuables she has saved to ensure a joint future, hides those valuables in a vessel that she keeps secret. In contrast to "Du Shiniang," "Zhao Chun'er" ends happily. After waiting fifteen long years for her beloved to mature and mend his ways, the courtesan accompanies her husband to the capital. There, using the silver she had buried in a porcelain jar beneath her loom, he purchases an appointment and begins his official career. We might expect that the order of the two stories would be reversed, that the reassuringly familiar comedic ending of "Zhao Chun'er" would follow the tragic example of "Du Shiniang." The fact that "Zhao Chun'er" precedes "Du Shiniang" suggests that it was meant to provide a set of instructions for reading "Du Shiniang."

"Du Shiniang" and "Zhao Chun'er" share several details that link the plots beyond these shared circumstances. In both stories, the young literatus visits his relatives to ask for funds to make a journey, but all decline to help. The courtesan then offers to seek aid from her sworn sisters to raise funds for her lover's journey, while secretly tapping into the funds she has saved for him. In "Zhao Chun'er," the moment in which Chun'er mentions her sworn sisters feels tacked on belatedly; we never glimpse these friends, as we do in "Du Shiniang." It is quite possible that Feng Menglong inserted this detail in "Zhao Chun'er" to further the parallelism between the two stories.

After reading "Zhao Chun'er," readers would suspect that Du Shiniang's mysterious box contains not gifts from her sister courtesans but wealth that she has wisely stored for the couple to live on in later years, and that Du Shiniang has kept the contents of the box a secret because she cannot yet trust that Li Jia has abandoned his dissolute ways. There is a signal difference between the two stories, however. The narrator of "Zhao Chun'er" informs readers that the courtesan is loyal to her lover by divulging her private thoughts. In contrast, the narrator of "Du Shiniang" never speaks of the courtesan's thoughts or motivations. Perhaps, because in "Zhao Chun'er" the characters' thoughts are not obscured, there is no need for a figural equivalence between the courtesan and a signal object to govern our interpretation.

THE BOX AND THE COURTESAN

The metaphorical equivalence that Feng Menglong establishes between Du Shiniang and the box guides us as readers, but the equivalence is complex and becomes increasingly difficult to map. The notion of an equivalence between Du Shiniang and the dressing case is first broached by Sun Fu, which suggests that perhaps we should not trust it. When Li Jia tells Sun Fu that Du Shiniang has agreed to Sun Fu's plan, he says, "It is an easy matter to exchange the silver, but I must have the beauty's dressing case as a token of trust" (兌銀易事，須得麗人妝臺為信).[13] The box stands in for Du Shiniang as the silver is exchanged. Of note, Sun Fu calls the box "the beauty's dressing case" (*liren zhuangtai* 麗人妝臺), a term that has not previously been used. He presumably has not seen the box, but simply assumes that such a box would be the courtesan's most valuable possession.

Sun Fu's suggestion that the object serves as a token of trust speaks to the way in which objects typically function in the vernacular fiction of the Ming. As we saw in chapter 1 with *The Plum in the Golden Vase*, objects are typically not emblematic of particular characters, but rather circulate, and in so doing bind characters together. We might think here of Feng Menglong's "Jiang Xingge Reencounters His Pearl Shirt," often anthologized with "Du Shiniang." There the pearl shirt of the title is an heirloom whose wayward circulation provides the clue that unveils an adulterous affair. Du Shiniang's box can be seen as such an object;

it circulates until she puts an end to its circulation (and her own) by plunging with it to her death. This ending ensures that she is forever collocated with the box.

After Sun Fu's silver has been inspected and found to be of the right color and weight, Du Shiniang asks that the box be returned so she can retrieve a travel pass allowing Li Jia to return to his hometown. Only at this point does the object begin to function in an unprecedented fashion. Li Jia unwittingly becomes Du Shiniang's assistant when she asks him to open each of the drawers in turn; she then proceeds to toss the contents of the drawers one by one into the river. For the first time, readers catch a glimpse of the contents of the box:

> At Shiniang's bidding, Li drew out the first drawer. Lo and behold, it was filled with pieces of expensive jewelry worth hundreds of taels of silver. She picked them up and tossed them in the river, to the astonishment of Li Jia, Sun Fu, and everyone else on the two boats.
>
> She then told Li to pull out another drawer, which was seen to contain jade flutes and golden pipes. Yet another drawer was filled with jade and gold objects of art worth thousands of taels of silver. Shiniang tossed them all into the water in full view of the wall of spectators now gathered on the shore. "What a pity!" they exclaimed in unison, wondering what on earth could have made this woman do such a thing.
>
> The last drawer was pulled out to reveal a small box. When it was opened, there, for all to see, was a large handful of luminous pearls as well as emeralds, cats'-eyes, and other precious objects, the likes of which none had ever seen and the value of which none could determine. Amid thunderous cheers from the onlookers, Shiniang was about to throw them in the river when Li Jia, overcome with bitter remorse, flung his arms around her and broke into wails of grief.

> 十娘叫公子抽第一層來看, 只見翠羽明璫, 瑤簪寶珥, 充牣於中, 約值數百金, 十娘遽投之江中。李甲與孫富及兩船之人, 無不驚詫。又命公子再抽一箱, 乃玉簫金管; 又抽一箱, 盡古玉紫金玩器, 約值數千金。十娘盡投之於水。舟中岸上之人, 觀者如堵。齊聲道: "可惜, 可惜!" 正不知什麼緣故。最後又抽一箱, 箱中復有一匣。開匣視之, 夜明之珠約有盈把。其他祖母綠, 貓兒眼, 諸般異

寶, 目所未睹, 莫能定其價之多少. 眾人齊聲喝采, 喧聲如雷. 十娘又欲投之於江. 李甲不覺大悔, 抱持十娘慟哭 . . .[14]

As the contents of the box are displayed, Du Shiniang finally reveals her thinking; this simultaneous unveiling reinforces the metaphorical correlation between her thoughts and the box's contents:

> "I opened the box and showed its contents in public so that you'll know that a mere thousand taels of silver are of little importance to me. I am not unlike a jewel box that contains precious jade, but you have eyes that fail to recognize value. Alas, I was not born under a lucky star. Having just freed myself from the tribulations of a courtesan's life, I find myself abandoned again. All those present will testify, by the evidence of their eyes and ears, that I have not failed you in any way. It's you who have betrayed me!" There was not a dry eye among the onlookers, all of whom cursed Li for being the fickle ingrate that he was. Ashamed and exasperated, Li shed tears of remorse and was about to apologize to Shiniang when she threw herself into the middle of the current, the jewel box in her arms.

> "今日當眾目之前, 開箱出視, 使郎君知區區千金, 未為難事. 妾櫝中有玉, 恨郎眼內無珠. 命之不辰, 風塵困瘁, 甫得脫離, 又遭棄捐. 今眾人各有耳目, 共作證明, 妾不負郎君, 郎君自負妾耳!" 於是眾人聚觀者, 無不流涕, 都唾罵李公子負心薄倖. 公子又羞又苦, 且悔且泣, 方欲向十娘謝罪. 十娘抱持寶匣, 向江心一跳.[15]

This speech has given rise to the critical convention that the box is a figure for Du Shiniang. Here, for the first time, the box becomes a metaphor as Du Shiniang employs a term for box, *du* 櫝, that not only calls attention to itself as a homonym for her surname but literally contains the components of the character for the surname Du 杜 among its constituent parts. The term *du* refers to an ornate wooden box; it is used in the *Analects* to refer to boxes that contained turtle shells used for divination.[16] Du Shiniang's use of this term in the phrase, "I am not unlike a jewel box that contains precious jade, but you have eyes that fail to recognize value" (妾櫝中有玉,恨郎眼內無珠), draws upon a

64 *Du Shiniang's Jewel Box*

four-character idiom, "one who buys the box and returns the pearls" (*maidu huanzhu* 買櫝還珠), which refers to an anecdote in a philosophical text of the Warring States period, the *Han Feizi* 韓非子. A man buys an ornately decorated box containing pearls, and then returns the pearls to the astonished vendor, saying that he had wanted only the box.[17] Feng Menglong rewrites Song Maocheng's text to embed the allusion to the *Han Feizi*. When Du Shiniang accuses Li Jia of having no eyes with which to see, Feng Menglong replaces Song Maocheng's term for eyes, *tong* 瞳, with *zhu* 珠, cleverly making use of the fact that the character for "pearls" (*zhu* 珠) in the anecdote in the *Han Feizi* could refer to "eyeballs" (*yanzhu* 眼珠) in this context. The idiom "one who buys the box and returns the pearls" describes someone who cannot judge value; the translation here recognizes and incorporates its buried presence with the phrase "you have eyes that fail to recognize value." Sun Fu and Li Jia, in other words, lack judgment because they view Du Shiniang as a decorative box, and do not value her internal qualities, the gems within.

In the Chinese literary tradition, there is no history of equating women and boxes (as there is of equating jade with loyalty and romantic steadfastness); readers must be trained to perceive the analogy between the courtesan and the box and to elicit something from it. The reference to the story from the *Han Feizi* does precisely this. Even though the idiom "one who buys the box and returns the pearls" speaks to the lack of judgment of Sun Fu and Li Jia, who see only Du Shiniang's superficial qualities, there is a less obvious aspect of this reference. The anecdote from the *Han Feizi* also speaks to the puzzlement of ordinary minds, such as that of the vendor, when faced with the notion that an empty box might have value. This potentially overlooked aspect of the reference, then, directs us to consider the value of an empty box.

The emptiness of the box is key to the metaphorical mapping of courtesan and box.[18] At first glance, we might assume that the equation of the jade and gems in the box with Du Shiniang's fidelity creates a space in which her inner qualities have been described. The gems, however, stand in the way of seeing the very space of potentiality in the interior of the box. In fact, the metaphor is enlivened not so much by the objects within the box, but by the space around them. As Du Shiniang jumps into the depths of the river clasping the box, it is the empty space within the box, rather than a simple equation between Du Shiniang's fidelity and the value of the gems within, that makes the metaphorical mapping possible. To use the terms *xu* and *shi* that we explored in chapter 2, the equation between the jade and Du Shiniang's loyalty is concrete and actualized (*shi*), while the emptiness of the final box is *xu*, a space of imaginative potential.

Du Shiniang, of course, is not simply a box. The equation between two elements of a metaphor—the tenor (the subject whose properties are elaborated by the metaphor) and the vehicle (whose properties are used to describe the subject)—is never exact; the tenor can never be precisely described by the vehicle. A metaphorical mapping is thus never merely a one-to-one mapping. Most important, the material properties of the box itself are suggestive of this lack of satisfaction with a one-to-one mapping, as the narrative's successive turn from one drawer to the next indicates.

The drawers organize the final part of the narrative. In the final scene, as Du Shiniang opens the drawers, we expect to encounter gems of ever-increasing value, as though in a fable. We do not know what the contents of the next drawer will be, but can hazard a guess, because the narrative is training us to anticipate its next move. The drawers also organize the way in which we think of the metaphorical mapping of courtesan and box. Since the value of the contents of the drawers is gradated, the equation between Du Shiniang's inner qualities and the contents of the box changes with the unveiling of each drawer. It is as though the first protestation of her worth were partially eclipsed by the second and then the third. Each step acknowledges and also partially cancels out the previous one. The progression leads inexorably to the conclusion that the courtesan is worth more than the contents of the last drawer, more than the accumulated contents of the entire box. The staggered, sequential unveiling of the drawers creates a momentum that takes us beyond the box itself.

The last scene is one of gradual unveiling, as each drawer is revealed to hold gems of increasing value, the purple gold (*zijin* 紫金) of the second tier trumping the gold flutes of the first. The internal radiance of the purple gold and the luminosity of the pearls create a suggestion of Du Shiniang's own interiority.[19] In other words, her interiority has not been present from the beginning and simply been masked. Rather, this final scene makes possible the premise of interiority, insofar as it is defined not only in terms of thoughts articulated, but also thoughts unarticulated and even unperceived. We could not project interiority onto Du

Shiniang were it not for the opacity of the locked box, nor could we maintain the fiction of her interiority were it not for the box with which she jumps into the waters.

SEVENTEENTH-CENTURY BOXES

At this point we should question how the physical contours of seventeenth-century boxes might affect the metaphorical mapping between Du Shiniang and the box, as well as the potential of the box to structure the narrative. The restless quality of the metaphorical mapping can be seen in the inconsistency in the descriptions of the box itself. The discrepancies exploit an inherent vagueness in the Chinese terms for boxes. As is the case with the word "casket" in English, the Chinese terms for boxes designate *shape* rather than size. Each of the terms used to describe the box, such as *xiang* 箱 and *xia* 匣, can describe boxes of a wide variety of sizes. We must look to the surrounding text for hints regarding the size, shape, and weight of the box.

The first indication of the heft of the box occurs when Li Jia tells Shiniang that Sun Fu has requested her box as pledge. "Li reported back to Shiniang, who said, pointing at her gold-traced jewel box, 'Take it'" (公子又回復了十娘，十娘即指描金文具道："可便擡去").[20] The conventional translation of *baibao xiang* as jewel box might lead us to think that the box is relatively small in size, but the phrase translated as "take it" (擡去) suggests that it is a box of some weight, more like a trunk than a toiletry box. The black lacquer box with gold tracery shown in figure 3.2 dates from the Wanli reign, which ended four years before this story was published. Made in the imperial workshops, it was two feet by two feet eight inches, large enough that a serving boy might need to exert effort to lift it.

From the phrase "gold-traced box for writing implements," we can deduce that the box has a lacquered exterior. Gold tracing was a technique for ornamenting lacquer. Any box containing drawers required either lift-off panels or hinged doors to hold the drawers in place, since seventeenth-century drawers had no slides or guides. Hinges, however, caused wear to lacquer, and hence lacquer boxes with inner compartments had lift-off front panels held in place by vertical grooves, as we see in figure 3.3.

FIGURE 3.2 Black lacquer with gold and silver inlay with mother-of-pearl, Wanli reign (1572–1620), Ming dynasty. *Source*: Provided by the Palace Museum.

FIGURE 3.3 Carved red-lacquer box for writing implements, Ming dynasty. *Source*: Provided by the Palace Museum.

In such lacquer boxes, the interior arrangement of the box, whether drawers or a series of nested smaller boxes, was concealed. The front panel fortified the sense of an interior. This is a particularly important point for modern readers of "Du Shiniang," who would assume that the series of drawers would be apparent. The front wall gave the effect of total opacity when it was sealed in the grooves, an opacity critical to creating the space of potential that delineates the space of interiority. We can confirm that Du Shiniang's lacquered box has just such a lift-off front concealing tiered drawers when we read the line, "Shiniang took out her key and unlocked it to reveal a stack of small drawers" (十娘取鑰開鎖,內皆抽替小箱).[21] The sequential unveiling of the contents of these tiered drawers will structure not only the remaining events in the narrative but also the metaphorical mapping between Du Shiniang and the box.

Here the modern term for drawer, *chouti* 抽替, functions as an adjective ("pull-out") that can be paired with the terms employed elsewhere in the story to describe boxes, *xiang* 箱 and *xia* 匣; a drawer is literally a "pull-out box" (*chouti xia* 抽替匣 or *chouti xiang* 抽替箱). This conflation between "drawer" and "box" is not a literary device but rather indicates that seventeenth-century drawers were in essence boxes without lids, since the technology for the modern drawer did not exist. The drawers, themselves described as boxes, contain more boxes within. Du Shiniang's box itself thus has a recursive or involuted quality. These boxes are not nested miniatures of each other, however, and in that sense are not equivalent or fungible.

The Song-dynasty philologist Zhou Mi's 周密 (1232–1308) notation book *Miscellaneous Gleanings from Guixin Street* (*Guixin zashi* 癸辛雜識) described an early arrangement of drawers for organization:

> I once heard Li Shuangxi (Xianke) say, "When Li Renfu wrote his *Continuation of the Comprehensive Mirror in Aid of Governance*, he had ten wooden cabinets made, and for each cabinet made 20 boxes that could be pulled out. Every box was marked with one of the celestial ten stems; whenever he heard of something that happened during a certain year, he would make sure to store it in one of the boxes, so that he could clearly distinguish the sequencing of events. This was very orderly, and can definitely be adopted as a method."

余嘗聞李雙溪獻可云: "昔李仁甫為'長編', 作木廚十枚, 每廚作抽替匣二十枚, 每替以甲子志之, 凡本年之事, 有所聞必歸此匣, 分月日先後次第之, 井然有條, 真可為法也。"[22]

The ten wooden cabinets, each containing twenty drawers, became an organizational tool for ordering the notes Li Renfu (李仁甫, 1115–1184) made as he prepared to write the *Continuation of the Comprehensive Mirror in Aid of Governance* (續資治通鑒長編). Here the neologism *choutixia* 抽替匣 designates a box that can be pulled out—in other words, a drawer. The term *xia* 匣 is defined by the late-Ming bibliophile Gao Lian 高濂 (ca. 1527–1603) as a box with three or four layers (*ge* 格) carried on a pole and used to store implements or utensils (*qi ju* 器具). Gao Lian adds in a prescriptive tone, "there is no need to have them carved or inlaid in an effort to make them more unusual; to use *huanghuali* wood for them is sufficient."[23] Yellow pear wood (*huanghuali* 黃花梨) was an expensive wood; in his light-hearted and snobbish fashion, Gao Lian makes the point that carving or inlay could be less elegant.

The late-Ming painter and arbiter of taste Wen Zhenheng, whose paintings were plagiarized on the fans depicted in Ling Mengchu's story of chapter 2, wrote about tiered boxes in his *Superfluous Things* (*Zhangwu zhi* 長物志, 1620–1627). Clear from his phrasing is that a "box for writing implements" (*wenju xiang* 文具箱) is an object of privilege, housing curios and antiques as well as writing implements such as small inkstones, brushes, notebooks, and brush rests. Wen Zhenheng suggests that aside from those writing implements one might fill a box of three tiers or drawers (*ge* 格) with a Xuande inkstick and a Japanese black lacquered box (*xia*) of ink. In the bottom drawer he suggested placing a small box (once more using the term *xia*) of Japanese lacquer holding a tortoiseshell comb, as well as a box (*xia*) for books and curios such as a pair of small cups made of rhinoceros-horn jade.[24] Here again, the term *xia* speaks to shape rather than size. Boxes rest within other boxes, creating a structure of compartments within the tiers. The potential confusion resulting from the capaciousness of the terms for boxes and drawers makes it harder to visualize Du Shiniang's box.

In order to retrieve the box from Sun Fu, Du Shiniang claims that Li Jia's travel papers—the papers that grant permission for a student at the imperial university to return home—are in the box. When Sun Fu asks for the box, he calls it a dressing case; the narrator in the same passage tells us it is a box for writing implements. Such distinctions means less than we might assume. Terms like "dressing case" and "box for writing implements" are catch-all terms; "dressing cases" could be used to store documents and valuables as well as combs, mirrors, and ornaments. The box shown in figure 3.4 is identified as a dressing case in the collection of the Victoria and Albert Museum in London; identical boxes are labeled as document boxes in other collections.

"Du Shiniang" over-supplements its description of the box: it is a storage trunk, a box for writing implements, a dressing case with mirror stand. We can attempt to iron out the discrepancies. Perhaps

FIGURE 3.4 Dressing case made of *huanghuali* (yellow pear) wood, ca. 1550–1700. *Source*: Victoria and Albert Museum.

Sun Fu viewed the box as a dressing case rather than a box for writing implements, in keeping with his interest in Du Shiniang as a famed beauty. Perhaps he did not think that Du Shiniang would have a box for writing implements, further proof that he has misunderstood her. But the inconsistency is inherent in the terms, and crucial in underwriting the implicit relation between Du Shiniang and the box.

The examples above show us that terms for "casket" and "box" are inherently unspecific, and that moreover, terms that we might believe to be widely disparate such as "document box" and "dressing case" are interchangeable. The metaphorical mapping with Du Shiniang thus lends the box a cohesion it would not otherwise have. Du Shiniang's person lends an imagined specificity to the box, which is depicted with the lack of specificity inherent in the Chinese terms for boxes themselves. At the same time, it is the box that teaches us how to read the narrative, especially the metaphorical mapping of courtesan and box. The recursive, involuted quality of the description of the box suggests that the metaphorical mapping is both agglutinated and imprecise.

Readers often imagine the box that Du Shiniang's fellow courtesans give her to be a small casket filled with jewels. But as we have seen, that box is more like a trunk that the servants require effort to lift. Du Shiniang's final words and actions cement the confusion among boxes. The text describes the box with which Du Shiniang plunges into the water as a *baoxia* 寶匣, not as a *baoxiang* 寶箱. Du Shiniang plunges to her death not with the box of the title—the larger trunk (*xiang* 箱) whose contents she has poured into the water bit by bit—but with the final box (*xia* 匣) within the last drawer (*xiang* 箱). The hazy relation in the reader's mind between the box transferred between Sun Fu and Du Shiniang's boats and the smaller casket that she clasps as she jumps serves the metaphorical relation between Du Shiniang and the box. In effect, she becomes identified with whichever box preserves the greater degree of mystery.

SONG MAOCHENG'S "THE FAITHLESS LOVER"

Feng Menglong revised the ending of Song Maocheng's "The Faithless Lover" to better establish the equivalence between the courtesan and the box. In "The Faithless Lover," Du Shiniang jumps to her death holding not the box but a fistful of gleaming pearls. Song Maocheng closes by relating that the ghost of Du Shiniang appeared to him as he was writing her story. He remarks that he dreamed of "a figure with long hair hanging down who spoke to me in a woman's voice" (夢被髮而其音婦人者謂余曰), employing a distorted syntax that emphasizes the indistinct quality of the ghostly figure. The figure threatened him should he continue to write, saying, "I feel grieved that I was so bad a judge of character, and I would be ashamed to have other people know of it. Lately, by the mercy of the gods of the underworld, I have been permitted to govern the winds and waves and visit good fortune or bad upon mankind. If you write my story, be sure that I shall bring your illness back" (姜自恨不識人，羞令人間知有此事. 近幸冥司見憐，令姜稍司風波，間豫人間禍福. 若郎君為姜傳奇，姜將使君病作).[25] Because of this threat from Du Shiniang's ghost, and because the next day he did fall ill, Song Maocheng put the unfinished story into a bamboo box. Seven years later, while traveling along a stretch of river, he came across the incomplete story in the box and finished writing it. Not several days passed before his maidservant fell into the river and drowned.

If the Du Shiniang of Song Maocheng's text had her way, the part of the story where she bares her soul as she spills the contents of the jewel box would never have been written; she appeared to Song Maocheng to instruct him to stop writing before he reached that scene. When, in defiance of her instructions, Song took the story out of the bamboo box and finished it, Du Shiniang, like a vengeful river goddess, took the body of his maidservant. The body of the maidservant in effect substituted for Song Maocheng's; the maid lost her life simply because of her proximity to Song Maocheng. But the drowning of the maidservant also oddly recalls Du Shiniang's own watery death. As Rania Huntington has observed, the actions of ghosts that seek substitutes are particularly frightening because there is no rationale to their targets beyond contiguity, and so one has no notion of whom the ghost will approach or attack next; she has simply provided an example of her power.[26] The metonymic reach of Du Shiniang's ghost terrifies because it is governed by logic and illogic in equal parts.

"The Faithless Lover" appears under the section on biographies in Song Maocheng's collection. The tale is presented as nonfiction, and the maid's death verifies Du Shiniang's ghostly appearance to Song Maocheng. Song Maocheng wrote two separate requiems (*jiwen* 祭文) for the maid Lu Tao, who drowned after his dream of Du Shiniang, and both testify to his ongoing remorse. Lu Tao's husband was Song Maocheng's servant as well, and we sense that Song Maocheng's regrets were spurred in part by witnessing the husband's grief. In one of the requiems, Song Maocheng informs the drowned maidservant that he has put her tablet with those of his own ancestors; in a highly unusual gesture, he remarks that she will be fed with his own ancestors' spirits and need not fear being a hungry ghost.[27] The second requiem is written after some years have passed; in it, Song Maocheng asks Lu Tao's spirit whether she is caught in karmic entanglements or has progressed yet to the great void.[28]

The hidden ellipsis of the vernacular story's revision of the classical biography is the excision of Song Maocheng's ending. Feng Menglong substitutes an entirely different ending for Song Maocheng's encounter with Du Shiniang's ghost. Feng Menglong's new ending, which adheres to the logic of reward and recompense that so often structures the vernacular story, both renders "Du Shiniang" a better pairing with the preceding story in the collection and reinforces the equation between Du Shiniang and the box. In Feng Menglong's revision, after Du Shiniang jumps into the water holding the "precious box" (*baoxia* 寶匣), Li Jia and Sun Fu meet their just deserts: Li Jia goes mad; Sun Fu is haunted by the ghost of Du Shiniang until he dies. Liu Yuchun, the friend of Li Jia's who gave him 150 taels to buy Du Shiniang out of the brothel, is rewarded by her ghost. He is traveling by boat near the place where Du Shiniang threw herself into the river when, leaning over the water to wash his face, he accidentally drops his wash basin into the river. A fisherman, trying to help him fish it out, brings up a small casket (*xiaoxia* 小匣) instead, and gives it to Liu Yuchun, who finds that it is full of priceless gems. Liu Yuchun leaves the casket by the head of his bed. That night, Du Shiniang appears to him in a dream, and tells him that she has sent him this casket to thank him for the 150 taels he spent to buy her out of prostitution. The correlation between Du Shiniang and the casket of jewels is strengthened when readers are told that Liu Yuchun left the casket by the head of his bed "to play with" (留於床頭把玩).

The figural relation between the box and Du Shiniang, however, ultimately is subject to the same contingent structure of displacement and substitution that we saw as the maid's body fell into the water in "The Faithless Lover." The casket that Liu Yuchun recovers is presumably the small casket Du Shiniang was holding when she jumped into the water.

Earlier in the story, when Du Shiniang likened herself to a box, she used the character *du* 櫝 for box; the term *du* was a homonym for her own surname and contained the character for her surname within it. Here, the character for the casket (*xia* 匣) contains the character for Li Jia's given name (*jia* 甲), as though Li Jia himself were contained in the box. The relationship between Liu Yuchun and Li Jia is potentially foregrounded. Just as the narrative seemed to settle on a means of uniting Du Shiniang with Liu Yuchun, the one who recognized her true worth and sacrificed his own funds to achieve her match with Li Jia, it inserts Li Jia in the casket, in the place that the metaphorical equivalence between Du Shiniang and the casket suggests that Du Shiniang should occupy. The repeated use of the character *xia* 匣 in this passage suggests that the thematic metaphor that equated Du Shiniang and the box is coming undone. There are no simple equations here, and consequently, no sense that Du Shiniang has been laid to rest.

CONCLUSION

"Du Shiniang" is the vernacular short story that establishes the potential for an equivalence between character and object in the tradition of vernacular fiction. An integral part of Du Shiniang's persuasiveness is that she never protests her worth. She herself is an enigma; it is the box that translates for her and says what she cannot say. Clearly, the contents of the box are a metaphor for Du Shiniang's fidelity and strength of character. But as the ambiguity between descriptions of the box such as "dressing case" and "box for writing implements" suggests, the box itself is an unstable term on which to rest a metaphorical mapping. The box contains other boxes, not nested within each other but scattered among the different tiers, or drawers. Thus the metaphor does not suggest a one-to-one mapping, but rather a conglomeration of mappings that are connected via contiguity, or metonymy.

Although the box makes Du Shiniang memorable, a thematic reading that compares Du Shiniang's unseen loyalty and value with the box's concealed jade and jewels ultimately has a certain flatness.[29] In such a reading, Du Shiniang as a character is effectively contained by the box. In fact, the analogy between the properties of the jade and gems within the box and Du Shiniang's own steadfastness is neither reinforced nor negated in the narrative, but simply bypassed. That these collocations are not dwelt upon becomes clear as the contents of each drawer are tossed into the river only to be superseded by the contents of the next drawer. The progression from one drawer to the next creates ever-increasing expectations, not just for the value of the jewels but also for the yoking of tenor and vehicle in the metaphor, for a more precise collocation between the contents of the box and Du Shiniang's inestimable value.

Rather than focusing on the contents of the box in conceptualizing this mapping, we should look to the empty space of potential within the box. The sense of an interior—a sense fortified by the fourth wall of the lacquer box, which renders the box impenetrable—makes the metaphorical map more than an equation of jade with fidelity and gems with value. The fourth wall of the box, which renders the contents invisible, creates a space of potential within the box that is signaled not by the contents of the box but by the space around them. Turning to the terms we used in chapter 2, it is the *xu* of the space inside the box, not the *shi* of its contents, that makes the metaphorical mapping resonant. Such a space of potential exists not only within the box, but also in the translation from the classical biography to the vernacular story.

In closing, I want to emphasize that the material form of the box points to the formal properties of metaphorical mapping as it operates in this story. The box as metaphor speaks to the ways the courtesan is like the box. But it also points to the ways in which she is *not* like the box. The boxlike nature of metaphorical mapping means that the metaphorical identification of Du Shiniang with the box will always remain incomplete.

CHAPTER FOUR

Li Yu's Telescope

The lens maker Gao Yun 高雲 (fl. 1796), who lived in the Xiling 西泠 area of Hangzhou, made telescopic lenses through which "one suddenly saw that drifts of snow resembled mountains, the peaks and ranges piling on top of each other. When one put down the lens and looked at the mounds of snow themselves, they were no bigger than piles of salt or millet" (忽見疊雪如山, 峰巒矗起, 撤鏡視之, 鹽黍許也).[1] Viewing through a telescope creates a radical shift in perceptions of scale. Setting down the telescope, however, does not restore ordinary reality. Instead, the drifts of snow look far smaller than they are in actuality, revealing the effort of the eye (and brain) to adjust to the instrument. This effect is all the more palpable because it is ephemeral.[2]

In Li Yu's story "A Tower for the Summer Heat," published in his collection of stories *Twelve Towers* (*Shi'er lou* 十二樓, 1658), the telescope produces a different sort of short-lived illusion: it purportedly allows the user to read minds, permitting Li Yu to experiment with the narration of thought. The telescope thus acts as a prosthesis for Li Yu as much as for his protagonist, a young licentiate named Qu Jiren 瞿吉人, who happens upon the telescope in an antique shop and decides he will use it to acquire a wife. As with the box of chapter 3, the material properties of the fictional object provide an opportunity to play with techniques of narration. Here the question becomes: How might the monocular telescope as the central, organizing object of Li Yu's story have facilitated his experiment with point of view?

Li Yu's interest in the telescope focuses in part on its single eye. Historical and anecdotal accounts of the telescope in seventeenth-century China note that the experience of viewing with a single eye through a tube that frames and delimits the field of vision potentially enlivens the object perceived. A number of scholars have speculated that the advent of the Western lens may have had consequences for traditional Chinese notions of visuality and visual experience.[3] The art historian Jennifer Purtle, who describes the telescope as having "pride of place" among the "optical baubles" that circulated in late-Ming elite visual culture, suggests that monocular devices may have influenced the development of single-point perspective in China.[4] As Hsu Hui-Lin notes, however, in this story Li Yu casts the new technology of the telescope in traditional terms: the telescope resembles a magic mirror that transports the viewer to an object of desire.[5] It is an instrument of magnification and of selection, one that Jiren uses to find a wife. I would add that in Li Yu's hands, the telescope furnishes a premise for placing before the reader a single character's extended train of thought. The text repeatedly suggests that the telescope is a charismatic object with unexpected powers, but then demystifies it, revealing it to be an instrument whose capacities are limited. Despite the demystification, the telescope's radical adjustments to perception persist. As the anecdote about Gao Yun's telescope suggests, readers may perceive differently even when the telescope is not in use.

MONOCULAR VISION AND THE TELESCOPE AS ORACLE

The first text to be written on the telescope in Chinese was *Yuanjing shuo* 遠鏡說 (*On the Telescope*, prefaced 1626), by the Jesuit missionary Adam Schall von Bell (adopted Chinese name Tang Ruowang, 1592–1666).[6] In it, Schall introduces the monocular capacity of the instrument by pointing to the enhanced clarity gained by concentrating rays of light through a single lens. He teaches Chinese readers how to assemble and use a telescope, telling them to take a convex glass lens and place it at the entrance of a tube, and then to place a small concave lens at the side of the tube nearest the eye. He instructs readers to check the strength of the two lenses to see if they match, and to place the lenses at the ends of the tubes rather than between. The tubes can then be extended or retracted to adjust the magnification.[7] Schall emphasizes that viewers need use only one eye to look through the lens:

> Take the telescope and position it on a stand or lean it against something stable, ensuring that it doesn't sway. To look through the lens, use only one eye; the capacity of the eye will be focused. The more concentrated the rays of light, the clearer the object.
>
> 將鏡置諸本架, 或倚著實落處, 使不搖動. 視鏡止用一目, 目力乃專, 光益聚而象益顯也.[8]

Schall claims that closing one eye concentrates the efforts of the remaining eye; moreover, utilizing this technique clusters the rays of light and renders the image more vivid. This notion is bolstered by his inclusion of illustrations that show a single eye receiving rays of light refracted through the combination of convex and concave lenses that were used to make the Galilean telescope. According to Schall, viewing through the telescope encourages distant objects to reveal themselves: "When you use it [the telescope] inside a room to look at all the distant objects, both their shape and form reveal their original aspect in a lively manner" (居室中用之則照見諸遠物, 其體其色活潑潑地各現本相). It is as though narrowing the visual purview enlivens the object.[9]

Schall's *On the Telescope* initially addresses celestial observation, but after discussing how the telescope can aid observation of the moon, Venus, and Jupiter, he turns to its terrestrial and nautical applications—it could be used for spying on military encampments to determine the number of enemies and their military readiness, or for identifying the number of men on pirate ships. The biography of the earliest known Chinese maker of telescopes, Bo Jue 薄珏 (style name Bo Zijue 薄子珏), relates that he attached glass telescopic lenses to cannons in 1635:[10]

In the fourth year of the Chongzhen reign (1630), there was a pirate invasion in Anqing. He received an invitation from the Vice Censor-in-Chief Zhang Guowei to cast cannon. His gunpowder could blast for 30 leagues.... Every time he set up a cannon, he would equip it with a telescope to discern the distance of the bandits. The two ends of the telescope each held glass [lenses]. One could see for 40 or 50 leagues, and it was as though [the object sighted] were only a foot away.

崇禎四年, 流寇犯安慶, 中丞張國維禮聘公為造銅炮, 炮藥發三十里.... 每置一炮, 即設千里鏡以偵賊之遠近, 鏡筒兩端嵌玻璃, 望四五十里外如咫尺也).[11]

The use of glass for telescopic lenses clearly ties Bo Jue to Western knowledge of lens-making; Chinese lens-making was focused on the use of rock-crystal rather than glass. As Qu Dajun 屈大均 (1630–1696) wrote in his late seventeenth-century notation book *A New Account of Guangdong* (*Guangdong xinyu* 廣東新語), "Glass comes from ships from overseas. Westerners use it to make spectacles" (玻璃來自海舶.西洋人以為眼鏡).[12]

Bo Jue's biography portrays him as a deeply learned man with a knowledge of astrological prognostication. A savant in possession of esoteric knowledge, he will not answer if spoken to in common vernacular speech. He can commit books to memory with a single reading and then recite them in reverse, as if the characters formed a palindrome:

> His name was Jue, style name Zijue, a man of Suzhou. He went to take the examinations in Zhejiang and received a licentiate degree from the county of Jiaxing. His knowledge was vast and profound, and we don't know from whence it was transmitted to him. He had a deep knowledge of astrological prognostication. He made forays into making various instruments with water and fire. When he had read a book only once he could recite it entirely, and then recite [the book] from the end back to the beginning without being mistaken in a single word. Those who heard him thought it most strange. He had an imposing physique and a square countenance. He would sit alone as though dozing, as though he were about to

fall asleep. If one spoke to him in common vernacular speech he would grunt and be unable to answer.

公名玨, 字子玨, 蘇州人也. 就試浙江, 補嘉興縣學生. 其學奧博不知何所傳. 洞曉陰陽, 占步, 製造水火諸器. 讀書一過成誦, 又從尾誦至顛亦不誤一字, 聽者異之. 偉軀方面, 獨坐昏昏如欲睡. 興言世俗語, 唯唯不能答.[13]

The biography makes clear that Bo Jue was a literatus, having passed the lowest level of the examinations and earned a licentiate degree.[14] His knowledge, however, is portrayed as vastly exceeding that of a licentiate; his agile memory for texts is far from that of the common run. His work is grounded in the study of *yin yang* 陰陽 and the Five Elements, which significantly underscores the degree to which astronomical calculation and astrological prediction were related in thinking about the telescope.[15] This notion of the maker of the telescope as a savant with knowledge of prognostication establishes a path to the representation of the telescope as an oracular instrument in Li Yu's "A Tower for the Summer Heat."

The telescopic sights that Bo Jue devised were fashioned only one year after the publication of Schall's *On the Telescope*, and it is more than likely that Bo Jue, a native of Hangzhou, gained the knowledge to make telescopic lenses directly or indirectly from Jesuits stationed in Hangzhou.[16] Hangzhou was the center of domestic lens-making through the latter half of the seventeenth century. In fact, Li Yu wrote "A Tower for the Summer Heat" during a ten-year residence in Hangzhou that began in 1648; the story hails his friend Zhu Sheng (諸升, b. 1618) of Hangzhou as the premier lens maker of his day.[17] Zhu Sheng, a well-known artist particularly recognized for his paintings of bamboo in snow, mentored a young maker of lenses from Suzhou named Sun Yunqiu 孫雲球 (1650?–after 1681), and composed a preface for Sun's *History of Lenses* (*Jingshi* 鏡史). Zhu Sheng probably introduced Li Yu to this treatise, which Li Yu would ultimately cite (without attribution, naturally) in "A Tower for the Summer Heat." The undated Xiaoxianju edition of the story contains a disquisition on lenses that draws heavily from Sun Yunqiu's *History of Lenses*.[18] In order to better demonstrate the effect of the addition of this new material, I first analyze the story as it was published in the late 1650s, and then examine the addition of the passage in which Li Yu drew on *History of Lenses*, which was most likely added to the story in the late 1670s, just before Li Yu's death in 1680.

THE MONOCULAR TELESCOPE

Li Yu wrote "A Tower for the Summer Heat" half a century after the telescope was invented in Europe and a few decades after Jesuit missionaries introduced the telescope to the court in Beijing.[19] It features the young licentiate Qu Jiren, who devises a plan to use the telescope to find a wife. As in the case of the shell and the box of chapters 2 and 3, the trope of recognition plays a role in conceptualizing the telescope's capacities. Jiren is rewarded by the telescope for recognizing its true potential; it selects scenes for him that enable him to convince his intended that he is clairvoyant. His pretense of clairvoyance is undermined, however, when the telescope's limitations as an instrument become apparent.

Jiren's unusual surname, Qu 瞿, has two "eye" (*mu* 目) radicals, signaling the role he gives the telescope as prosthetic eye.[20] He rents a room in a monastery on a hill, and proceeds to survey the surrounding landscape, including the secluded women's quarters of various estates, which, although they cannot be penetrated from the level of the street, are now open to his observation. One day Jiren's eye is caught by an odd scene in the women's quarters of a gentry family surnamed Zhan 詹. A group of young serving maids has stripped to lark about in a lotus pond. Suddenly, the daughter of the house steps out and proceeds to discipline the young girls in a judicious manner. Struck by her perspicacity as well as her beauty, Jiren sends a matchmaker to inquire further. The girl, named Xianxian 嫻嫻 (in Patrick Hanan's translation, "Serena"), becomes persuaded of the match when Jiren, with the privileged knowledge he has gained by spying on her through the telescope, convinces her (via the matchmaker) that he knows her every thought.

Li Yu, however, never mentions the telescope in the story's first chapter. How Jiren comes to his privileged knowledge of Xianxian's thoughts is a mystery to readers until the second of the story's three chapters. At that point, Li Yu pulls back the curtain hiding the telescope, revealing how Jiren was able to deduce Xianxian's thoughts. The limitations of the telescope are underscored as its capacities as an instrument are foregrounded. Revealed to be simply a device rather than a charismatic object, the role of telescope as *mechanism* for the narration of thought becomes clear, not only on the level of Jiren's knowledge of Xianxian's thoughts, but also on the level of the readers' knowledge of Jiren's and Xianxian's thoughts. The addition of a new passage that lists the telescope as merely one among a number of visual devices in the undated Xiaoxianju edition of the story further undermines the portrayal of the instrument as a charismatic object.

With each retrospective retelling of events, readers are able to gain information that previously was not communicated about the telescope's role. In the third and final chapter, after Xianxian and Jiren marry, Xianxian insists on an explanation for Jiren's clairvoyance, and Jiren confesses to the aid of the telescope. That leads the couple to trust in the telescope's preternatural power of selection, and they hang it in a shrine, where they worship it. The couple consults the telescope whenever they encounter a problem, treating what they see through the lens as an oracle. The telescope's powers of selection are taken as a kind of prognostication, such that the telescope once again is subject to mystification. After describing the couple's investment in the telescope's powers, however, Li Yu once again demystifies the telescope. He explains that the concentrated attention of the observer lends a numinous, animating quality (*ling* 靈) to the objects of wood and clay, adding that worship of deities "amounts to worshipping one's own mind."

With Li Yu's characteristic invention, he grafts the telescope's capacity for revelatory sight onto his long-standing interest in voyeurism.[21] "A Tower for the Summer Heat" opens with six lyrics that feature girls picking lotuses, poems that the narrator proclaims were written by Li Yu himself in his youth.[22] The trope of lotus-picking is inextricably linked to voyeurism in the poetic tradition, and these poems thus introduce the theme of voyeurism that is so prominent in the first chapter. The fourth lyric features a male observer on the riverbanks undetected by the girls picking lotuses in the water:

> Sing but the lotus-picking songs,
> And tell no wild, indecent lies.
> A man on the bank admires the lotus,
> And on the lotus-pickers spies.

採蓮只唱採蓮詞,
莫向同儕浪語私.
岸上有人閒處立,
看花更看採花兒.²³

In contrast to the monocular quality of vision of the telescope, here a bifurcated envisioning is introduced as readers watch the voyeur watching the lotus pickers. That, in turn, prepares readers to watch Li Yu's voyeur Jiren with a similar quality of vision, in essence training readers to be both within and without the diegesis. While *Jin Ping Mei* describes a sociality based on stolen objects, in Li Yu's story of the telescope, a sociality between narrator and readers develops from stolen glances.²⁴ The readers stand with the narrator to observe not just the girls picking lotuses, but the voyeur as well.²⁵

In Li Yu's fiction, the narrator is typically extremely gregarious, and virtually indistinguishable from Li Yu himself.²⁶ Li Yu's narrator frequently breaks the diegesis to comment on the ingenuity of his techniques of narration while also inserting space for readers to pause and marvel at his capacity for invention. In this sense, the trope of voyeurism could be said to extend to the readers' observations of Li Yu's techniques of narration. At the close of the introduction, Li Yu states, "I shall now tell a remarkable story, and because I started off talking about lotus-picking, I shall take that subject as my lead-in, to avoid the danger of picking the wrong tree and finding that the graft doesn't take" (如今敘說一篇奇話, 因為從採蓮而起, 所以就把採蓮一事做了引頭, 省得在樹外尋根, 到這移花接木的去處, 兩邊合不着笋也).²⁷ The metaphor of the graft is worth lingering over. It marks the contrast between the sensual voyeurism of the lotus-picking poems and the story's recasting of voyeurism as the perception of another's thoughts.

In the first chapter, readers are puzzled as to how Jiren acquires his knowledge of the inner workings of the Zhan household. Several days after Xianxian disciplines her maids for cavorting naked in the lotus pond beneath her private apartment, a marriage proposal arrives for her from Jiren. From this point to the close of the chapter, events are focalized through Xianxian, and her hesitations, doubts, and bewilderment are foregrounded. Li Yu focuses on Xianxian's thoughts—not only what she knows, but how she knows—to a degree that is unprecedented in Chinese vernacular fiction.²⁸

How the voyeur has been able to intuit the thoughts of a young woman living in a secluded tower ringed by willows so thick that no light can penetrate is the puzzle that dominates the first chapter. Xianxian falls ill with longing after seeing that her suitor has topped the list of successful graduates.[29] When Qu Jiren sends her a message through the matchmaker urging her to take care, Xianxian is flabbergasted. "I'm the only one who knows about my illness," she thinks. "Even my personal maids have been kept in the dark. He's just back from a long journey, so how could he possibly know about it and send her over to ask?" (我自己生病, 只有我自己得知, 連貼身服事的人都不曉得. 他從遠處回家, 何由知道, 竟着人問起安來?).[30]

The telescope brings the action to Jiren as he sits in his room, much as a work of fiction brings the action to the reader. Because events are initially told from Xianxian's point of view, Jiren's knowledge of Xianxian's illness appears to be proof that he knows her every thought, when were the chapter focalized through Jiren, the reader would know that he has merely observed her physical wasting away and guessed at its cause. To Xianxian's challenge—"Supposing I were sick, how could he possibly know?"—the matchmaker replies:

> I don't understand how he does it, but he knows everything that goes on in your mind, as if you and he were Siamese twins. And not just your thoughts either, but everything you do—you can't hide anything from him. You've never seen him, but he knows exactly what you look like; in fact he gave me a description that fits you perfectly. I imagine you two must have been husband and wife in some previous existence and that that is the reason. . . . He claims he has the eyes of a god and can see anything, no matter how far away it is.

> 不知甚麼原故, 你心上的事體他件件曉得, 就像同腸合肺的一般. 不但心上如此, 連你所行之事, 沒有一件瞞得他. 他的面顏你雖不曾見過, 你的容貌他却記得分明, 對我說來, 一毫不錯. 想是你們兩個前生前世原是一對夫妻, 故此不曾會面就預先曉得. . . . 他說自己有神眼, 遠近之事無一毫不見.[31]

In the matchmaker's phrasing ("And not just your thoughts either, but everything you do—you can't hide anything from him"), thoughts are more easily discerned than actions. The reader, who has been privy to Xianxian's longing all along, falls for the trick as readily as Xianxian does. In a further twist, the matchmaker's phrasing suggests that knowing what transpires in someone's mind is a matter of seeing *with*, sharing the parameters of vision. As she tells Xianxian, "He knows everything that goes on in your mind, just as though you were Siamese twins." The telescope, which has never been mentioned, has led Jiren's observation to be mistaken for clairvoyance. There is no attention to ocular perception at this point in the narrative, no suggestion of the distortion that comes with magnification. The sensual voyeurism of the lotus-picking poems is recast in the story as a more cerebral form of voyeurism involving the capacity to know another's thoughts.

Both Jiren and the narrator model a process of deduction from data that is known to be partial. At the end of the first chapter, the narrator teasingly goads us to put our knowledge to the test:

> Having come this far, gentle reader, please put aside all other concerns and focus on the question of how Jiren knew what was going on in the Zhan household. Was he man or ghost? Was it dream or reality? By all means try to guess the answer and then, when you find you cannot come up with it, turn to the next chapter for the explanation.
>
> 看官們看到此處, 別樣的事都且丟開, 單想詹家的事情, 吉人如何知道? 是人是鬼? 是夢是真? 大家請猜一猜. 且等猜不著時再取下回來看.[32]

In traditional vernacular fiction, the narrator typically intrudes at the end of a chapter to urge readers to turn the page to find out what happens next. The request from Li Yu to narrow the purview in order to speculate more productively is unprecedented. The narrator first alerts readers that selective attention paired with deduction will be crucial to piecing together the significance of events, and then claims that such an attempt will be futile.

Effacing the technology by which Jiren observed Xianxian in the first chapter makes him seem omniscient, but in the second chapter, readers discover that the telescope is the source of that omniscience. Once the telescope is introduced as an instrument, Jiren's abilities are shown to have limits. The monocular lens of the telescope first grants a seeming omniscience to Jiren and then restricts the scope of his understanding.

As the lens of the telescope, omitted in the first chapter of the story, becomes a presence in the second chapter, Li Yu's play with point of view becomes more evident. The extension of purview in chapter 2 is both spatial, as the telling of events moves beyond the Zhan household, and temporal, as the narrator engages in a flashback to Jiren's purchase of the telescope in an antique store. The narrative now launches into a discussion of lenses that extends the parameters still further, taking us out of the story and into the rhetorical mode of the gazetteer and notation book. Referring to the telescope by the vernacular term for a thing, *dongxi* 東西, Li Yu explains how the mysterious object allowed Jiren to cast himself as an immortal with the capacity to intuit other's thoughts:

> I expect you have been unable to guess how Jiren came to know these things, so let me explain. The incident was the work neither of man nor of ghost, and the account given you was neither a complete fabrication nor the complete truth. It was the work of a certain device (*dongxi*) that served Jiren as an eye, a device that allowed a flesh-and-blood human being to impersonate a disembodied immortal without any fear that people would doubt his word.
>
> 吉人知道事情的原故，料想列位看官都猜不著。如今聽我說來。這個情節，也不是人，也不是鬼，也不全假，也不全真，都虧了一件東西替他做了眼目。所以把個肉身男子假充了蛻骨神仙，不怕世人不信。[33]

In the passage from *The Plum in the Golden Vase* in which Ximen Qing spoke of "that thing that likes to move," the "thing" had a kind of volition that was associated with its capacity to circulate. Here it is animated because it is supplemental and prosthetic.

> Although the device (*dongxi*) did not originate in China, it was something that lovers of exotica were able to collect; it was certainly no figment of the imagination. Unfortunately everybody looked upon it as a mere toy and ignored its potential value. Only this man knew enough to conceal its usefulness and not put it to work in other areas, but to keep it for selecting a beautiful wife. For that

purpose, he built an altar, appointed the device his commander-in-chief, and asked of it a great service. It proved capable of picking up a great beauty ensconced in her boudoir, placing her right in front of him, and capable also of taking the rare blooms from another man's garden and setting them in all their glory before his eyes.

這件東西的出處,雖然不在中國,却是好奇訪異的人家都收藏得有,不是甚麼荒唐之物.但可惜世上的人都拿來做了戲具,所以不覺其可寶.獨有此人善藏其用,別處不敢勞他,直到遴嬌選豔的時節,方才築起壇來,拜為上將;求他建立膚功,能使深閨豔質不出戶而羅列於前,別院奇葩才着想而爛然於目.[34]

Here Li Yu, perhaps ironically, draws on the trope of recognition so prominent in the literature of connoisseurship. In contrast to the shopkeeper and the customers who see the telescope as a toy, only Jiren has a true understanding of the object; only he is suited to be its owner. The lack of clarity regarding the object itself underscores the brilliance of Jiren's recognition of the object's capacity. At the same time, the trope of recognition not only elevates the object but also places Jiren, who recognizes its potential, in a surprisingly submissive position. Jiren takes an abject position with regard to the object, literally saluting it as his commanding general (*bai wei shang jiang* 拜為上將). Li Yu gestures toward unveiling the mystery of the object in a lyric that personifies the telescope:

Not only does it have the dazzling cleverness of Lu Ban,
But it is aided by Lilou's designs.
A subtle thread of light thin as silk,
Can make those with eyes sprout wings.

At first, its body makes no distinction between near and far,
All depends on the differences in its use.
Don't scorn its single eye at which others laugh,
Those blind in one eye have always been keen of sight.

非獨公輸炫巧,
離婁畫策相資.
微光一隙僅如絲,
能使瞳人生翅.

制體初無遠近，
全憑用法參差.
休嫌獨目把人嗤，
眇者從來善視.³⁵

The lyric underscores that the telescope is "single-eyed" and "blind in one eye"—monocular rather than binocular. At the same time, the poem obfuscates whether the telescope is person, charismatic object, or mere instrument. With Li Yu's typical wit, the unnamed object is first cast as an aid to Lilou 離婁, described by Zhuangzi as well as Mencius as capable of seeing the infinitely small, and then compared with the famous inventor Lu Ban 魯班, also known as Gongshu Ban 公輸班.³⁶ The object, then, has not only powers of magnification but also the powers of invention so prized by Li Yu himself.³⁷

Li Yu has put to novel use a turn of phrase that we find in a letter written by Lu Jun 陸雋 (n.d.) to a friend of Li Yu, the artist Zhu Sheng, who as mentioned earlier, was a well-known maker of lenses in Hangzhou. Zhu Sheng produced the illustrations for the sections on bamboos and orchids for the *Mustard Seed Garden Manual of Painting* (*Jiezi yuan huazhuan* 芥子園畫傳) published by Li Yu's son-in-law. The letter was published in 1667 in a collection of exemplary letters, Wang Qi's 汪淇 (b. 1604) *A New Account of the Anatomy of Letters* (*Fenlei chidu xinyu* 分類尺牘新語).³⁸ The latter half of the letter reads:

> When it comes to the making of Western lenses, your intelligence and skill surpass all others; somehow you make the near-sighted able to see far, and those dim of sight able to see clearly. That which is infinitesimally small one can see as though it were gigantic. Even if one is separated by rivers and lakes or must jump over cliffs and hills, as soon as you peer through, the hair in people's beards and brows will become perfectly clear. How magical it is. It's almost like letting us steal Lizhu's [Lilou's] eyes and Lu Ban's fingers.

即如西鏡之制，慧巧絕倫，何以近視可遠，昏視可清，渺小者可視為鉅麗.
雖隔江湖，踰嶺阜，閒一窺測，鬚眉了然. 神哉至此乎. 幾令奪離朱之目，搶公輸之指矣.³⁹

This letter, included in an epistolary collection that furnished models of well-written letters, was presumably a private communication that in the context of the collection became a public advertisement for Zhu Sheng's lenses for the near- and farsighted.[40] It is the earliest document that implies a community of Chinese lens makers exists in Hangzhou, and its phrasing ("When it comes to the making of Western lenses") clearly suggests that those lens makers had access to the optics introduced by the Jesuits. The letter shares with Li Yu's story the allusions to Lu Ban's fingers and Lilou's sight. Given Li Yu's friendship with Zhu Sheng, as well as the widespread popularity of this collection of letters, it is quite possible that Li Yu plucked this language from Zhu Sheng's letter, providing in miniature an example of how nonliterary genres infiltrated the boundaries of fictional texts.

THE TELESCOPE AS INSTRUMENT

In the version of "A Tower for the Summer Heat" published in 1658, the lyric on the telescope is followed immediately by Jiren's purchase of the telescope in a shop that sells antiques and curiosities. Having spied a strange object in the shop whose function he cannot fathom, Jiren goes to examine it and notices a slip of gold paper attached to the object, on which is written in tiny characters "thousand-league lens from the west" (*xiyang qianli jing* 西洋千里鏡). The paper recalls the custom of labeling objects in the imperial collections with thin strips of yellow paper, suggesting that this telescope originated in the Forbidden City in Beijing. The diminutive characters, which enhance the sense of mystery regarding the instrument's origins, call attention to the object's own play with scale and magnification.

Jiren views the telescope as an instrument of selection, a conception of the telescope that echoes the Qing emperors' use of the telescope in military observation and the hunt.[41] The Kangxi 康熙 emperor (r. 1661–1772) wrote of an occasion on a military campaign when he told his attendants to give him privacy, and he climbed a hill alone to use a telescope to search for the enemy. Not seeing a soul through the lens of the telescope, he deduced that the rebels were firmly in position and that they planned to fight to the death.[42] His grandson, the Qianlong emperor, used the telescope in the hunt. The telescope has a prominent place in the Jesuit artist Giuseppe Castiglione's (Lang Shining 郎世寧, 1688–1766) painting *Portrait of the Emperor Troating for Deer* (*Shaolu tu*, 哨鹿圖, 1741), which commemorated the Mulan Autumn Hunt (*Mulan qiuxian*, 木蘭秋獮) that took place annually near the summer residence of the Qing emperors in Jehol. The painting shows a procession of Qianlong and his entourage traveling through the hills on horseback at a deer hunt, a telescope strapped to the back of a black horse.[43] The telescope, protected by an enormous case the length of the horse, is so cumbersome to transport that it almost qualifies as an additional member of the expedition.

The telescope that Jiren finds in an antique shop is a long way from Beijing and, whatever its origins, has become no more than a curiosity. When Jiren's friends ask what the instrument is for, the shopkeeper tells them that if they were to take it to the top of a hill, they would see the surrounding landscape for dozens of leagues, surveying its entirety with a sweep of the eye (*yi lan er jin* 一覽而盡). The crowd voices incredulity, and the shopkeeper suggests a demonstration. He takes a piece of scrap paper, a failed examination essay that has somehow found its way to his shop, and tacks it to the gate across the street, saying, "How about testing the telescope?" (就把他試驗一試驗). In contrast to the examination essay, the telescope passes with flying colors. Jiren and his friends are amazed to find that when they peer through the telescope, not only can they read the characters, but the strokes look thicker than before (筆畫都粗壯了許多).[44]

For the first time, the narrative displays an interest in the way that the telescopic lens might convey an image rather than simply transport a scene to the viewer. What the telescope sees is not just what the paper says. The words of the failed examination essay have no currency; they have become mere marks used to test the powers of this instrument, much like the letters on a modern optician's chart. The Western origin of the telescope underscores the irrelevance of the characters as calligraphy (in which one might read the personality of the calligrapher through the strokes of the brush) or even as script.

In the first chapter, which chronologically takes place after this flashback, the telescope magically transported Jiren (and the readers) into a scene that Jiren was able to view as though he were present. There was no particular attention given to the lens, nor to Jiren; both the observer and the instrument of observation were omitted. In the scene in the antique shop, the telescope is cast as an instrument for the first time. We see that in the hands of an ordinary shopkeeper, the telescope is merely an agent of magnification. In Jiren's hands, the telescope will have the capacity to illuminate Xianxian's internal qualities and indeed her thoughts.

The events of chapter 1 are retold after this scene, now focalized through Jiren so as to underscore the role of the telescope as his possession. We learn that after he purchased the telescope, Jiren tucked it into his sleeve and returned home (*xiu zhi er gui* 袖之而歸). Once the telescope is integrated into Jiren's person in this way, his thoughts become visible to us. In a long internal monologue, Jiren conjures up a plan to take the telescope to a high place, the pagoda of a temple, to see if he can spy into the homes of distinguished families and find himself a mate. "It's not only for looking at distant scenery," he thought. "It can also make people in the distance look clearer than if they were close at hand. It's not a telescope, it's a pair of long-distance eyes!" (這件東西既可以以高望遠，又能使遠處的人物比近處更覺分明，竟是一雙千里眼，不是千里鏡了).[45]

The telescope transports Jiren to the scenes he will need to interpret, and Jiren proves that he has the capacity of deduction that the narrator tried to encourage in the readers at the end of chapter 1. Xianxian's thoughts are not communicated to Jiren via the telescope, but after he views her wasting away, he deduces that she is ill with longing for him. The telescope is indistinguishable from the magic mirror of classical Chinese fiction; it enables Jiren to see a scene as though he were standing before it.[46] But the information it gives him would be useless if Jiren did not know how to interpret it; his capacity to supply missing context allows him to appear clairvoyant.

In the second chapter, the telescope's charismatic powers are demystified, and Jiren's clairvoyance is debunked once it is known that the telescope allowed him to pose as a false immortal (*jia shenxian* 假神仙). The incident of spying on Xianxian and sending a matchmaker over to inquire about her illness is now referred to as a "trick." As the telescope's limitations are exposed and it becomes apparent that Jiren did not have the ability to read Xianxian's thoughts, her thoughts are no longer foregrounded. Instead, the narrative turns to Jiren's thought process and his capacity for invention. Readers learn that after Jiren dispatched the matchmaker to Xianxian, he picked up the telescope again and saw Xianxian writing a poem. She appeared startled and hid her writing. Jiren initially suspected that she somehow saw him observing her. A space appears between Jiren's partial vision and the narrator's omniscience that widens when Xianxian's father comes into view and Jiren deduces that her startled look was a response to her father's tread on the stairs. The limitations of the telescope are foregrounded: the telescope cannot hear.

Xianxian's restricted purview reinforced the sense of mystery as to the telescope's clairvoyance. Jiren's, by contrast, exposes the limitations of the telescope. The narrative's play with the formation of partial knowledge thus enables both the mystification of the telescope as charismatic object and its subsequent demystification as mere instrument or device. The third chapter then turns to a more traditional mode of omniscient narration where thought is not foregrounded. Li Yu emphasizes this transition with an unorthodox break between chapters. As before, the author insists on a delay in the unfolding of events: "Like Serena's [Xianxian's] poem, which was broken off before it was completed, the story will be far more interesting than if it were told all in one piece" (猶如詹小姐做詩, 被人隔了一隔, 然後聯續起來, 比一口氣做成的又好看多少).[47] The comment recalls the transition from introduction to first chapter, where Li Yu used the metaphor of the graft to describe the shift in diegetic levels from preface to story proper.

The telescope is put to one final test when Xianxian's father states that he will write a petition to her dead mother to ask which of Xianxian's suitors he should accept. Xianxian is initially quite concerned that the result will not bode well for her match with Jiren. But once again Jiren employs the telescope to read words that were privately written in the Zhan household, this time a petition from Xianxian's father to her dead mother. Jiren copies the words and transmits the information to Xianxian, who then recites the petition to her father, word for word, to persuade him that her mother has appeared in her dreams with the instruction that she is to marry Jiren.

After the couple marries, Xianxian realizes that Jiren is no immortal and asks how he was able to provide the text of the petition and provide a solution to their quandary. Jiren reveals that he hung the telescope high and begged its aid. When he then took it down and looked through it, he saw Xianxian's father composing the petition to his dead wife. Jiren, realizing that the telescope had selected this scene on his behalf, copied the text of the petition and conveyed it to Xianxian. The telescope has been transformed from mere instrument back to charismatic object. Its monocular capacity to view selectively, which was cast as a limitation in the scene where Xianxian wrote the poem, is now the source of its revelatory power.

By story's end, the telescope's power of selection entirely replaces its capacity to magnify. Jiren and Xianxian, now married, treat the telescope as an instrument of divination. The pair place the telescope, now referred to as a magical object (*fabao* 法寶), within the tower and pay obeisance to it. Whenever they encounter difficulties, they consult the telescope, taking whatever they randomly chance to see as a portent. The telescope has become an oracle; its unknowable interiority exceeds its instrumentality.

Li Yu, however, engages in a further demystification. The narrator comments: "From this we can see that where the mind is concentrated, objects of clay and wood can work miracles. The worship of gods and buddhas means worshipping our own minds; it does not mean that gods and boddhisattvas really exist" (可見精神所聚之處, 泥土草木皆能效靈. 從來拜神拜佛都是自拜其心, 不是真有神仙, 真有菩薩也).[48] This is a bit of a surprising turn; the telescope is once again revealed to be a mere device. It is the mental investment of the user that renders the telescope an oracle. Li Yu simultaneously underscores the telescope's materiality and robs it of its numinous potential. From the narrator's point of view, the con man has conned himself into believing in the telescope.[49]

"A TOWER FOR THE SUMMER HEAT" AND SUN YUNQIU'S *HISTORY OF LENSES*

Li Yu's voice is so idiosyncratic, and his authorial presence so marked, that scholars were surprised to discover that a section of the second chapter of Li Yu's story appearing only in the undated Xiaoxianju edition drew heavily from Sun Yunqiu's *History of Lenses*. The historian of science Sun Chengsheng's discovery of *History of Lenses* in 2007 solved a long-standing problem in the history of the telescope in China, showing that the early lens makers Bo Jue and Sun Yunqiu knew of Western learning regarding the telescope and did not invent the telescope.⁵⁰ At the same time, Sun Chengsheng's discovery raised a problem in the textual history of Li Yu's story. The descriptive passage on lenses in chapter 2 shares many phrases with Sun Yunqiu's *History of Lenses*, and the question naturally arises as to whether Li Yu was copying Sun Yunqiu, or vice versa.

In the spring of 1672, Sun Yunqiu paid a visit to Zhu Sheng to ask his advice regarding some points in Schall's *On the Telescope*. Sun Yunqiu was a scion of a once well-established family. His father succeeded in the highest level of the civil service examinations as an imperial scholar (*jinshi* 進士) of 1643, and was magistrate of Putian province in Fujian as well as administrator of Zhangzhou. After the fall of the Ming, the family returned to their place of origin, Suzhou, where Sun's mother tutored him in the histories and classics. When Sun's father died, mother and son were left destitute. They moved to Tiger Hill in Suzhou, where Sun Yunqiu sold medicinal herbs and began a side business in grinding lenses out of rock crystal for the near- and farsighted. He had been consulting Schall's *On The Telescope* but was having difficulty understanding the optics. Zhu Sheng described Sun's visit:

> In the spring of 1672, he [Sun Yunqiu] got Matteo Ricci and Adam Schall von Bell's book about the geometry of making lenses [i.e., optics] and came to Hangzhou to ask me about the study of lenses. At that time, because I had the obligation of finishing some painting, I couldn't afford much time. We knelt by the window, rain streaming outside, and I sketched out a few pointers for him; Sun caught on unbelievably quickly and could take one piece of information and extrapolate the rest, never showing any confusion.

> 壬子春, 得利瑪竇, 湯道未造鏡幾何心法一書, 來遊武林, 訪余鏡學. 時余為筆墨酬應之煩, 日不暇給. 雨窓促膝, 略一指示, 孫生妙領神會, 舉一貫諸, 曾無疑義.⁵¹

Zhu Sheng's description of Schall's *On the Telescope* as a work about optics rather than as an introduction to the telescope suggests that the illustrations of the workings of convex and concave lenses were perplexing to Sun Yunqiu. Several years after that first visit, Zhu Sheng had the opportunity to pass through Suzhou and paid a return visit to Sun, who brought out lenses he had recently made to show his mentor. Sun also showed Zhu a short work he had written called *History of Lenses*, totaling some three thousand characters. Despite the title, it was not a historical account of lenses but rather a catalogue of the various lenses he was capable of making—among them lenses for the near-sighted (*jinshi jing* 近視鏡), lenses that preserved the sight of children so that their eyes did not fail later in life (*tongguang jing* 童光鏡), portable cosmetic mirrors (*duanrong jing* 端容鏡), and lenses that concentrated the sun's rays in such a way as to cause incense placed beneath it to burn (*fenxiang jing* 焚香鏡). Zhu Sheng recalled:

> Master Sun took out his *History of Lenses* and the lenses he had made to show me. His lenses were very cleverly made, and his craft had reached the ultimate heights. On the night of the Mid-Autumn moon, we discussed these topics very diligently and I told him all I knew. Among those who are manufacturing various lenses now, there is likely no one who is his superior.... He is the only person making lenses who understands Ricci and Schall's optics and can expand upon what they sketched.... I know a number of professionals making lenses. Sixty or seventy percent can make their lenses look like his in externals, but not twenty or thirty percent have his understanding of principles, and Master Sun is the only one who has a thorough conceptual grasp. Even if Matteo Ricci and Adam Schall von Bell were to check my claims, I daresay they wouldn't change my words.
>
> 孫生出鏡史及所製示余, 造法馴巧, 並臻絕頂. 中秋月夜, 相對討論, 亹亹不倦, 予亦罄厥肘後以述. 今製諸鏡, 迨無出其右矣.... 即造鏡一藝, 獨得利, 湯幾何之秘, 啓發則舉一知三.... 造鏡家, 余亦閱歷數子, 得其形似者十有六七, 會其神理者十無二三, 拈花微笑, 惟孫生一人, 即起利, 湯而証之, 恐不易吾言.⁵²

Sun Yunqiu made a telescope that was mentioned in the 1691 gazetteer of Suzhou's Tiger Hill. The gazetteer incorporated the foreword to the *History of Lenses* in the context of a long list of the local products from Suzhou. (The entry previous to the one about Sun Yunqiu's devices described a kind of *mille-feuille* pastry, made only in Tiger Hill, that alternated myriad layers of leaf lard and flour.) The gazetteer lauded

Sun Yunqiu as a maker of self-chiming clocks and spectacles; the object that took pride of place among the list of Sun's products was not the telescope but the sundial.[53] In addition, the gazetteer mentioned Sun Yunqiu's use of rock crystal to make lenses to aid those afflicted with near- and farsightedness. Another gazetteer for the district of Suzhou related that when Sun Yunqiu took a near-sighted friend to the top of Tiger Hill, his friend found that, with the aid of the telescope, he could see clearly for miles around, such that Suzhou's towers and platforms, temples and gardens, seemed "as close as his table and mat."[54] Although the telescope was just one among many local products that the gazetteer mentioned with pride, it enabled the enjoyment of the local sights of Suzhou and reinforced the gazetteer's emphasis on their worthiness.[55] The Suzhou gazetteer adopted Schall's phrasing regarding the student of the histories whose nearsightedness would eventually prevent him from seeing beyond his table and mat; the phrasing likely entered the gazetteer via Sun Yunqiu's citation of Schall's text in the *History of Lenses*—without attribution, as was the custom.

The *History of Lenses* is richly illustrated, with a woodblock print accompanying the description of each kind of lens. Some of the prints depict the lenses themselves. The illustration that accompanies the text on the cosmetic mirror, for example, shows a young woman holding a mirror in her right hand and gazing at it.[56] More often, however, the illustrations are interpretive; they offer comment as to how it might feel to use the lens rather than rendering a portrait of the lens described in the text. As a case in point, the illustration following the text on lenses for nearsightedness is of a rock that is a "supplement to Heaven" (*butian shi* 補天石), the rock presumably the rock crystal from which the spectacles would be carved. The colophon to the illustration mentions "glass cages for the eyes" (*liuli longyan* 琉璃籠眼), or spectacles; the "supplement to Heaven" is perhaps rock crystal.[57]

In this manner, the illustration for the text on the telescope is not of a telescope but of the artist's sense of what it might be like to look through the telescope (see figure 4.1). The round eyepiece of the telescope is suggested by the curvature of the trunks of the trees, which form a near circle framing the image. Within the midst of the circle are several Dutch or Flemish houses by a lake. This monocular framing is what signals the presence of a telescope; there is no suggestion of magnification.

FIGURE 4.1 Illustration from *A History of Lenses* by Sun Yunqiu. Rare manuscript, Shanghai Library.

At first glance, the illustration resembles a perspectival drawing, but the perspectivalism is superficial and restricted to the lines of the buildings. The reference in the drawing to Western techniques of copperplate engraving, such as horizontal and vertical striations to depict clouds and reflections in water, creates an even greater suggestion of what it is like to look through a Western lens. The feeling of unfamiliarity regarding these cues for shadows and volume presumably gave a sense of the visual adjustment readers would feel when using the device.[58]

Sun Yunqiu enumerates the lenses available in his shop—twenty-two different strengths of lenses for the nearsighted, twenty-two different strengths for the farsighted, and specialties such as the microscope, incense-burning mirror, cosmetic mirror, flint, and telescope. The text introduces the telescope to those who have opportunity to encounter it as a physical object for the first time. Earlier manuals of style such as Wen Zhenheng's *Superfluous Things*, whose description of elegant boxes appears in chapter 3, or Li Yu's own *Casual Expressions of Idle Feeling* (*Xianqing ouji* 閒情偶寄, 1671), give the impression that the author entertains his readers by describing the proper storage and use of luxury items they might never encounter. In Sun Yunqiu's text it is evident that the telescope has become a commodity, and that the intended readers of the *History of Lenses* are the sort of people who might enter his shop to acquire it.

Clearly assuming that readers can easily obtain a telescope, Sun goes on to make sure that they know how to manipulate and care for the instrument:

> This instrument is suitable for use in high places like towers and platforms to look at mountains, rivers and lakes, forests and villages in the distance. They will be as if before your eyes. If something is several dozens of leagues away, or over a few hundred or a few thousand paces away, you can use it to look at people and observe objects. They will be even clearer than if they were before your eyes. There are many uses, which are all written of in Tang Daowei's [Adam Schall von Bell's] *On the Telescope*, so I won't list them here. The pair of tubes can be extended and retracted. If the object is near, the tube must be extended; if the object is far, the tube must be retracted; if it is accordingly extended and retracted,

you may stop as soon as the image becomes clear. Adjusting for a distance of one or two leagues is rather the same as adjusting for a distance of 20 or 30 leagues; it's only within one league that you will have to adjust it more frequently.

此鏡宜於樓臺高處用之, 遠視山川河海, 樹木村落, 如在目前. 若十數里之內, 千百步之外, 取以觀人鑒物, 較之覿面, 更覺分明. 利用種種, 具載湯道未先生《遠鏡說》中, 茲不贅列. 筒筒相套者, 取其可伸可縮也. 物形彌近, 筒須伸長; 物形彌遠, 筒須收短; 逐分伸縮, 象顯即止. 若收至一二里, 與二三十里略同, 惟一里以內, 收放頗多.[59]

Sun Yunqiu's text was a user's manual as well as a not-so-thinly veiled advertisement for his lenses. He spoke directly to the adjustment of seeing with one eye:

Bo Zijue advised that one must ordinarily practice seeing through the telescope for a number of days, going from the obvious to the minute, from the near to the far, extending and retracting the draws, gradually becoming familiar, then later if you happen on occasion to take a look through it, you will be able to see. If you are just a hair off, the light will be diminished, and this is the fault of the instrument. People who are farsighted should stand behind the telescope and extend the tube, people who are nearsighted should stand behind the telescope and retract the tube. No two people's eyesight will be alike, so everyone must adjust it. Do not touch the lenses with sweaty hands and soil them. If they get dusty, use a clean cloth to wipe them lightly, and the strength of the lenses will be as before. Don't rub them with silk. One should avoid doing so with all lenses.

薄子珏云, 須平時習視數日, 由顯之微, 自近至遠, 轉移進退, 久久馴熟, 然後臨時舉目便知. 倘一毫未合, 光明必減, 奚鏡之咎. 衰目人後鏡略伸, 短視人後鏡略縮, 目光亦萬不能同, 自調為得. 鏡面勿沾手澤. 倘蒙塵垢, 以淨布輕輕拂拭, 即復光明. 勿用綢絹揩摩. 諸鏡仿此.[60]

Li Yu was by far Sun Yunqiu's senior, so we might imagine that Sun Yunqiu imitated Li Yu. When we look at the borrowing, however, we see that in the opening section of chapter 2 Li Yu's story splices a passage of Sun Yunqiu's that existed in *History of Lenses* as an integrated whole into his descriptions of several different lenses. He carefully mixes and matches short phrases from *History of Lenses* rather than copying the passages from Sun Yunqiu outright.[61] Sun Yunqiu's language is quite similar to that of Schall's *On the Telescope*, and in fact he inserts phrases from Schall's text into his own.

Sun Yunqiu's commercial tone focuses on the practical advantages of his devices. His cosmetic mirror, for example, is "not as cumbersome as a bronze mirror, and one can avoid [being sneered at for] having one's robe and cap out of order" (既不如銅鏡之累贅, 可免衣冠不飾之譏). Li Yu follows Sun Yunqiu's wording almost exactly, making only insignificant changes. The similarity in style is remarkable. I suspect that Sun Yunqiu, born a generation after Li Yu, was an admirer of Li Yu's *Casual Expressions of Idle Feeling* (*Xianqing ouji* 閑情偶寄, 1671) and adopted its style, allowing Li Yu in turn to suture in Sun's passages with nary a seam. We saw that Li Yu's friend Zhu Sheng wrote in a preface to *History of Lenses* that Sun Yunqiu had showed him a draft; it is quite possible that Zhu Sheng shared the draft with Li Yu, and that Li Yu then incorporated the section from *History of Lenses* into the version of the story that appeared in the undated Xiaoxianju edition.

Purporting to answer the riddle of how Jiren has gained revelatory sight, the passage of Li Yu's story that draws on Sun Yunqiu's text begins:

> The device in question is known as a thousand-li glass and comes from the West. It demonstrates the same intelligence as the minute-revealing glass, the incense-burning glass, the makeup glass, and the lighting glass, all of which are capable of numerous strange and ingenious effects.
>
> 這件東西名為千里鏡, 出在西洋, 與顯微, 焚香, 端容, 取火諸鏡同是一種聰明, 生出許多奇巧.[62]

The selective focus on the telescope in the earlier version of Li Yu's story here gives way to the distributed attention of the list. No longer is the telescope enlivened by a singular quality of attention. Of note, the five lenses—the microscope, incense-burning mirror, cosmetic mirror, flint, and telescope—are all described as having an internal intelligence that produces "ingenious effects." The passage concludes with a mock historical explanation of the telescope that mentions the artist Zhu Sheng's success in fashioning lenses "of a superior quality, on a par with the finest products of the West" (皆不類尋常，與西洋上著者無異).[63] Within the passage, the description of the microscope precedes that of the telescope:

> Somewhat bigger than a coin, it is supported on a tripod. When the tiniest object is placed beneath the tripod and observed from above, it is transformed into something huge. Lice and nits appear almost as big as dogs and sheep, and mosquitoes and flies as large as cranes and herons. The hairs on the louse's body, like the specks on the fly's wing, are so distinct you can count them. That is why it is called the minute-revealing glass—because it can reveal the most minute objects and set them before the eye with brilliant clarity.
>
> 顯微鏡大似金錢，下有三足. 以極微極細之物置於三足之中，從上視之，即變為極宏極鉅. 蟣蝨之屬，幾類犬羊; 蚊虻之形，有同鸛鶴. 並蟣蝨身上之毛，蚊虻翼邊之彩，都覺得根根可數，歷歷可觀. 所以叫做顯微，以其能顯至微之物而使之光明較著也.[64]

The microscope initiates the fiction of empiricism evident in the statement about seeing the hair of lice through the microscope. Lice have no hair. The claim that the microscope could make visible even the hair (presumably the cilia) on a louse's body appears in Robert Hooke's *Micrographia,* published in January 1665.[65] Astoundingly, it resurfaces in Li Yu's text, written less than fifteen years later. Here writ large is an example of the capacity of the lens to set before our eyes that which literally cannot be seen, to make us believe in the existence of that which does not exist.

This disquisition on the five lenses in chapter 2, a brief foray in the vein of the treatise on things, creates a marked interruption in the diegesis of "A Tower for the Summer Heat." Li Yu invites the reader to see if we are as perspicacious as Jiren:

> This glass employs several tubes of different thickness, of which the smaller ones fit inside the larger. To adjust it, you extend or retract the tubes. The reason it is called a thousand-*li* glass is that the lenses are set at the ends of the tubes, and when you use it for looking into the distance, nothing is beyond its range. Although the term *thousand li* is an exaggeration—you can't really see from one kingdom to another [literally, Wu to Yue, or Qin to Chu]—if you try it out inside that range, you will find the claim not at all fraudulent. If you use it for looking at people or things at a distance of several hundred yards to a few *li*, you'll find them more distinct than if they were sitting opposite. It is a genuine treasure.

> 此鏡用大小數管，粗細不一. 細者納於粗者之中，欲使其可放可收，隨伸隨縮. 所謂千里鏡者，即嵌於管之兩頭，取以視遠，無遐不到. 千里二字雖屬過稱，未必果能由吳視越，坐秦觀楚，然試千百里之內，便自不覺其誣. 至於十數里之中，千百步之外，取以觀人鑒物，不但不覺其遠，較對面相視者更覺分明. 真可寶也.[66]

The influence of Schall's *On the Telescope* is clear in this description of the instrument and its use. The telescope is a set of tubes and lenses; its range is limited and it has no fantastic powers. Anyone might use it—the connoisseur's recognition of the potential of the instrument is no longer at issue. But Li Yu grafts onto this description a more traditional claim, that the telescope can in effect transport the viewer to people and things: "You'd find them more distinct than if they were sitting opposite." Li Yu continues:

> The glasses described above were all produced in Western countries. Two hundred years ago they were brought to China only by tribute emissaries and thus were rarely seen and virtually unobtainable. From the Ming dynasty onward, some outstanding scholars from those countries, choosing not to restrict their activities to their own lands, chanced to come and establish their teaching in China. They knew how to manufacture these glasses and gave

them to people as presents, and so collectors of exotica were able to obtain them. Wishing to extend this knowledge, the scholars also taught people how to manufacture the glasses. But China was unable to match the foreigners in this kind of intelligence, and few men were able to master the techniques.

以上諸鏡皆西洋國所產, 二百年以前不過貢使攜來, 偶爾一見, 不易得也. 自明朝至今, 彼國之中有出類拔萃之士, 不為員幅所限, 偶來設教於中土, 自能製造, 取以贈人. 故凡探奇好事者, 皆得而有之. 諸公欲廣其傳, 常授人以製造之法. 然而此種聰明, 中國不如外國, 得其傳者甚少.[67]

In this passage, Li Yu adopts an ethnographic tone that will be familiar to readers of his earlier collections of stories, a tone that suggests the close relation between Li Yu's fiction and the notation book. The added passage hints at a commercialization of the telescope that was absent in the earlier version of the story. The culmination of this passage is a promotion of the lenses of Li Yu's friend Zhu Sheng of Hangzhou, the lens maker who mentored Sun Yunqiu and likely shared the draft of his *History of Lenses* with Li Yu. Li Yu depicts Zhu Sheng as a scholar who is the equal of Western lens makers:

In the last few years only Zhu Sheng, cognomen Xi'an, of Hangzhou, a scholar well known in literary circles, has succeeded.[68] His minute-revealing, incense burning, makeup, lighting and thousand-li glasses are all of superior quality, on a par with the finest products of the West, while his eyeglasses for near- and farsightedness are even better. Those in possession of his products look on them as rare and remarkable treasures.

數年以來, 獨有武林諸曦庵諱□者, 係筆墨中知名之士, 果能得其真傳. 所作顯微, 焚香, 端容, 取火及千里諸鏡, 皆不類尋常, 與西洋上著者無異, 而近視, 遠視諸眼鏡更佳, 得者皆珍為異寶.[69]

In the space between Li Yu's writing of the original story in 1657 and the writing of the passage added to the Xiaoxianju edition of "A Tower for the Summer Heat," the significance of the Western origins of the telescope had changed: now the West is invoked as a certification of authenticity, and the invocation of foreignness has a kind of instrumentality.

There are some similarities between the wording of the description of the telescope in Li Yu's story and that in *History of Lenses*, but it is the description of the cosmetic mirror that makes it clear that Li Yu has redacted Sun's text.[70] Sun's text reads:

> The mirror is small as a coin, and can be used to examine one's countenance, to ensure that one's beard and eyebrows are all in order. Since it is not as cumbersome as a bronze mirror, one can avoid having one's robe and cap out of order. It's even more suitable for the beauty, and can hang from her fan, or be tied into the corner of her handkerchief, so that she can smooth her hair at any time, or prettify her countenance on the spot, looking at her image and becoming more charming. It is a rare treasure for the fragrant boudoir.
>
> 鏡小如錢，用以鑒形，須眉畢備。既不如銅鏡之累墜，可免衣冠不飾之譏。更與美女相宜，懸之扇頭，系諸帕角，隨時掠鬢，在處修容，顧影生妍，香閨異寶。[71]

In Li Yu's version, the use of the cosmetic mirror for men has been omitted, and the entire section has been abbreviated. Li Yu has also omitted the comparison with the size of a coin, which he had borrowed to describe the microscope and incense-burning glass:

> This is even smaller than the preceding two. It is used to check one's appearance and see that one's hair is in order. Ladies on an outing will find it most convenient. Attached to a fan or kerchief, it is readily available for titivating along the way, and they need have no worries about their hair being out of place.
>
> 此鏡較焚香、顯微更小，取以鑒形，鬢眉畢備。更與游女相宜，懸之扇頭或繫之帕上，可以沿途掠物，到處修容，不致有飛蓬不戢之慮。[72]

The notion that a cosmetic mirror could become a fan pendant is the sort of ingenious touch that we would associate with Li Yu, and it is this

106 *Li Yu's Telescope*

sort of correspondence between Li Yu and Sun's text that made Li Yu's borrowing from Sun's text hard to detect. Zhu Sheng's preface to *History of Lenses* presents Sun Yunqiu as not only possessed of an inventive mind but dedicated to the new in a way that is reminiscent of Li Yu himself. "From time to time he would make an unusual instrument (*qiqi* 奇器), and if it wasn't unusual, he would think it mediocre (*yong* 庸)."[73]

Such unacknowledged, unmarked citations as Li Yu's borrowing from Sun Yunqiu were common in writing of this period in both China and Europe.[74] The text of Sun Yunqiu's *History of Lenses* depends heavily on that of Adam Schall von Bell's *On the Telescope*, which in turn incorporates portions of Galileo's *Sidereus Nuncius* (1610). The personal connections among Zhu Sheng, Sun Yunqiu, and Li Yu, however, complicate the significance of Li Yu's borrowing from Sun Yunqiu's text. As I noted, Li Yu pays homage to Zhu Sheng in the passage that introduces the list of lenses borrowed from Sun Yunqiu; Zhu Sheng is identified as the only person who can make such complex Western lenses. Zhu Sheng's preface to Sun Yunqiu's *History of Lenses* states in turn that Sun Yunqiu viewed Zhu Sheng as a mentor and had traveled from Suzhou to Hangzhou to ask Zhu Sheng to explain aspects of Schall's text. When Li Yu borrowed from the draft of Sun Yunqiu's *History of Lenses* in order to praise the lenses of Zhu Sheng, Sun Yunqiu could hardly object.

CONCLUSION

In "A Tower for the Summer Heat," the monocular focus of the telescope gives rise to Li Yu's experiments with perspective, involving both selective presentation of events from a single character's point of view and an extended focus on an individual character's process of thought. The monocular lens enlivens the original appearance of the objects selected, as Adam Schall von Bell noted in his instructions to new users of the telescope. Li Yu's telescopic lens provides the premise that permits the reader to hear Xianxian's extended thoughts. His experiment with representing thought enhances the sense that his characters have subjective experience. If events can be told from a character's point of view, it would stand to reason that the characters *have* a point of view. Just as seventeenth-century discursive writing on magnifying lenses delivers a consolidated version of the partial understanding the lenses provide, "A Tower for the Summer Heat" allows us to hear what the mind cannot directly perceive—a single, uninterrupted train of thought. That this was an experiment in the narration of thought is lost on us now. To modern-day readers, the selective narration of events from the perspective of a particular character might not seem noteworthy, but in the context of the omniscient narration of Ming-Qing vernacular fiction, it is an invention as newfangled as the telescope itself.

CHAPTER FIVE

The Plate-Glass Mirror in *The Story of the Stone*

This chapter and the next are devoted to Cao Xueqin's mid-eighteenth-century novel *The Story of the Stone* and its thinking about perception and perspective. In the criticism generated by the novel, the plate-glass mirror in the chambers of the novel's protagonist, Baoyu, has become an emblem of the character himself.[1] As we shall see, mirrors of this type, which combined European plate glass and a Chinese standing-screen frame, were not only unique to China but a rarity within Beijing itself. These full-length mirrors were fashioned in the imperial workshops and then bestowed as a measure of the emperor's favor; they were also commissioned by members of the royal family and high-ranking officials. In this chapter I ask how the material properties of the plate-glass mirror and its frame might affect its significance in *The Story of the Stone*. How might our understanding of the mirror shift when we ask how eighteenth-century readers experienced the technical marvel of plate glass? How might the plate-glass mirror enable the novel's questioning of the singular perspective associated with the notion of an "I," and how might it further the novel's interest in the "grand view" associated with the Grand View Garden (*Daguan yuan* 大觀園) in which Baoyu lives?[2] Finally, how might the plate-glass mirror speak to the interest of late-imperial fiction in describing the phenomenal world as simultaneously actual and illusory?

FIGURE 5.1 Bronze mirror in frame of table screen; frame bears the date 1776.
Source: Provided by the Palace Museum.

In 1763, the Qianlong emperor composed a poem titled "On the Mirror" (*Jing yu* 鏡喻) that examines the technical marvel of mirrored plate glass. Qianlong explains the process of applying the tain, the coating of quicksilver and tin that turns a transparent sheet of glass into a mirror. Unlike the bronze mirror, which oxidizes and must be polished, the glass mirror has the capacity to reflect accurately and with constancy (see figures 5.1 and 5.2). From that prosaic beginning Qianlong launches in a

FIGURE 5.2 Glass mirror in frame of standing screen, red sandalwood, Qing dynasty. *Source*: Provided by the Palace Museum.

different direction, exclaiming over the capacity of the glazed windows of his pavilions to reflect as though they were mirrors when lit by the glow of the setting sun.

"ON THE MIRROR"

Once the bronze mirror was polished with felt,
It was already able to reflect forms without leaving any aspect behind.
A recent method of the West,

The glass mirror is even more novel and ingenious than the bronze.
It is all achieved with the aid of human craftsmanship,
By spreading mercury across the mirror's back.
Before the mercury is applied,
The plain piece of glass gleams.
If one installs it in a window frame,
Objects outside can be seen quite clearly.
My mountain pavilions occasionally use this glass,
Solely because I wanted to see the silhouettes of the peaks.
Who knew that there would be some additional virtues?
Permit me to tell you of its novel charms.
The pavilion darkens although the world outside is still bright,
Lit by the glow from the western hills.
In the transparent glass windows,
The western peaks encounter their reflection and drape across it.[3]
I did not use a mirror, but I still harvested a mirror image,
This is truly hard for others to imagine.
From my veranda, I can count the people walking past my pavilion,
Amidst the tall trees, I look down and see the birds flying.
One could call them illusions, but illusion is also not illusion,
One can say that it is real, but real is also not real.
The buildings of the palace are suspended in vastness like the Guanghan Palace on the moon,[4]
The city towering like that of the Gandharvas.[5]
Even the most skilled debater could not distinguish one from the other,
Who could have initiated this all?
The cosmos has long been this way,
And heavenly design is truly impartial.

《鏡喻》

青銅摩以旃,
照形已無遺.
近代泰西法,
玻瓈更新奇.
然均藉人工,

水銀塗抹資.
其未塗水銀,
素片玻瓈輝.
可以施窓檽,
外物瞭然窺.
山亭偶用此,
徒緣觀峯姿.
孰知別有得,
新趣請言之.
亭暗而外朗,
承以西峯暉.
通徹玻瓈窓,
西峯觸影披.
不鏡而獲鑑,
實匪伊所思.
迴廊數人行,
喬樹瞰鳥飛.
曰幻幻即否,
曰真真又非.
宮疑廣寒懸,
城似乾闥巍.
炙轂莫能辨,
椎輪誰所爲.
宇宙此有素,
造物誠無私.[6]

Plate glass was of particular interest to Qianlong. In 1735, the first year of his reign, he began to install glass windows in his living quarters in the Chonghua palace, commencing with small glass "window eyes" (*chuanghu yan* 窗戶眼) inserted within conventional paper or silk window panes.[7] Here, he suggests that as night falls the windows of his pavilion become mirrorlike in their capacity to produce reflections (and indeed, the title of the poem could be translated as "Analogy for a Mirror"). One might assume that the emperor would see the reflection of the objects *within* the pavilion once dusk fell and candles were lit. The poem describes the opposite. The glow of the sunset renders the world outside brighter than the darkened pavilion. Under those conditions of lighting, the plate-glass windows act as mirrors, reflecting the features of the landscape outside the pavilion. In that way, the western hills outside the pavilion see their own reflection in the glass. In Qianlong's words, this effect is an "additional virtue" or novel charm of the plate-glass window. In an intriguing couplet that becomes a turning point in the poem, Qianlong remarks, "I did not use a mirror, but I still harvested a mirror image / This is truly hard for others to imagine."[8]

Qianlong uses the unusual verb *kan* 瞰, which means to look up or down into a vast expanse, to describe his view of the birds flying among trees as they are reflected in the glass. The verb *kan* often describes the soaring perspective of birds in flight. The mirror image of the birds in the glass thus permits Qianlong to view the birds themselves with a bird's-eye view. The play with reflection grants him freedom from an ordinary corporeal viewing position, and he begins to acquire a panoramic perspective that renders his vision gradually more comprehensive.

The window as mirror becomes a kind of charismatic object rather than a mere technological instrument, allowing Qianlong to inhabit space in a new way. When Qianlong tells us that he installed the plate-glass windows because he wanted to see the silhouettes of the peaks, or when he writes that the "objects outside can be seen quite clearly," he is implicitly positioned inside the pavilion. When he describes the reflections in the window of the darkened pavilion, however, he is outside the pavilion. Subtly, the speaker abandons a singular position, adopting instead a twinned set of positions in consonance with the notion of reflection.

The play on perception afforded by a sudden breadth of vision was a quality that Qianlong sought in the architectural spaces he built in later life, such as the Fuwangge (Belvedere of Viewing Achievements, 符望閣) and the Juanqinzhai (Studio of Exhaustion from Diligent Service, 倦勤齋) of the Qianlong gardens in the northeast corner of the Forbidden City. In the Fuwangge, the largest structure of the Qianlong gardens, the emperor passed through a warren of cellular rooms on the first two floors and ascended a staircase to reach a grand hall for meditation with a panoramic view of the Forbidden City on all four sides. Similarly, in the Juanqinzhai, the retirement lodge Qianlong built across the courtyard from the Fuwangge, he crossed from a small and cramped antechamber into the sweeping vistas of a room decorated from floor to ceiling with illusionistic paintings. With such sudden shifts, he created the experience of an abrupt and radical shift toward an all-encompassing perspective.

In the final section of the poem, the play on perspective takes a more philosophical turn. The reflections in the plate-glass windows that appear when dusk falls grant Qianlong a commanding view. Looking at the reflections of birds flying and people walking below, he turns to wonder whether the illusory quality of images reflected in the window points to the way in which the world around him is both real and not real. Contemporary readers might imagine the birds to be real and their reflections to be illusions, whereas the poem suggests that the birds, the people walking, the palace, and the city below are simultaneously illusions and not illusions. Otherwise put, the phenomenal world is illusory in that it is constructed through our senses and our cognitive apparatus, but it is not illusory in the sense that there is no world more real than the one we see. Qianlong conveys this not-real-and-yet-real quality in part with the internal mirrorlike reflection within the next lines. From the perspective of the plate-glass window acting as mirror, opposing formulations coexist without tension. The forms of this world are there and not there: "One could call it illusion, but it is also not illusion, / One can say it is real, but it is also not real" (曰幻幻即否 / 曰真真又非). As with the oft-cited phrase from the first chapter of *The Story of the Stone*, "Truth becomes fiction when fiction is true" (假作真時真亦假), this structure of repetition and reversal creates an impression that the formulation is all-encompassing. It also gives weight to the intermediary spaces between the terms, reinforcing the sense of being in suspension between two extremes.

We see here how symmetrical rhetorical structures create an intentional confusion that allows readers to intuit, rather than grasp, the proposition that the phenomenal world is both real and unreal. The play in the middle of the poem with formal structures that incorporate mirroring and reflection suggests an impartial perspective free from the trap of a singular and subjective position.[9] That prepares the ground for Qianlong's concluding lines. From his seemingly aerial vantage point, the relation of the glass to the forms it holds within is not simply mimetic. Rather, as objects encounter their mirror images in the glass, the conversation regarding accuracy of reflection, or verisimilitude, quickly turns to a consideration of how the glass might reveal the illusory (and yet not illusory) quality of the surrounding world. This distinction is central to the mirror scenes in *The Story of the Stone*.

PLATE GLASS IN THE IMPERIAL WORKSHOPS

As we saw in the poem "On the Mirror," plate glass appealed to the Qianlong emperor because it temporarily disrupted established modes of perception, in particular spatial perception.[10] The play with the potential of sheet glass as an artistic medium during the mid to later years of Qianlong's reign can be seen in such objects as the red sandalwood screen (figure 5.3) and the throne (figure 5.4), each of which incorporates sheet glass in an innovative way.[11]

The art historian Nancy Berliner has observed that the glass of the screen and throne is simultaneously transparent and solid, allowing the carved reliefs to float within the frame.[12] Within its backrest and arms, the throne embeds decorative motifs made of jade in clear glass, so that the jade seems suspended in midair. This use of plate glass can be understood as yet another manifestation of the playful substitution of one substance for another in the imperial workshops of the Yongzheng and Qianlong emperors.[13] Artisans of the imperial workshops fired porcelain to look like bronze, wood, and lacquerware, and blew glass that resembled porcelain but had an even greater ethereal translucence.[14] Glass, which had been used as a substitute for jade since ancient times, was also crafted to resemble precious gems such as lapis, turquoise, carnelian, amber, realgar, malachite, crystal, and mother of pearl.[15] The Bolognese techniques of perspectival painting that the Chinese artists of the imperial workshops learned from the *quadratura* painters Giovanni Gherardini (1655–ca. 1729) and Giuseppe Castiglione were yet another facet of this technical exploration of the mastery of surface. Although these various exercises of wit often have been spoken of in terms of trompe l'oeil, or in terms that suggest fakery or forgery such as "true" (*zhen* 真) and "false" (*jia* 假), I would suggest that we speak of them in terms of the substitution of substance.[16] They were not seriously intended to fool the eye but rather to dazzle the initiated with technological mastery as one material substance impersonated another. In other words, they were meant to inspire a double-take rather than to

FIGURE 5.3 Screen, Qianlong reign period. *Source*: Provided by the Palace Museum.

deceive entirely, to trigger momentary misperception that could inspire further reflection.

For Qianlong's grandfather, the Kangxi emperor (r. 1661–1722), the possession of sophisticated glass-making technology was a sign of good governance. This was not simply a trope, as it is perhaps in the poem by

FIGURE 5.4 Throne of the Qianlong reign period with glass panels. *Source*: Provided by the Palace Museum.

Qianlong on the glass mirror, but spoke to the technological rivalry between China and Europe. The Kangxi emperor opened a glassworks in the imperial workshops in 1696 under the direction of Kilian Stumpf 紀理安 (1655–1720), a German Jesuit who had learned glassmaking in the Black Forest.[17] Kangxi's tutor Gao Shiqi 高士奇 (1645–1704) wrote of a visit he made in 1703 to the Changchun yuan 暢春園, the Summer Palace in Beijing.[18] There he visited the imperial library and saw a neighboring stage surrounded by two-story structures featuring glass windows and Western paintings.[19] Gao Shiqi reported that the emperor then took him to the imperial glassworks, where Kangxi presented him with a number of glass objects, including a floor screen inset with European glass:

> The Emperor ordered me to approach the area before his daybed to look at the newly made glass objects, which were of the utmost in refined translucence. I said to him, "Even though these are [merely] ceramic pieces, whether or not they can be achieved has to do with correct governance. What China can create now greatly surpasses the West." The Emperor gave me twenty different glass objects, as

118 *The Plate-Glass Mirror in* The Story of the Stone

well as a European mirror set in a screen frame. It was over five and a half *chi* 尺 (1.8 meters) tall.

上命近榻前, 觀新造玻璃器具, 精瑩端好. 臣云: "此雖陶器, 其成否有關政治. 今中國所造, 遠勝西洋矣." 上賜各器二十件, 又自西洋來鏡屏一架, 高可五尺餘.[20]

Gao Shiqi's remark to the emperor—"What China can create now greatly surpasses the West"—suggests that glassmaking technology was a matter of global rivalry. The historian Yang Boda, who pioneered the study of Qing-dynasty glass, noted that a great deal of foreign glass was present in late-Ming Canton, but the literati of Canton considered glassware to be of little interest.[21] It was the global circulation of glass in gifts presented by diplomatic missions from Europe that lent a new urgency and rigor to Chinese glassmaking.[22] When the Kangxi emperor did a southern tour in 1689, the Sicilian missionaries Emmanuel Laurifice 潘國良 (1646–1703) and Prospero Intorcetta 殷鐸澤 (1626–1696) presented to him a cosmetic mirror, a small telescope, and two glass vases, as well as a colored glass sphere.[23] A papal legation of 1721 presented Kangxi with Venetian glass.[24] Such gifts spurred technical development in the imperial glassworks, whose artisans drew inspiration from gifts of glass from the Dutch East India Company, France, Portugal, and Russia, as well as Jesuit missionaries.

Even after the imperial glass workshop in Beijing gained the technical expertise to make plate glass in the mid-eighteenth century, European glass mirrors were prized, as the poem by Yuan Mei that concludes this chapter suggests.[25] European gifts of mirrored glass to the imperial court and to lower-ranking officials continued for decades after the imperial glass workshop is thought to have gained the capacity to make sheet glass.[26] The plate glass that entered China via gifts from European emissaries was so precious that the secondary recipient was often of higher rank than the first. Maritime customs officials in Canton sent Western sheet glass to the emperor as tribute.[27] During the Yongzheng reign (1722–1735), mirrors, glass screens, and lanterns were a common feature of the presentation lists of officials posted in Canton, who offered tribute on imperial birthdays, the New Year's festival, the Duanyang festival, and the change of seasons.[28]

As I mentioned in the introduction, *The Story of the Stone* is the work of fiction that literary scholars, art historians, and historians turn to for illustrative example; it offers an encyclopedic rendering of the material culture of the mid-eighteenth century. Its author, Cao Xueqin, was the scion of a formerly wealthy family close to the Kangxi emperor. Three generations of the Cao family served as textile commissioners in Nanjing from 1663 to 1728 before Kangxi's successor, the Yongzheng emperor, charged the family with financial mismanagement. For this reason, the Cao family was deeply familiar with the material culture of the Kangxi and Yongzheng courts. Much of the scholarly writing about the objects of *The Story of the Stone* delves into the records of the imperial workshops to develop a picture of the material surroundings of the fictional Jia family. This archival turn is premised on the notion that Cao Xueqin drew on his own family's experience in his depiction of the Jias.

Documentation of the gifts from the Cao family to the Kangxi and Yongzheng emperors shows that Western glass passed through their hands; as textile commissioners, they had the responsibility of forwarding tribute gifts from foreign emissaries as well as presenting their own gifts to the throne. Of the five extant presentation lists of gifts from high-ranking officials to the Kangxi emperor, three are from the Cao family: two from Cao Xi 曹璽 (1619–1684), Cao Xueqin's great-grandfather; and one from Cao Fu 曹頫 (ca. 1696–after 1735), Cao Xueqin's uncle.[29] The Cao family's lists of gifts presented to the throne contain a number of objects of Western origin, some of which appear in *The Story of the Stone*. For example, in 1696 Cao Yin presented Kangxi with liquid essence of roses (*meigui lu* 玫瑰露) in a glass bottle, which had been given to him by Portuguese emissaries. Such a bottle appears in *The Story of the Stone* in chapter 34, when Baoyu's mother sends him essence of roses contained in a glass bottle with a tiny yellow label signaling that it came from the palace, and in chapter 60, when Baoyu passes the bottle on to the cook who serves his apartment, hoping that it will improve her ailing daughter's health.[30] Mirrors set with European glass often entered the imperial workshops after having been sent in tribute by foreign dignitaries or by customs officials in the south. Such a plate-glass mirror in a standing screen frame can be seen in the former residence in Beijing of Ji Yun 紀昀 (1724–1805), head compiler under the Qianlong emperor of *The Complete Library in Four Branches* (*Siku quanshu* 四庫全書).[31]

When glass mirrors in foreign frames arrived at the imperial workshops, the original frames were discarded in favor of those used for Chinese standing screens. In other words, mirrors with foreign frames were simply treated as a source of raw glass. In 1733, Mao Keming 毛克明, the superintendent of tax revenue at customs in Canton, sent the Yongzheng emperor a plate-glass dressing mirror that had been set in a carved lacquered frame in the Japanese style, as well as four sheets of mirrored glass without frames. The notes of the imperial workshops on the treatment of this gift are revealing. The Yongzheng emperor ordered that the mirror in the lacquered frame be stripped of its frame and then reframed as a single-sided "half-legged" mirror (*ban tui jing* 半腿鏡), its legs spliced in half vertically to allow the screen to stand flush against the wall (figure 5.5).[32]

When officials in Canton refitted European glass into Chinese screen frames and then sent the freestanding mirrors to Beijing as gifts for the emperor, they were forwarded directly to the imperial workshops. For example, in 1731, the superintendent of maritime customs in Canton, Zu Binggui 祖秉圭 (1684–1740), presented the Yongzheng emperor with a standing mirror (*chaping* 插屏) more than five Chinese feet (1.6 m) tall and framed in Chinese cedar. He also sent a large piece of glass of the same length protected by a sleeve of white wool in a wooden case. Both framed and unframed mirrors alike were received simply as a source of raw glass and delivered to the imperial workshops straightaway.[33]

The process of reframing European glass in frames for Chinese standing screens resulted in a constellation of features in the Chinese plate-glass mirror that was unique in the world.[34] The custom of placing plate-glass mirrors in full-length standing screens likely developed from the earlier practice of setting bronze mirrors in frames for table screens. In eighteenth-century Europe, glass mirrors were handheld or mounted on walls; they were not freestanding. Several characteristics of the glass mirror set in a standing screen reinforced the mirror's potential to surprise and confuse the characters of *The Story of the Stone*. First, the screen frame was full body in height, so that those who walked toward the mirrored glass encountered their reflection at eye level, an unfamiliar sensation to eighteenth-century Chinese accustomed to the bronze mirror, which was held in one's hand or placed on a small stand. Second, the glass mirror could be left

FIGURE 5.5 Half-legged mirror, Yangxin dian (Hall of Mental Cultivation), Forbidden City. *Source*: Provided by the Palace Museum.

uncovered; in contrast, bronze mirrors were kept covered to prevent oxidation. This presented a possibility of encountering the glass mirror unexpectedly. Lastly, double-sided standing screens were customarily inset with different materials in front and back, whether patterned marble, decorative carving, or painting, but mirrored screens held glass on both sides of the screen, so that viewers did not know which side they were approaching.[35] The unexpected encounter with a full-length, uncovered glass mirror was understandably disorienting for the characters of *The Story of the Stone* who happened upon the unaccustomed expanse of plate glass.

THE DOUBLE-SIDED MIRROR

Scholarly criticism of *The Story of the Stone* has paid considerable attention to the scenes in which various characters encounter the plate-glass mirror. I consider those scenes again to imagine how the mirror's material properties might have set in motion imaginative possibilities that affected not only the depiction of the glass mirror but also the portrayal of the bronze mirror of this novel, the "mirror of the romantic" (*fengyue baojian* 風月寶鑑) of chapter 12. The Qianlong emperor's poem showed us that as night fell, the reflections that appeared in plate-glass windows granted a sudden vision of a vast and redoubled expanse. This notion of a broad, encompassing quality of vision is in fact encapsulated in the name of the garden in which the young protagonists of *The Story of the Stone* live, the "Grand View" or "Prospect" Garden. The double-sided mirror is perhaps the object within the garden that Cao Xueqin returns to describe most often, and so it makes sense to ask how this glass mirror, which stands in the doorway between Baoyu's public reception room and his private chambers, might amplify our understanding of *daguan* 大觀, a term often translated as "grand view" or "prospect" that might also be translated as "total vision."[36]

In chapter 12 of *The Story of the Stone* a signal scene featuring the bronze mirror establishes the parameters for later encounters with the plate-glass mirror. A Daoist arrives at the deathbed of Jia Rui, a minor male relative of the Jia family. Jia Rui's cousins have dumped nightsoil on him in punishment for ogling his cousin's wife, Xifeng; drenched in this nightsoil, he spends the night locked out of the house in the cold. Severely weakened by both the punishment and his unfulfilled desire, he is desperate for a cure when the Daoist arrives. The Daoist offers Jia Rui a two-sided mirror that can save his life if he looks at it every day—but only if he looks at the back of the mirror, never at the front.

This scene draws on the complicated cultural associations of the bronze mirror, which within the Confucian tradition is a venerable figure for the self-examination of both ruler and polity.[37] Mencius (ca. 372–289 BCE) warned that "the mirror of Yin"—the example of the decline of the Shang dynasty—was close at hand.[38] The mirror served as a reminder to consider one's character and actions with a view to the figurative mirror of historical example. This notion of the mirror as an inspiration to self-reflection on the part of the sovereign played a role in the interior decoration of the imperial precincts of the Qing dynasty, where standing screens containing plate-glass mirrors often stood to either side of the throne and served as silent reminders of the need for examination of one's thoughts and behavior.

Jia Rui naturally ignores the opportunity the mirror affords for self-reflection. As instructed, he consults the back of the mirror, where he is confronted by a skull. In horror he promptly flips to the front, and upon doing so sees the object of his lust, Xifeng, beckoning him. He slips into the mirror, where Xifeng engages in intercourse with him before ushering him out. As the mirror turns of its own accord in his hands, he sees the skull and becomes aware of a trickle of semen he has ejaculated. This sequence repeats—Jia Rui turning the mirror so that he can enter the side from which Xifeng beckons, the mirror flipping back to reveal the skull—until two figures approach him inside the mirror, enchain him, and cart him away. The two sides of the mirror are not equally balanced; they are weighted toward the verso side, as is suggested when the mirror turns of its own accord in Jia Rui's hands to show him the skull. In fact, the mirror could have provided a cure for Jia Rui had he used it as instructed.[39]

Bronze mirrors were not typically double-sided; one side was ornamented, the other polished as a reflective surface. It is possible, then, that the double-sided glass mirror might have influenced the conception of the magical bronze mirror in this scene. The nineteenth-century Yao commentary notes succinctly after Jia Rui has intercourse with Xifeng inside the mirror, "The Land of Illusion" (Taixu huanjing 太虛幻境). The mid-nineteenth-century commentator Zhang Xinzhi 張新之 (fl. 1828–1850) adds, "Is it illusion or reality? Illusion is reality" (是幻是真, 幻即真也). Jia Rui's last words as he expires in a pool of cold semen are "Wait! Let me get the mirror and then go!" (讓我拿了鏡子再走). Zhang Xinzhi comments sarcastically, "Who is 'me'? And where is the 'mirror'?" (我是誰? 鏡子何在?).[40] In Zhang Xinzhi's view, the skull on the verso side of the mirror should have revealed to Jia Rui that there was no "I"—no subject and no object, no "me" to hold the mirror, and no "mirror" to hold.[41]

Zhang Xinzhi likely invokes the long history of a figural equivalence between mind and mirror in the Chinese Buddhist tradition and in Daoist philosophy. Xiaofei Tian notes that as early as the Six Dynasties, the monk Hui Yuan 慧遠 (334–416) spoke of the form (*ti* 體) of a "vacuous mirror" (*xu jing* 虛鏡) that when contemplated allows the meditating subject's mind to become clear.[42] We find the image of "mind as mirror" as well in the seventh of the inner chapters of the *Zhuangzi*, "Fit for Emperors and Kings" (Ying di wang 應帝王), which uses the mirror as a figure for the imperturbable tranquility of the sage, stating "The Perfect Man uses his mind like a mirror—going after nothing, welcoming nothing, responding but not storing. Therefore he can win out over things and not hurt himself" (至人之用心若鏡, 不將不迎, 應而不藏, 故能勝物而不傷).[43] In the *Zhuangzi*, dust on the mirror becomes a metaphor for that which prevents the mind from seeing clearly, a metaphor that later surfaces repeatedly in Chinese Buddhist texts, as dust on the mirror becomes associated with the desires that cloud the mind.[44] The metaphor of mind as mirror on which dust might settle anchors the opening of The Platform Sutra, in which two poems by the rivals for the title of Sixth Patriarch debate the significance of the metaphor.[45] In the Laṅkāvatāra Sutra, an important text in the development of Chan Buddhism, the perceiving mind is cast as a mirror that mistakes the reflections on its surface for reality.[46] In those texts, the mirror is a figure for an understanding unadulterated by preconception or desires. In *The Story of the Stone*, the notion of the mirror as a figure for perfect comprehension coexists, and indeed undergirds, the more superficial capacity of the plate-glass mirror to occasion misperception. As with the witty substitutions of substance executed in the imperial workshops, the double-take as characters come across reflections in the mirror that momentarily fool the eye creates the potential for a deeper understanding of the way in which the forms of the everyday world are both real and not real.

THE PLATE-GLASS MIRROR IN *THE STORY OF THE STONE*

In chapter 17 of *The Story of the Stone*, Baoyu's father Jia Zheng confidently leads a group of friends through Baoyu's future lodgings, which are under construction in the garden. Once inside the apartment that will become Baoyu's, the group quickly becomes lost:

> He led them inside the building. Its interior turned out to be all corridors and alcoves and galleries, so that properly speaking it could hardly have been said to have *rooms* at all. The partition walls which made these divisions were of wooden paneling exquisitely carved in a wide variety of motifs: bats in clouds, the "three friends of winter"—pine, plum, and bamboo, little figures in landscapes, birds and flowers, scrollwork, antique bronze shapes, "good luck" and "long life" characters, and many others. The carvings, all of them the work of master craftsmen, were beautified with inlays of gold, mother-o'pearl and semi-precious stones. Shelving was concealed in the double thickness of the partition at the base of these apertures, making it possible to use them for storing books and writing materials and for the display of antique bronzes, vases of flowers, miniature tray-gardens and the like. In addition to being paneled, the partitions were pierced by numerous apertures, some round, some square, some sunflower-shaped, some shaped like a fleur-de-lis, some cusped, some fan-shaped. The overall effect was at once richly colorful and, because of the many apertures, airy and graceful. The trompe l'oeil effect of these ingenious partitions had been further enhanced by inserting false windows and doors in them, the former covered in various pastel shades of gauze, the latter hung with richly-patterned damask portières. The main walls were pierced with window-like perforations in the shape of zithers, swords, vases and other objects of virtù. The literary gentlemen were rapturous: "Exquisite!" they cried. "What marvellous workmanship!"

> 說著, 引人進入房內. 只見其中收拾的與別處不同, 竟分不出間隔來的. 原來四面皆是雕空玲瓏木板, 或流雲百蝠, 或歲寒三友, 或山水人物, 或翎毛花卉, 或集錦, 或博古, 或萬福萬壽, 各種花樣, 皆是名手雕鏤, 五彩銷金嵌玉的. 一槅一槅, 或貯書, 或設鼎, 或安置筆硯, 或供設瓶花, 或安放盆景. 其槅式樣, 或圓或方, 或葵花蕉葉, 或連環半璧. 真是花團錦簇, 玲瓏剔透. 倏爾五色紗糊, 竟係小窗; 倏爾彩綾輕覆, 竟如幽戶. 且滿牆皆是隨依古董玩器之

形摳成的槽子. 如琴, 劍, 懸瓶之類, 俱懸於壁, 却都是與壁相平的. 衆人都贊: 好精緻, 難為怎麼做的!"[47]

The ornament of these partitions suggests the dizzying referential excess that so many critics have observed in *The Story of the Stone*.[48] Like the novel itself, these partitions condense many cultural references into a single space. There is a certain sleight of hand at work, however. The zithers, swords, and vases of the last lines of the passage are described in terms of *negative* space. They are carved apertures that issue an invitation to the viewer to enter their recesses visually, a point I will return to shortly when I discuss Grannie Liu's encounter with the mirror.

The narrative describes Baoyu's chambers as being different from other places (與別處不同) in that the intricate carvings of the partitions create confusion as to how the rooms are divided (分不出間隔來的). The sensation of being unable to place the self in space is reinforced by the vertiginous luster of the materials inlaid in the partitions, which momentarily affects stability of perception and fools the physiological sense of the body in space. To better understand this disorientation regarding the body's position in space, we could look to the Fuwangge of the Qianlong gardens, which I mentioned briefly in the discussion of the Qianlong emperor's poem on the mirror. The neighboring building, the Juanqinzhai, has received greater scholarly attention, and consequently has often been mentioned in conjunction with *The Story of the Stone*. The Fuwangge, however, was famous for its maze-like quality.[49]

Designed and built by Qianlong during the early 1770s, the Fuwangge has been described by architectural historians as a Milou 迷樓, a labyrinth in the tradition of the palace of Emperor Yang of the Sui.[50] An interior story that is not visible from the outside (*xianlou* 仙樓) enhances a sense of mystery. Like the inlaid partition of Baoyu's chambers above, the wooden partitions of the Fuwangge are inset with expanses of gemstones and mother-of-pearl. A technique that recently had been developed in Yangzhou for inlaying jade in furniture was used, in an unthinkable luxury, to adorn the architectural partitions themselves, rendering the carved partitions between rooms lustrous with inlaid jade. The sheen of the silk gauze panels that covered the interior windows of the partitions was enhanced by techniques now lost, such as the pasting of gold on silk. The gauze panels, moreover, were embroidered using a technique called "double-sided embroidery" (*shuangmian xiu* 雙面繡), which hid all trace of workmanship. Because there were no visible knots to indicate the back side of the embroidery, whichever side the viewer approached the partitions from seemed to be the front. Those embroidered panels quietly and wittily referenced the notion of spatial disorientation.

The carved partitions surrounding the full-length plate-glass mirror in Baoyu's chambers similarly reference a loss of orientation regarding the spatial positioning of the body.[51] The commentator Zhang Xinzhi suggests that Baoyu's chambers themselves recall the labyrinthine palace, "It is as if it were a Milou. If desire for material things is like this, then Baoyu, the stone that has numinousness, will also be like this" 隱然一座迷樓, 物欲如此, 通靈亦如此.[52] Unlike the aspiration of trompe l'oeil to represent three dimensions on a flat surface, this play with space suggests an effort to elude any sense of dimensionality. As the partition's lustrous surfaces disorient newcomers to Baoyu's chambers, the body loses a sense of where it is in space, and thus of the "I" as a point of orientation.

This diminished capacity to perceive space from the viewpoint of the "I" prepares the way for Jia Zheng's lack of self-recognition in the mirror.

> Jia Zheng, after taking no more than a couple of turns inside this confusing interior, was already lost. To the left of him was what appeared to be a door. To the right was a wall with a window in it. But on raising its portière he discovered the door to be a bookcase, and when looking back, he observed—what he had not noticed before—that the light coming in through the silk gauze of the window illuminated a passage-way leading to an open doorway, and as he began walking towards it, a party of gentlemen similar to his own came advancing to meet him, and he realized that he was walking towards a large mirror. They were able to circumvent the mirror, but only to find an even more bewildering choice of doorways on the other side.
>
> 原來賈政等走了進來, 未進兩層, 便都迷了舊路, 左瞧也有門可通, 右瞧又有窗暫隔. 及到了跟前, 又被一架書擋住. 回頭再走, 又有窗紗明透, 門徑可行;

> 及至門前，忽見迎面也進來一群人，都與自己形相一樣，卻是玻璃大鏡相照. 及轉過鏡去，一發見門子多了。[53]

The dizzying effect of seeing one's own image in the mirror is part of the overall sensation of being disoriented and losing one's way in Baoyu's quarters, which at this point are not yet inhabited.[54] Qiancheng Li has observed in the context of this passage that the character *mi* 迷, translated below as "lost," refers in Buddhist terminology to "an unenlightened state of loss and disorientation, the opposite of awakened perception."[55] The spatial disorientation signals the possibility of a productive confusion. Jia Zheng's lack of self-recognition before the Western mirror conceivably creates the potential for a fleeting recognition of the notion that there is no enduring essence to the self.[56] The opportunity for realization passes, however, as Jia Zheng and his party circumvent the mirror without remark; the very sophistication that allows them to recognize the technology of the mirror forecloses the possibility of deeper realization.

GRANNIE LIU'S MIRROR IMAGE

In chapter 41, Grannie Liu, an unlettered woman from the countryside whom the Jia family hosts as a jester of sorts, mistakes her own image in the mirror for that of her son-in-law's mother. Having only just arrived from her farm in the countryside, she is bewildered by the opulence of the Jia mansion. She has left a drinking party in the vicinity of Baoyu's quarters to relieve herself when she loses her way. Drunk and confused, she approaches the mirror through a portal covered by a green-flowered curtain. She is dazzled by the carvings on the partitions surrounding the mirror:

> She lifted this [the curtain], stepped through and looked around. The four walls here were paneled with cunningly carved shelves on which were displayed lyres, swords, vases, and incense-burners. They were hung moreover with embroidered curtains and gauze glittering with gold and pearls. Even the green glazed floor-tiles had floral designs. More dazzled than ever she turned to leave.

> 劉姥姥掀簾進去，擡頭一看，只見四面墻壁，玲瓏剔透，琴劍瓶爐皆貼在墻上，錦籠紗罩，金彩珠光，連地下踩的磚，皆是碧綠，鑿花，竟越發把眼花了。[57]

As Grannie Liu lifts the curtain to reach the interior of Baoyu's apartment, the narrative gives us a condensed version of the first lines of the long descriptive passage on the partition in chapter 17 that I examined earlier. The two passages describing the partition in chapters 17 and 41 repeat the same phrases but with a sly reversal: the empty apertures now appear to be solid forms. The recessed apertures in the shapes of lyres (in Hawkes's translation, "zithers"), swords and vases are now described as actual musical instruments, swords and vases affixed (*tie* 貼) to the wall. The term *affixed*, which did not appear in chapter 17, might refer to the wall-mounted illusionistic painting known as "affixed hanging" (*tieluo* 貼落) that I discuss in chapter 6; if so, perspectivalism is here used to create painted forms that rise dynamically from the flat surface of the wall. However we interpret the term *tie*, the quiet play—in which the shapes described in chapter 17 as apertures are described in chapter 41 as being affixed to the wall—suggests an inconstant quality to phenomenal form. This inconsistency in the description of the partition subtly disorients the readers, reinforcing the confusion created by the dazzling surfaces of the partition itself.

The play with symmetry and reversal in the twinned passages describing the carving of the partition sets the stage for Grannie Liu to mistake her own image in the mirror for that of her son-in-law's mother (*qing jia mu* 親家母). The term, which does not exist in English, encapsulates the reflection and reversal of a mirror image. Grannie Liu mistakes herself for her symmetrical opposite in the familial structure:

> She turned to leave—but where was the door? To her left was a bookcase, to her right a screen. She had just discovered a door behind the screen and stepped forward to open it when, to her amazement, her son-in-law's mother came in. "Fancy seeing you here!" exclaimed Grannie Liu. "I suppose you found that I hadn't been home these last few days and tracked me down here. Which of the girls brought you in?" The other old woman smiled and did not answer.

找門出去,那裏有門,左一架書,右一架屏。剛從屏後得了一門,才要出去,只見他親家母也從外面迎了進來。劉姥姥詫異,忙問道:"親家母,你想是見我這幾日沒家去,虧你找我來。那一位姑娘帶你進來的?"他親家只是笑,不還言。[58]

This scene presents us with a comic version of the earlier scene in which the more sophisticated Jia Zheng quickly recognizes his image in the mirror. Grannie Liu's misrecognition is more specific: she misperceives the old woman in the mirror as her son-in-law's mother, that is, her "mirror image" in the map of the family structure. As the old woman in the mirror smiles and does not answer, we see an interest in perception from the point of view of the mirror image. There are two optic axes: the perspectives of Grannie Liu and her son-in-law's mother, symmetrical but reversed. This prepares us for the biaxial symmetry of the dreams of Jia Baoyu and Zhen Baoyu in chapter 56.

> "How little you've seen of the world," chuckled Grannie Liu. "The flowers in this garden are so fine, you just had to go picking some to stick all over your own head—for shame!" Again the other made no reply. Suddenly Grannie Liu recalled having heard that rich folk had in their houses some kind of full-length mirror. It dawned on her that this was her own reflection. She felt it with her hand and looked more carefully. Sure enough, it was a mirror set in four carved red sandalwood partitions.
>
> 劉姥姥笑道:"你好沒見世面,見這園子裡的花好,你就沒死活帶了一頭。"他親家也不答應。便忽然想起:"常聽見大富貴人家有一種穿衣鏡,這別是我在鏡子裏頭呢罷。"說畢,伸手一摸,再細一看,可不是四面雕空紫檀板壁,將這鏡子嵌在中間。[59]

When Grannie Liu extends her hand to touch the mirror, the action follows her realization that the surface is indeed flat. In chapter 6, a series of anecdotes suggests that the act of touching a painted wall is what allows the viewer to realize the scene is painted, not real. The significance of the touch in such anecdotes is often read via Hawkes's translation of this scene, which I do not use here because it is not faithful to the original. Hawkes adds a vignette in which Grannie Liu engages in a comic skirmish with her counterpart in the mirror. She finally grasps that the image is her own when she reaches out to touch the face of the old woman and finds her "cold and hard as a block of ice."[60] But in the passage quoted above we see that Grannie Liu realizes she is standing in front of a mirror *before* she reaches out to touch her own image. The touch is not what causes her to realize she stands in front of a flat surface. We should notice as well that Grannie Liu does not simply accept that she was deceived but examines the frame that delimits the mirror as well as its surface.

As the scene closes, we are reminded that the mirror is not just a reflecting surface but also a three-dimensional object, and we discover that, as an object, it is not stable. Just prior to the passage above, Grannie Liu passed a standing screen (presumably inset with something other than mirrored glass) when she arrived at the full-length mirror, which is now described as mounted in the wooden partitions that separate Baoyu's private and public rooms. When she accidentally presses a Western mechanism hidden in the frame, she activates a technology by which the mirror suddenly slips to the side and a door appears in its place; she walks through and finds herself in Baoyu's bedchamber. This vision of the mirror as a trick door mounted in a partition is in direct contrast to its earlier depiction, when Jia Zheng walked around a mirror set in a freestanding screen in order to enter Baoyu's private rooms. The various depictions of the mirror are not congruent. That inconsistency reinforces the mirror's potential to disorient and confuse; I will return to this point later.

MIRROR AND DREAM

For the rustic Grannie Liu, the mirror is literally a portal, opening to permit her entrance into Baoyu's bedroom. For Baoyu, the mirror is a portal in a more figurative sense. It opens the possibility of thinking about the self from a perspective other than that of the singular, corporeal "I" as Baoyu journeys into the mirror to meet his counterpart, Zhen Baoyu 甄寶玉.[61] This scene builds on Jia Rui's encounter with the magic mirror in chapter 12, as Jia Baoyu repeatedly encounters opportunities to reflect on the impermanence of his body. As the similarity in their first names suggests, Zhen Baoyu is initially positioned as the double of Jia Baoyu. But their last names—Zhen (a homonym for "true") and Jia (a homonym for "false") suggest they are, like mirror images, symmetrical but also reversals of one another.

It is fitting that Baoyu's waking moments before he enters the mirror in his dream in chapter 56 are preoccupied by thoughts of a double. Troubled by the news that the Zhen family of Nanjing have a boy named Baoyu whose appearance exactly matches Baoyu's own, Baoyu argues with his cousin Shi Xiangyun 史湘雲 that he cannot possibly have a double of the same name and same appearance:

> "You don't believe that rubbish, do you?" said Baoyu. "How *could* there be another Baoyu?"
> "There was a Lin Xiangru in the Warring States period and a Sima Xiangru under the Former Han," said Xiangyun.
> "Yes, but this one's supposed to *look* the same as well," said Baoyu. "That's not something you can find precedent for, surely?"
> "What about when the men of Kuang mistook Confucius for Yang Huo?" said Xiangyun.
> "Confucius and Yang Huo may have looked the same," said Baoyu, "but they didn't have the same name. Lin Xiangru and Sima Xiangru had the same name but they didn't look alike. We are supposed both to have the same name and to look the same. It isn't possible."

寶玉道："那裡的謊話你也信了，偏又有個寶玉了。" 湘雲道："怎麼列國有個藺相如，漢朝又有個司馬相如呢。" 寶玉笑道："這也罷了. 偏又模樣兒也一樣，這是沒有的事。" 湘雲道："怎麼匡人看見孔子，只當是陽虎呢。" 寶玉笑道："孔子陽虎雖同貌，卻不同名姓；藺與司馬雖同名，而又不同貌；偏我和他就兩樣俱同不成？"⁶²

Initially, Baoyu is confident that he is unique; his sense of "I" is based on his conviction that no one resembles him. How could there be two people who simultaneously hold the same name and the same appearance, he asks? This is exactly what the technology of the mirror permits. Baoyu's confusion here produces a moment in which the reader overhears Baoyu's thoughts, in a manner reminiscent of the momentary transparency of Jia Zheng and Grannie Liu's thoughts before the mirror:

But Baoyu's confidence was shaken. Had he a double? When he told himself that he couldn't possibly, he now began to feel that perhaps after all he had. On the other hand how could he be sure that he had when he had never seen him? Brooding on this uncertainty, he went back to his room and lay down on his bed to ponder it in silence. Soon he had drifted into sleep.

寶玉心中便又疑惑起來: 若說必無, 然亦似有; 若說必有, 又並無目睹。心中悶悶, 回至房中榻上, 默默盤算, 不覺就忽忽的睡去。[63]

Although the English translation adds the pronoun "he" to the phrase "Had he a double?," the original elides all pronouns, so therefore the phrase could be voiced in Baoyu's mind or by a third-person narrator. The phrase "Baoyu's confidence was shaken" serves as an entry to his thoughts, while the elision of pronouns achieves a lack of orientation in the Chinese text that anticipates the diffusion of the boundaries of the self within the dream. What is important about these moments is that they shimmer between two possibilities; it is not clear whether the words are voiced by the omniscient narrator or by Baoyu. At stake here is the notion that readers might overhear a character's thoughts. *The Story of the Stone* thus engages in formal experiment with new means of representing thought even as it explores the possibility that the self has no intrinsic substance. Like the telescope, the mirror serves as a foil for experimentation in techniques of narration.

By the famed scene in which Baoyu enters the mirror in dream, Cao Xueqin has established that the mirror is double-sided. In chapter 41, as in the earlier chapters, the mirror faces Baoyu's public spaces; Grannie Liu spies her reflection as she approaches Baoyu's private chambers from the main room. In chapter 51, however, it becomes clear that the mirror also faces Baoyu's private apartments—the maids argue sleepily about who will cover the mirror, and Baoyu resolves the argument by rising from his bed to do so.

The double-sidedness of the freestanding mirror is crucial to interpreting the journey of Jia Baoyu into the mirror to meet his alter ego, Zhen Baoyu. In his dream in chapter 56, Jia Baoyu slips inside a mirror to enter a courtyard just like his own. There he meets Zhen Baoyu, who coincidentally has just had a dream in which he has entered Jia Baoyu's courtyard. Jia Baoyu overhears Zhen Baoyu telling his maids that he has had a dream in which he has just been chastised by Jia Baoyu's maids.

In *his* dream, Jia Baoyu has just been harassed by Zhen Baoyu's maids (as is common in the late-imperial trope of the shared dream, the dream is not precisely shared).[64] The mutual excitement of Zhen Baoyu and Jia Baoyu at first meeting creates a fiction that their identification is substantive. Zhen Baoyu exclaims, "So you too are Baoyu! This cannot be a dream" (原來你就是寶玉. 這可不是夢裏了). Jia Baoyu replies, "How could this be a dream? It is more real than real!" (這如何是夢, 真而又真了).[65] Their identification animates the fiction of the self that the commentator Zhang Xinzhi pointed to when he remarked on Jia Rui's failure to understand the lesson of the bronze mirror of chapter 12: "Who is 'me'?"

As several scholars have observed, Baoyu's dream quite evidently draws on an anecdote in the *Zhuangzi*, in which Zhuangzi dreams that he is a butterfly dreaming that he is Zhuangzi.[66] The historian Michael Nylan notes that Zhuangzi's butterfly dream implies it is only possible to "be in one state at one time ... either Zhuangzi dreaming he is a butterfly or a butterfly dreaming it is Zhuangzi."[67] In the *Zhuangzi*, there is no indication that Zhuangzi could inhabit both positions at once.[68] In other words, the dream itself does not illustrate a freedom from a singular subjective position. Cao Xueqin re-envisions the butterfly dream so that the dreams of Zhen Baoyu and Jia Baoyu are not only simultaneous, but also mutually permeable. Jia Baoyu, for example, overhears his double Zhen Baoyu lament that when he had tried to visit Jia Baoyu, he saw only a sack of skin (*pi nang* 皮囊) on a bed—Jia Baoyu's dreaming self. The term *sack of skin*, by this point in the literary tradition a shopworn convention, is a reminder of the transience of the physical body.[69] Within the biaxial perspective of the dream, Baoyu is freed from a corporeal perspective—as the reference to his body as a sack of skin might suggest.

Jia Zheng mistook the mirror for a door; for Grannie Liu, the mirror mysteriously slid open to become a door.[70] In Baoyu's dream, the mirror is explicitly a portal (as Zhen Baoyu's exit through the mirror at the end of the dream makes clear).[71] Inside the mirror, Baoyu can intuit truths foreclosed upon awakening: the material forms of the garden and its environs are illusory, and so is consciousness itself. Rather than enabling an enduring sense of self, the mirror provides a corrective to it.

When Jia Baoyu wakes from his dream, the maid Aroma (Xiren) hears him calling after Zhen Baoyu. She laughs and asks, "Where is Baoyu?"

(*Baoyu zai nali* 寶玉在那裏). Aroma quickly establishes a conventional, prosaic way of thinking: "You were disoriented in your dream. Rub your eyes and look carefully; it is your image in the mirror" (那是你夢迷了。你揉眼細瞧，是鏡子裏照的你的影兒).[72] Aroma's question "Where is Baoyu?" reminds us that the ephemeral reflections in the mirror have suggested all along that there is no inherent essence to the self. Her thought that Baoyu could orient himself by regarding his own image reveals that she does not understand the lesson that Baoyu should have learned in his dream: that there is no "me" to be reflected in the mirror. The commentator Zhang Xinzhi indicated as much when he commented sarcastically "Who is 'me'?" after Jia Rui said, "Let me take the mirror with me" in chapter 12. Here Zhang Xinzhi notes tartly, "Grannie Liu has come back" (*Liu laolao laiyi* 劉姥姥來矣).[73] Hearing Aroma's instruction to regard his own image, Baoyu looks at the large mirror facing him, and simply laughs: "Baoyu peered and looked forward. There was the mirror, tucked in its frame, regarding him back. He also laughed" (寶玉向前瞧了一瞧，原是那嵌的大鏡對面相照，自己也笑了).[74] The laugh indicates Baoyu's comprehension of a philosophical conundrum that cannot be articulated in words.

Aroma's presence at Jia Baoyu's side as he wakes links this dream to the erotic dream he had in the Land of Illusion in chapter 5, where the fairy Disenchantment (Jinghuan xiangu 警幻仙姑) introduced Baoyu to her younger sister "Two in One" (Jianmei 兼美). Her name, which literally means "Beauties Combined," has been understood as a figure for the collective charms of Baoyu's cousins Baochai and Daiyu. The dreams of chapters 5 and 56 both play with the notion that no individual character is an independent entity, and that in some fundamental sense the ontological substance of the characters is indivisible. The overlap between the names of Baochai, Daiyu, and Baoyu can be seen in this light; each contains some part of the other.

THE MIRROR AND ITS HISTORICAL ANALOGUES

With the visual turn in the study of *The Story of the Stone*, several scholars have suggested historical analogues for the mirrored trick door that Grannie Liu walks through by happenstance in chapter 41.[75] Zhang Shuxian of Beijing's Palace Museum has proposed a likeness to a mirrored screen set as a door within a partition for display of curios (*duobaoge* 多寶格) in the Yonghe Temple, the residence of the Yongzheng emperor prior to his ascension to the throne.[76] Zhang Shuxian and Shang Wei have suggested as well a potential correspondence between the mirrored trick door of chapter 41 and the mirrored door that grants entry to the theater room of the Juanqinzhai (shown closed in figure 5.6 and open in figure 5.7). The mirrored door is one of a pair of mirrored screens in the half-legged style with heavy, red sandalwood frames standing in parallel against the wall of the anteroom of the theater.[77] The mirror on the left is mounted on a door that has a small cloisonné handle decorated in brilliant colors, and leads to a narrow passage into the theater. The pair of mirrored screens are unusually slim and small, perhaps because mirrors of ordinary size would have been too heavy to rest easily on hinges.

To my mind, the mirrored door of the Juanqinzhai cannot function as an analogue for the mirrored trick door of the partition in Baoyu's rooms because it cannot be read in isolation from the door with which it is paired. In eighteenth-century parlance, the mirrored door of the

FIGURE 5.6 The "true and false doors" of the Juanqinzhai. *Source*: Courtesy of Zhang Shuxian, Palace Museum.

FIGURE 5.7 The "true and false doors" of the Juanqinzhai (left door open). *Source*: Courtesy of Zhang Shuxian, Palace Museum.

Juanqinzhai was not considered a false door but rather the true (or operable) door in a pairing of "true and false" doors (*zhen jia men* 真假門).[78] The false (or inoperable) door (*jia men* 假門) of the Juanqinzhai is the half-legged mirror affixed to the wall. In the Forbidden City, "false doors" were always paired with true doors, the pairing of true and false perhaps a vestige of the pairing of painted and actual features in Italian *quadratura*, which I discuss in chapter 6.

These proposed analogues to Baoyu's plate-glass mirror allow us to consider the question of historical referents in a broader sense. The inconsistency in the way the plate-glass mirror is portrayed in *The Story of the Stone* presents a stumbling block to scholarly attempts to find a match. In chapters 17, 26, and 51, Baoyu's mirror is depicted as set in a standing floor-length screen, and alternatively in chapter 41, as set into the wooden partition that divides his private from his public chambers. We could pursue historical analogues for each depiction of the mirror, but a more literary reading would suggest that we take this inconsistency into account.

The portrayal of the mirror is not meant to give a sense of historicity, but rather underscores the mirror's role in creating illusionistic spaces. The inconsistency in the depiction of the partition that appears in chapters 17 and 41 subtly disorients us; the lack of constancy in the mirror's depiction works in much the same way. In chapter 17, Jia Zheng approaches the mirror from the main room in Baoyu's apartments and sees the image of himself and his party. He walks around the mirror, suggesting that the mirror is set in a floor screen. In chapter 26, the minor cousin Jia Yun 賈芸, approaching the mirror from the entrance to the main room, is first dazzled by his surroundings, then mesmerized by the sight of two girls appearing from behind the mirror as they exit Baoyu's private chambers. Here again, the mirror is set in the frame of a standing screen. In chapter 41, the mirror is hung amidst four wood panels. The text informs us after Grannie Liu strokes the mirror that it is not set in a screen but rather into the partition between the main room and the private chambers. It disappears behind the panels, presumably into grooves, when Grannie Liu accidentally presses the trick mechanism.

Thus we must hold two mutually exclusive depictions of the mirror in suspension. The very form of the mirror is not static but dynamic, changing over time as the reader progresses through the pages of the book. The incongruity in depictions of the mirror reinforces the sense that there is a dynamic whole that is interior to the text and only partially captured on the page. The mirror's shape-shifting thus helps create the impression that the illusory world of the novel is, in Jia Baoyu's words, "more real than real."

THE DISCERNING GLASS MIRROR: YUAN MEI'S POEM ON THE WESTERN MIRROR

In 1794, the poet Yuan Mei 袁枚 received a rectangular Western glass mirror from Zhang Chaojin 張朝縉 (1744–after 1794?), the provincial administration commissioner in Zhejiang. It was so large that he had difficulty bringing it through the door. In the preface to "A Poem in Gratitude for the Mirror" (*Xie jing shi* 謝鏡詩), which Yuan Mei wrote to commemorate the gift, he remarked with exuberant self-mockery, "I am obsessed with mirrors. I have over 30 ancient bronze mirrors and glass mirrors stored at my house. Whenever I light a lamp, the effect is dazzling, and I feel that I cut a fine figure" (余有鏡癖. 家藏古銅, 玻璃三十餘種. 每一張燈, 熒煌炫赫, 自以爲豪矣).[79] Referring to the old trope that the first emperor of the Qin dynasty had a rectangular mirror that revealed the thoughts of his consorts and courtiers, Yuan Mei writes in the poem's last line that when his internal organs were reflected in the mirror, the mirror revealed the word "gratitude" inscribed on them.[80] The latter part of Yuan Mei's poem reads:

> As one might expect, this fine screen with a surface clear as mica,[81]
> Reveals a truer world in the glass.[82]
> Three thousand volumes of books suddenly multiply in the mirror,
> The gold hairpins of the twelve beauties gently brush against their raven tresses.
> The array of green peaks opposite the mirror considers its own image,
> The white cranes ascending to the hall mistakenly hold the flowers in the mirror in their beaks.
> My guests are surprised at my ingenuity,
> In bringing the mirage from the sea into my home.
> Old and young delightedly bemoan having seen this so late,
> Guests and friends cluster round composing poems on the mirror.
> Even before the mirror beckons the flowers, they insist on entering it,
> My buildings and terraces—the mirror knows them all.
> Winds cannot disturb it and clouds cannot cover it,
> For how many generations will it cast its glance upon my descendants and reflect their images?
> For a thousand gold it would be hard to buy this rarity that has been given me,
> People near and far convey the news of the notable who sent me the mirror.
> They are only aware of the flowers blossoming within my four walls,
> Who realizes that the tortoise carries the weight of the three immortal islands?[83]
> One has long heard tell of the ancient mirror of the Qin palace,
> I say that my western mirror is even finer.
> When the mirror is shone on this old man's heart,

The two characters for gratitude, *gan'en* 感恩, most clearly appear.

果然雲母好屏風,
現出琉璃真世界.
三千書卷斗然加,
十二金釵掠鬢鴉.
對面青山齊弄影,
升堂白鶴誤銜花.
客來多怪先生巧,
海市蜃樓帶到家.
老幼欣欣恨見遲,
賓朋簇簇共題詩.
鏡無招引花偏入,
我有樓台鏡盡知.
風不能搖雲不掩,
看照兒孫到幾時.
千金難買奇珍供,
遠近多傳顯者送.
但覺花開四壁榮,
誰知鰲載三山重!
秦宮古製久聞名,
我道西洋鏡更精.
照到衰翁心膽上,
感恩兩字最分明.[84]

Yuan Mei famously claimed that his garden in Nanjing had been the site of the garden of *The Story of the Stone*.[85] "A Poem in Gratitude for the Mirror" refers indirectly to that claim. The twelve beauties in gold hairpins in the glass recall *The Story of the Stone*'s alternative title, mentioned in its first chapter: *The Twelve Hairpinned Beauties of Nanjing* (*Jinling shi'er chai* 金陵十二釵). Yuan Mei's phrase "truer world made of glass" (*liuli zhen shijie* 琉璃真世界) similarly hearkens to the phrase "a world of glass" (*liuli shijie* 琉璃世界) used to describe the radiant array of glass lanterns attached to the bare wintry branches of the trees of the garden in chapter 18.[86]

As Qianlong does in his poem "On the Mirror," Yuan Mei refers to the peaks opposite the glass encountering their own reflections as well as the flight of birds as captured in the mirror. He arrives quickly at a similar conclusion regarding the illusory quality of the phenomenal world, but with a twist: the mirror does not beckon the "flowers in the mirror" so much as the flowers "insist on entering it." We might remember that Baoyu was drawn to enter the mirror via his interest in the possibility of a double in the dream scene of chapter 56. With the phrase "flowers in the mirror," Yuan Mei draws on a conventional trope—"flowers in the mirror and moon [reflected] in water" (*jinghua shuiyue* 鏡花水月)—that designates the quality of seeming to have form (*se* 色) and yet having no substance. Cao Xueqin used that very phrase to describe his protagonists Lin Daiyu and Jia Baoyu: "One is moon in water, one is flowers in the mirror."[87] That phrase, from a song suite that discloses the eventual fates of the characters, warns readers at the outset of the novel that ultimately both protagonists are in fact mirages.

Of all the fictional objects that I have discussed, the mirror is most closely associated with fictionality. In *The Story of the Stone*, the double-sided plate-glass mirror becomes a sign of fictionality that points in two directions. On the one hand, the reflections in the mirror betoken fiction's capacity to provide verisimilitude. On the other, the forms within the mirror gesture toward a complex cognizance of the role of fiction in revealing the illusory quality of the everyday world.

CONCLUSION

In Qianlong's "On the Mirror," Yuan Mei's "A Poem in Gratitude for the Mirror," and *The Story of the Stone*, the mirror furnishes a reminder of the illusory nature of phenomenal form. There is no a priori reality that the mirror reflects. Rather, the mirror reveals the inherently illusory quality of that which stands before it. My analysis of the mirror scenes in this chapter drew on the globally unprecedented features of the eighteenth-century Chinese plate-glass mirror. European plate glass inserted into a Chinese standing screen engendered a mirror that was uniquely full-length, double-sided, and freestanding. In the Qianlong emperor's poem, the mirrorlike reflections in his pavilion's plate-glass windows illustrate the potential of a perspective that is no longer singular and subjective, and lead Qianlong to remark on the illusory quality of the phenomenal world in first spatial and then philosophical terms.

The mirror scenes in *The Story of the Stone* further this line of thought. In chapter 17, Jia Zheng mistakes the Western mirror in Baoyu's chambers for a door, and does not recognize the figures advancing toward him in the mirror as those of his own party. He quickly realizes his error and leads his party around the mirror. For a moment, the text suggests that the mirror might be a portal to a deeper understanding, but Jia Zheng, with his sophisticated recognition of the plate-glass mirror as an imported technology, literally circumvents that possibility. In chapter 41, Grannie Liu mistakes her own image in the mirror for that of her son-in-law's mother. Their relationship to one another in the family structure is symmetrical but reversed, in effect a mirror image, and for the first time, the text becomes interested in the perspective of the image within the mirror. Grannie Liu's encounter with her own reflection establishes a biaxial perspective in a comic mode. After Jia Baoyu enters the mirror to meet his double, Zhen Baoyu, in chapter 56, this biaxial perspective is fully realized in Cao Xueqin's rewriting of Zhuangzi's butterfly dream. Each of those scenes builds on the last, recasting the traditional association of the bronze mirror with self-reflection to ask whether the self is in fact a substantive entity. In that sense, the biaxial perspective permitted by the mirror grants the total vision that the name of the garden, *Daguan yuan*, suggests.

The same could be said of the various depictions of the mirror as a physical object; each is quite distinct, in fact incongruent, and yet they form a conglomerate (here we might be reminded of the conglomerate metaphorical mappings of Du Shiniang's box). At the end of chapter 56, the maid Musk (Sheyue 麝月) notes that the mirror typically is covered with a protective sleeve (*jingtao* 鏡套) that the servants must have forgotten to place over the mirror before Baoyu fell asleep. Those words suggest that the mirror is set in a freestanding screen, in contradiction to Grannie Liu's experience in chapter 41 of a mirror inlaid into a partition. That in a nutshell is the difficulty in finding a historical analogue to the mirror within Baoyu's chambers. The novel's representation of the mirror is not consistent across chapters. The initial encounter between Jia Baoyu and Zhen Baoyu can be seen as parallel in some ways to the imagined encounter between the literary object and the historical object—there is an expectation of affinity, an initial rejoicing at similitude between literary text and historical substrate. And yet, as the dream that takes place within the mirror tells us, similitude ultimately misleads.

Baoyu is not necessarily singular or double. He is also multiple and diffuse, closely identified not only with the jade with which he is born, but also with the stone stele that in chapter 1 becomes the novel itself. The rhetorical force of *The Story of the Stone*'s dualistic formulation of true and false masks the text's deeper interest in creating impossible morphological resonances that are conceptual conundrums. The material homologies of *The Story of the Stone* are impossible to map; the stone that is the protagonist inhabits the book that is written on the stone. Matter is always simultaneously there (*you* 有) and not there (*wu* 無). Our insistence on identifying it as there or not there is what artificially isolates the two states.

CHAPTER SIX

Historicizing Recession via *The Story of the Stone* and the Juanqinzhai

This final chapter brings my investigation full circle, asking how readings of historical artifacts might change when we bring to them the habits of mind cultivated in us by eighteenth-century fiction. A historian of China once asked me, "But why should we care about *literary* objects?" I respond in this chapter by showing how scenes concerning perspectivalism from Cao Xueqin's eighteenth-century novel *The Story of the Stone* might shift our understanding of a life-size painting of a lady with a clock affixed to the wall in the Qianlong emperor's retirement lodge, the Juanqinzhai.

Art historians and literary scholars have considered *The Story of the Stone* in tandem with the perspectival paintings of the Juanqinzhai since the end of the 1990s.[1] The scene in the novel in which Grannie Liu encounters a painting of a young girl has been understood to reflect the reaction of eighteenth-century Chinese viewers when they first encountered perspectival painting. How would our understanding change if, conversely, we were to take the novel not as illustrative, but as capable of providing terms for perspectivalism with which we might analyze the painting of the Juanqinzhai with fresh eyes? How might such a shift in turn affect our thinking regarding the eighteenth-century Chinese understanding of Italian *quadratura*, introduced to China by Giovanni Gherardini and Giuseppe Castiglione, the first European painters to work in Beijing?

GRANNIE LIU AND THE PAINTING

In chapter 5 I discussed the scene in *The Story of the Stone* in which Grannie Liu believes her own image in a mirror to be that of her son-in-law's mother. Just prior to that scene, Grannie Liu mistakes a painting of a young girl for the girl herself, and asks the girl in the painting to help her find her way:

> After she had crossed the bridge there was a raised cobbled path which, after a couple of right-angled bends, brought her up to the door of the house.
> The first thing she saw on entering it was a young woman smiling at her in welcome. Grannie Liu smiled back.
> "I'm lost, miss. The young ladies have left me to find my own way and I've wandered in here by mistake."
> Surprised that the girl did not reply, Grannie Liu stepped forward to take her hand and—bang!—hit her head a most painful thump on the wooden wall. The girl was a painting, as she found on closer inspection.

> 劉姥姥便踱過石去,順着石子甬路走去,轉了兩個彎子,只見有個房門,於是進了房門,便見迎面一個女孩兒,滿面含笑迎出來。劉姥姥忙笑道:"姑娘們把我丢下了,叫我碰頭碰到這裏來。"說了,只覺那女孩兒不答。劉姥姥便趕來拉他的手,咕咚一聲便撞到板壁上,把頭碰的生疼。細瞧了一瞧,原來是一幅畫兒。[2]

The bump on Grannie Liu's head is not just a sharp rebuke to her technological naïveté. It speaks to the materialization of figurative language. Grannie Liu refers to the fact that she has wandered to this spot with a colloquialism that David Hawkes leaves untranslated: "The girls left me behind, and told me to meet [literally, bump heads] here" (姑娘們把我丢下了,叫我碰頭碰到這裏來). Because the colloquialism in which "bump heads" serves as shorthand for "meet" is untranslatable, readers of the translation miss the materialization of the metaphor when, moments later, Grannie Liu painfully bumps her head on the painting (把頭碰的生疼). Sound becomes haptic as the figural and onomatopoeic bumping of heads is reenvisioned as an actual bump to the head. With the materialization of the metaphor, we see on the level of the text itself the dynamic relation between language and dimensionality that underlies the depiction of the painting. Grannie Liu's bump to the head is the materialized affordance of her words. It is as though there existed an involuntary or parasympathetic relation between Grannie Liu's language and the world of the Jia family, so that her colloquial metaphor inadvertently sparks a response in the lived world.

Hawkes translates the lines that follow with some liberty, describing the painting on the wall as done in the "foreign mode of light and shadow painting." That phrasing is of Hawkes's own coinage, added to the original text to explain Grannie Liu's confusion.

> "Strange!" she thought. "How can they paint a picture so that it sticks out like that?" Grannie Liu was ignorant of the foreign mode of light-and-shadow painting and was sorely puzzled to discover, on touching the picture, that it did not in fact "stick out" but was flat all over. Turning from it with a sigh and a shake of her head, she moved on to a little doorway in the wooden partition-wall, over which hung a green, flower-patterned portière. She raised the portière and went inside. . . .
>
> 劉姥姥自忖道:"原來畫兒有這樣凸出來的." 一面想,一面看,一面又用手摸去, 卻是一色平的, 點頭嘆了兩聲. 一轉身方得了一個小門, 門上掛著蔥綠撒花軟簾. 劉姥姥掀簾進去. . . .³

Hawkes's addition of the phrase "foreign mode of light-and-shadow painting" has led to the widespread perception that here Grannie Liu encounters European perspectival painting for the first time. In the original, the text moves directly from Grannie Liu's question, "How can they paint a picture so that it sticks out like that?," to the narrator's description of her response to the painting, which could be translated more literally as, "She pondered it, looked at it, and used her hand to stroke it in turn, but it was nothing but a flat surface." The passage initially suggests that its readers are more sophisticated than Grannie Liu. In a preceding passage Grannie Liu has been likened by Lin Daiyu to one of the hundred beasts that danced when the sages played music; her response to the aesthetic is characterized as involuntary and instinctive.⁴

But here, as in the scene with the mirror, Grannie Liu recognizes the technical accomplishment of the illusory surface and then turns to explore it via touch. Her mistaking a painting of a young girl for the girl herself, then, does not suggest that she must touch the painting to ascertain that it is real. Nor does it necessarily speak to the persuasiveness of European perspectival techniques, as is conventionally thought. Rather, the passage creates a distinction between Grannie Liu's naïveté and the sophistication of its readers, a distinction that is soon undone.

Hawkes's translation also obscures the significance of the sigh in this passage. In *The Story of the Stone*, the sigh often marks an intuition of deep philosophical truth, an opportunity to see beyond the illusory solidity of the material world. The phrase that Hawkes translates as "[t]urning from it with a sigh and a shake of her head" would more literally read, "she nodded her head and sighed twice" (點頭嘆了兩聲). This phrase recalls the idiom "the rocks nod their heads," a reference to Kumarajiva's disciple Daosheng 道生 (ca. 360–434), whose preaching so moved the unenlightened rocks at Tiger Hill that they bowed their heads.[5] In other words, Grannie Liu's realization that the girl is but a painting leads her, an unenlightened rock, to sigh and nod her head. Her initial misperception shifts to profound realization. We could liken her groping discernment that the young girl is an illusion to the reader's inevitable recognition that the characters of the novel do not exist beyond the flat surface of the page.

Scholars have assumed that Grannie Liu bumps against the figure of the girl herself. Logically, however, were Grannie Liu to be taken in by the illusion of volume in the figure of the young girl, she would in fact stop in advance of the painting. Most likely, she has bumped into the illusion of recessed space—in other words, she believed she could progress through what she perceived as emptiness surrounding the young girl, only to find it was a painted surface. This is particularly likely in that the text explains that she bumps against a wall. As I will explain, if the painting were in fact executed with the polyfocal perspective of Italian *quadratura*, it would likely have been a floor-to-ceiling painting on silk affixed to the wall. If this were the case, the successive resolution of vanishing points as Grannie Liu progressed toward the painting could have produced the appearance of recessed space behind the girl, and perhaps the consequent impression that the girl had moved forward and was about to step down from the painting in welcome.⁶

THE JUANQINZHAI

The panoramic paintings (*tongjing hua* 通景畫) of the Forbidden City drew on the techniques of Italian *quadratura*, using linear perspectivalism to create illusionistic architectural space.⁷ The Bolognese school of *quadratura* developed sophisticated techniques of perspectival painting that employed multiple vanishing points; this polyfocal perspectivalism was particularly suited to the illusory extension of recessed space in scenic design for the theater as well as in naves, halls, and other elongated architectural spaces. The use of multiple vanishing points created illusionistic realms far more complex than could be suggested by the use of a single vanishing point. For this reason painters of the Bolognese school were much sought after, and worked for the aristocracy across Europe, in sites as far-flung as Madrid, St. Petersburg, and Vienna. The first European painter to serve a Chinese emperor, Giovanni Gherardini (1665–ca. 1729), arrived in Beijing after studying in Bologna with the *quadratura* master Angelo Michele Colonna (1604–1687).⁸

Although Bologna may seem a long way from Beijing, we can in fact trace a fairly direct line from one to the other. The Bibiena family of Bologna was the first to use polyfocal schema in scenic design for the stage. But Agostino Mitelli (1609–1660) was credited by Count Carlo Cesare Malvasia with the invention of the use of multiple vanishing points in his *Lives of the Bolognese Painters* (*Felsina pittrice*), first published in 1678.⁹ Mitelli, who painted frescoes for Count Malvasia's residence, is best known for his decades-long collaboration with Gherardini's teacher Colonna. Colonna and Mitelli frescoed the Hall of Pompeius of the Palazzo Spada in Rome, the interiors of the Royal Alcazar in Madrid, and the reception rooms of the Palazzo Pitti for Ferdinando II de' Medici in Florence.¹⁰ Later, Colonna returned to Bologna, where he taught Gherardini the art of *quadratura*. Before Gherardini left Europe for Beijing, accompanying the Jesuit mission that sailed on the ship *Amphitrite* in 1698, he had been trained in Bologna in the use of the polyfocal techniques that we see in the painting of the lady with the clock in the Juanqinzhai. He then painted at the court of the emperor Kangxi from 1699 to 1704, where he taught Chinese court artists. When the Jesuit Matteo Ripa visited the imperial workshops in 1711, several years after Gherardini's departure, he saw the court artists at work and wrote of their use of European techniques.[11] The artists eventually were directed by Giuseppe Castiglione, who taught Chinese court painters from his arrival in 1715 until his death in 1766. Castiglione was trained in *quadratura* in his native Milan before proceeding to Portugal to await his transfer to China.[12]

The famed theater of the Juanqinzhai is a room of extraordinary scale, its walls, to which are affixed trompe l'oeil paintings on silk, measuring some 33 feet by 22 feet (see figure 6.1). The wall behind the stage, the western wall, features depictions of a mountain range reminiscent of those outside Beijing. This theater room is accessed from a small anteroom containing only a raised bed, where two mirrors of the "half-legged" style (see figures 5.6 and 5.7) stand flush against the wall. The mirrors are far less monumental than they seem in photos; each is likely little more than 20 inches wide and, with the frame, a little more than 5 feet tall. As I discussed in chapter 5, these mirrors are "true and false

FIGURE 6.1 Stage of the Juanqinzhai. *Source*: Courtesy of Wang Shiwei, Palace Museum.

doors"; the one on the left is in fact mounted on a door. To the right of the door after one passes through is a narrow staircase that the emperor would ascend to take his throne in a second-story balcony opposite the stage. The north wall, to the right of the stage when facing it, is hung with a panoramic painting that references the actual scenery outside the windows of the south wall, depicting the vermilion walls of the Forbidden City. A bamboo lattice fence contains a large moon gate that serves as a focal or organizing point of the painting. At the south wall, an actual lattice fence with a moon gate stands directly opposite to the moon gate of the painted fence at the north wall.

In the center of the east side of the room are two thrones, one on the first floor and one on the second-story balcony directly above it. When seated on either of these thrones, the emperor held within his frame of vision the north wall, with its painted bamboo lattice fence, and the south wall, with its actual lattice fence. He was positioned in such a way that he held the painted architectural features and the actual architectural features in tension, the former on the right and the latter on the left. This pairing is indebted to Castiglione's training in the Bolognese style of *quadratura*. At the same time, it recalls the dyadic relation of true (*zhen* 真) and false (*jia* 假) that we encountered in chapter 5.

As I mentioned briefly in chapter 5, the actual lattice itself plays games with substitutions of one substance for another that showcase the imperial workshops' technological mastery of surface. As is well known, the so-called bamboo lattice of the southern wall is not made of bamboo at all; although bamboo was the favored wood of the literati gardens of the south, it would crack in the extreme heat and cold of Beijing. Rather, the bamboo lattice is made of costly *nanmu* wood, which was treated to look like lowly bamboo.

The emperor would have encountered the now-iconic painting of a young lady beside a clock affixed to the north wall of the *xianlou* balcony of the theater room as he ascended the stairs to the balcony. (Here I should issue a quick caveat: the word "painting" suggests that the portrait of the lady and the clock is a discrete unit, when in fact it is merely a portion of the painted silk that stretches along the entire wall.) The second floor of the Juanqinzhai is currently barred to viewers, but we can get a sense of the sophisticated perspectival challenges the depiction presents by considering the shift in the shape of the ceiling when the wall is photographed from the right as opposed to the left. In a photograph taken from the top of the stairs and to the right of the lady and the clock, the ceiling is far more elongated (figure 6.2a). In a photograph taken from the left side (figure 6.2b), the shape of the ceiling seems closer to an equilateral trapezoid. The very shape of the ceiling seems to change depending on the angle from which the painting is viewed.

These variations from one viewpoint to another provide a clue as to the techniques of scenographic design that made their way from northern Italy to the Forbidden City with Gherardini and Castiglione. Perspectivally, the painting draws from the *scene teatrali vedute per angolo* (theatrical scenes viewed at an angle), the use of the oblique angle in stage design that the famed *quadratura* artist Ferdinando Galli Bibiena (1657–1743) introduced for the Italian stage in 1687. Figure 6.3 shows Bibiena's instructive drawing in an illustration titled "Perspectival Scenes Viewed at an Angle" in his *L'architettura civile preparata sú la geometria, e ridotta alle prospettive* (Civil architecture by means of geometry and rendered in perspective, 1711).[13] The illustration uses two-point rather than monofocal perspective.

If we consider the *tongjing hua* of the balcony in tandem with the illustration from Bibiena's *L'architettura civile*, we see that the three bays indicated by the painted arches in the *tongjing hua* correspond to the first three arches in the colonnade that occupies the center of the engraving (this is especially clear in figure 6.2b). The window to the extreme left of the *tongjing hua* corresponds to the window at the left of the colonnade in the engraving. This perspectival structure creates two resolutions in terms of viewing positions for the painting of the lady and the clock, one to the extreme left, where the emperor would encounter the painting walking from the throne toward the stairs, and one to the extreme right, where the emperor would view it from below as he ascended the stairs. Of note, only the central section of Bibiena's illustration is referenced; the actual vanishing points presumably would be beyond the frame of the painting. Thus the *tongjing hua* in the Juanqinzhai merely suggests bifocalism, and does not slavishly follow it.

In figures 6.2a and 6.2b we see how the polyfocalism of the *tongjing hua* operates. Figure 6.2a shows the painting as viewed from the top of the stairs. From that vantage point, the proportions of the table

FIGURE 6.2 Juanqinzhai: Contrasting views of the *tongjing hua* painting on the *xianlou* balcony, from (a) the top of the stairs and from (b) the left. *Source*: Provided by the Palace Museum and Wang Shiwei, Palace Museum.

FIGURE 6.3 Ferdinando Galli Bibiena, "Prospettiva scenica in veduta d'angolo," from *L'architettura civile: Preparata sú la geometria e ridotta alle prospettive: Considerazioni pratiche*. Parma, Paolo Monto, 1711. *Source*: Getty Research Institute, Los Angeles (2871-047).

legs are awkward, an ungainliness that presumably is resolved when the viewer approaches the painting from below (*di sotto in sú*, in the parlance of *quadratura*). The middle arch appears to contain a wall that angles inward, on which a clock is hung. Next to the clock is a door frame, suggesting a room from which the lady peeps. The vertical architectural columns fragment and layer the space, generating the optical illusion of a corridor before the tables. As the viewer walks past, a recessed chamber in which the lady stands emerges dynamically between the two tables just mentioned. This is seen most clearly in photographs taken from the extreme left (figure 6.2b).

The subject of the painting is neither the lady nor the clock; it is the appearance and disappearance of recessed space around the lady and the objects that surround her. As the viewer moves past the painting, hidden recesses appear and the planar surface acquires resonance and depth. Most important, the chamber containing the lady becomes prominent and then recedes. Space becomes fluid and dynamic, literally eluding our conceptual grasp. Italian techniques of scenography, then, provided the painters of the Juanqinzhai with ways of illustrating space as volumetric, but volumetric in a dynamic rather than a static sense. The appearance of illusionistic space is even more important than the depiction of illusionistic form, for it suggests a realm that the viewer might enter.

We can now return to Grannie Liu's exclamation, "How can they paint a picture so that it sticks out like that?" (原來畫兒有這樣凸出來的). We saw the fluid materialization of dematerialized surfaces at work in the material actualization of her metaphors (as with the bumping of heads). Reading the scene in tandem with the painting of the lady with the clock, we might imagine that as Grannie Liu walked past the painting in Baoyu's chambers, an empty recess appeared behind the girl in the painting—an empty recess that she believed she could enter. Italian *quadratura*, in other words, was pressed into the service of the dynamic appearance of recession and protrusion. The dynamism, or metamorphosis of space, is at least as important as static volumetrism, and it has a history in literary and anecdotal accounts of the painted wall.

TOUCHING RECESSION: THE PAINTED WALL

Eighteenth-century accounts document the urge to touch the *quadratura* paintings produced by Giovanni Gherardini and Giuseppe Castiglione for the Beitang and Nantang churches of Beijing. Scholars have understood this urge to touch the paintings in terms of the desire of Chinese viewers to make certain that the objects depicted are not real. In fact, I would argue that the desire to touch indicates not the moment when the viewer realizes that the painting is a worked material surface so much as the viewer's attempt to manipulate the illusion. As we will see momentarily, the touch marks the moment when the viewer, who has been in motion, stops to recalibrate, calling a halt to the dynamic experience of the painting.

In a letter written from Beijing, the missionary Pierre Jartoux mentioned Gherardini's *quadratura* altarpiece in the Beitang church:

> High above among the clouds, over a group of angels, the Heavenly Father holds the terrestrial globe in his hands.... The Chinese cannot believe that all this has been painted on one plane, and cannot be persuaded that the columns are not straight, as they seem to be.... This painting is by M. Gherardini, an Italian painter that Father Bouvet took with him when he went to China. The altarpiece is painted, too: both sides of it represent the continuation of the architecture of the church in perspective. It was amusing to see the Chinese visit that part of the church, which seemed as if it were behind the altar: when they arrived at it, they stopped, then stepped back a little, then forward again, and put their hands on it to find out that there really were no reliefs or hollows.[14]

The reliefs, the hollows, the depiction of recessed space in the wall are what interested the Chinese viewers. The appearance of recession would be produced by the viewers via anamorphic projection as they walked past the painting. I suspect that this is why the viewers stopped, stepped back, and then moved forward again: they wished to reproduce the effect of seeing the hollows appear. When the viewers stretched out their hands to touch the painting, they in effect called a halt to the dynamism of the space. The touch became a way of deliberately manipulating the illusion of depth. The eighteenth-century Chinese viewers who stopped, stepped back, and then moved forward again were not necessarily (as has been imagined by recent scholarship) naïve viewers who believed the altarpiece to be real, but rather potentially sophisticated viewers controlling the techniques of producing depth as they reached out to touch the illusionistic space behind the altar. As the visitors to the Beitang church moved forward and then back, they manipulated the technology that produced the recesses. Their experience of the painting was technological as much as aesthetic.

Eighteenth-century Chinese viewers understood *quadratura* painting in terms of the trope of the dynamic appearance and disappearance of recessed space in wall murals. In his *Notes of the Bamboo Leaf Pavilion* (*Zhuyeting zaji* 竹葉亭雜記), Yao Yuanzhi 姚元之 (1773–1852) wrote of Castiglione's wall painting for the Nantang church in the Xuanwu district of Beijing: "When you see the tables and desks from a distance, they seem lined up in rows; it is as though you could enter. When you approach close to it, it is no more than a wall" (室內几案遙而望之, 飭如也, 可以入矣. 即之, 則猶然壁也).[15] The phrase "seem lined up in rows" (*chi ru* 飭如) here speaks to verisimilitude as a kind of cosmetic similarity that does not fool the viewer with trompe l'oeil but rather cues an approach to an illusionistic space.

The response of these eighteenth-century viewers to the work of Castiglione in the Nantang church was profoundly traditional, drawing on a trope of long standing: the painted wall that contains an immortal realm. Speaking of the wall that Castiglione painted in *quadratura* fashion for the Nantang church, Zhang Jingyun 張景運 wrote:

> I stared at it for some time and had the intention of walking forward to enter it, but when I arrived at it and touched it, it was simply a wall. It must have been like the Jade Island of the immortals, which one can look toward but never reach. It left me bewildered for some time.
>
> 凝眸片晌, 竟欲走而入也. 及至其下捫之, 則塊然堵墻而已. 殆如神洲瑤島可望不可即, 令人恨惘久之.[16]

Zhang experiences a profound sense of loss when he realizes that the recessed space he hoped to enter was illusory. To better understand the significance of the recessed space that beckons viewers toward the wall, we might look to Pu Songling's late seventeenth-century classical tale "The Painted Wall" (*Huabi* 畫壁).[17] The tale relates the story of two literary men who happen to visit a Buddhist temple in Beijing while sojourning in the capital. The temple is relatively deserted, but an old monk shows them around the premises. In the main hall of the temple, the eastern and western walls are covered with marvelous paintings, such that the people and objects in the paintings seem alive (*renwu rusheng* 人物如生). The figure of the Heavenly Maiden Scattering Flowers (*tiannü sanhua* 天女散花) is painted on the eastern wall; she holds a flower in her hand, her lips about to smile. Her hair is done up in tufts, signaling her virginal status. Zhu fixes his eyes upon her for some time, when suddenly his spirit is shaken and his volition taken from him (*shenyao yiduo* 神搖意奪). His body floats up as though he were riding a cloud, and he enters the wall.

Once inside the wall, Zhu finds himself in a vast compound where an aged monk is teaching the Dharma. The Heavenly Maiden tugs at his sleeve, and he follows her into a small pavilion, where he flirts with her and eventually makes love with her for several days. The girl's friends then put up her hair in the style of a married woman. Once the friends depart, Zhu and the girl continue their lovemaking. Suddenly, an armored guard appears and asks whether someone from the world below has entered. The girl opens a side door in a wall (that is, a wall within the painted wall) and escapes; Zhu, at her instruction, hides under the bed. Zhu waits for some time under the bed in fear, barely daring to breathe, until eventually he can barely remember where he is from (竟不復憶身之何自來也).

At that moment, the narrative explicitly shifts from the events within the wall to Zhu's friend Meng Longtan, who is still standing with a monk outside the wall:

> At the time, Meng Longtan was in the great hall, and not having seen Zhu for some time, asked the monk where Zhu had gone. The monk smiled and said: "He has gone to hear the dharma." Meng asked, "Where?" The monk answered, "Not far from here." After a short while, he used his finger to strum the wall and called, "Donor Zhu, why have you been gone for so long?" At that moment, Zhu's silhouette appeared on the painted wall, his ear cocked as though he were listening closely to something. The monk called, "The friend who you were travelling with has been waiting for a long time." Then suddenly Zhu floated from the wall and descended, his mind like ashes and his body like wood, his eyes staring and his legs swaying.

時孟龍潭在殿中, 轉瞬不見朱, 疑以問僧, 僧笑曰: "往聽說法去矣." 問: "何處?" 曰: "不遠." 少時, 以指彈壁而呼曰: "朱檀越何久遊不歸?" 旋見壁間畫有朱像, 傾耳佇立, 若有聽察. 僧又呼曰: "遊侶久待矣." 遂飄忽自壁而下, 灰心木立, 目瞪足耎.[18]

Zhu has opportunity to listen to the Dharma but does not take advantage; rather than hear the Dharma, he consorts with the Heavenly Maiden.[19] The joke is that Zhu's concentrated contemplation of the girl has led him to a state reminiscent of meditation: his mind is like ashes and his body like wood. The tale implies an equivalence between listening to the Dharma and dallying with the girl. What seemed like a missed opportunity is not: by the time Zhu exits the wall, the horrific fright has altered mind and body in a way reminiscent of the effect of listening to the Dharma. Mentation, the sixth sense in Buddhist thought and thus as much a cause of desire and grasping as any of the other senses, has ceased. As is so often the case in late-imperial sources, here the text layers a reference to the *Zhuangzi* over a line of thought that is phrased explicitly as a Buddhist concern. The phrase "his mind like ashes and his body like wood" recalls *Zhuangzi*'s description of the mind of an infant who acts spontaneously and without intention: "body like the branch of a withered tree, his mind is like dead ashes" (形固可使如槁木, 而心固可使如死灰乎).[20]

The phrase translated here as "he used his finger to strum the wall" suggests that the monk is playing the wall like an instrument, and controls Zhu's experience. The commentary by Lü Zhan'en 呂湛恩 (d. 1840) asks readers to recall the Vimalakīrti Sutra (Weimo jing 維摩經) at this point.[21] The Heavenly Maiden is often a succubus in the anecdotal literature of eighteenth-century China.[22] But in her original form in the Vimalakīrti Sutra, first translated into Chinese in the fifth century CE, the Heavenly Maiden reveals the improper desire of some of the disciples of the bodhisattva Mañjuśrī. She lives in the home of the merchant Vimalakīrti, a layman skilled in debate, who bests Mañjuśrī in a climactic scene of the sutra, answering Mañjuśrī with a silence that has come to be known as "the lion's roar." The Heavenly Maiden causes flower petals to rain down on Mañjuśrī and his assembled disciples, petals that stick to some of the disciples and not others. When Mañjuśrī's attendant, the monk Śāriputra, tries to shake off the petals, stating that they are not proper for religious people, the Heavenly Maiden replies that the petals are proper; it is the thoughts that are improper. Śāriputra then challenges her, asking her why, if she is so advanced in her thinking, she occupies the body of a woman. She switches bodies with him to teach him a lesson. When she finally allows Śāriputra to return to his original form, she asks him, "Where now is the form and shape of your female body?" She then says, "All things are like that—they do not exist, yet do not not exist. And that they do not exist, yet do not not exist, is exactly what the Buddha teaches."[23]

This dialogue puts the dalliance with the Heavenly Maiden in "The Painted Wall" in a new light. By the time Zhu has emerged from the wall, mind like ashes, he presumably has an experiential knowledge of the Heavenly Maiden's words: "All things are like that—they do not exist, yet do not not exist." The Heavenly Maiden within the tale, however, is, like Zhu, so frightened and shocked when the guard comes to ask whether someone is hiding from the world of men that "she was greatly afraid, her face like dead ashes" (女大懼, 面如死灰).[24] She is no longer outside the human world, but rather is now bound by its desires and emotions.

In the sutra, the Heavenly Maiden sets in motion shifts from one epistemological level to another as she switches bodies with Śāriputra. In Pu Songling's story, the wall itself takes over this role. The entrance and exit into the wall inspire the shifts from one frame of reference to another; the experience of the wall teaches Zhu what the Heavenly Maiden taught Śāriputra. We can now understand why Zhang Jingyun, who wished to enter Castiglione's painted wall in the Nantang church in Beijing, felt such a sense of loss when he realized he would never be able to do so.

THE TERM *AOTU* IN *THE STORY OF THE STONE*

How could we use *aotu* 凹凸 (literally, "recession and protrusion"), the term that is conventionally understood to denote perspectivalism, to investigate the instability of form suggested by these painted walls? To answer that question, we might turn to a conversation between Baoyu's cousins Lin Daiyu and Shi Xiangyun in chapter 76 of *The Story of the Stone* regarding the significance of the terms "recession or concavity" (*ao* 凹) and "protrusion or convexity" (*tu* 凸) in Chinese aesthetics. Shi

Xiangyun and Lin Daiyu, the two orphans of the extended Jia family, find solace with each other during the Mid-Autumn Festival, a time for the gathering of family. Feeling abandoned, they wander to a part of the garden that has until this point remained obscure to readers, a spot where the creek runs into the lake below. Shi Xiangyun admires the names given to several scenic spots, among them the Concave Crystal (*aojing* 凹晶) hollow and the Convex Azure (*tubi* 凸碧) hill.[25] When Xiangyun remarks that the terms *concave* and *convex* (literally, "receding" and "protruding") are typically considered vulgar, and therefore seldom used in Chinese literature, Daiyu reveals that it is she who named the spots. She contends that the term *aotu* has a distinguished pedigree, and she proceeds to give a short history of its use, ending with an account of the monastery named Temple of Recession and Protrusion (Aotu si 凹凸寺) in Zhang Yanyuan's Tang-dynasty *Records of Painting* (*Huaji* 畫記).[26]

Despite Daiyu's defense of the literary pedigree of *aotu*, the term has not received much consideration, perhaps because the pictographic characters are somewhat simplistic and even vulgar.[27] After the advent of Buddhism, the term *aotu* was associated with a technique for the painting of ornament within the precincts of Buddhist temples that created the appearance of recession and protrusion on a planar surface. Gu Qiyuan (1565–1628), the author of the Wanli-period notation book *Idle Chatter in the Guest's Seat* (*Kezuo zhuiyu* 客座贅語, 1617) described it as a kind of secret knowledge that had entered China from India:

> The European from Rome, Matteo Ricci, spoke of the methods of rendering recession and protrusion in painting; nowadays no one understands this. The *Veritable Record of Jiankang* (*Jiankang shilu* 建康實錄) says that the lintel above the gate of the Yicheng temple had flowers painted in a protruding style. Tradition had it that they were done by the hand of Zhang Sengyou. His flowers were painted according to a method that had been handed down for painting such heavenly orchids. After they were painted, when one looked from far away, they had the aura of standing forth, but when one went closer to look, they were flat. Everyone found this quite curious, and the temple came to be called the Temple of Recession and Protrusion. Thus we know that in ancient times the western regions had this method of painting. Sengyou was one of the earliest to

grasp it. And so we know that it is necessary for one's learning to be vast.

歐邏巴國人利瑪竇者,言畫有凹凸之法,今世無解此者.建康實錄言: 一乘寺寺門遍畫凹凸花,代稱張僧繇手跡,其花乃天竺遺法,朱及青綠所成,遠望眼暈如凹凸,就視即平,世咸異之,名凹凸寺.乃知古來西域自有此畫法,而僧繇已先得之,故知讀書不可不博也.[28]

The "western regions" refer here not to Europe but to Central Asia. The technique used to paint the flowers on the lintel of the Yicheng temple likely originated in areas such as Dunhuang, where the influence of regions farther west along the Silk Road, such as Kizil, is palpable. The alternation of lighter and darker timbres was key to creating a sense of volumetrism, as was the play with scale.

The enameled porcelain tray in figure 6.4, purportedly made in the imperial workshops during the Kangxi reign, illustrates the capacity of such alternation to produce a sense of recession and protrusion. The surface of the tray is decorated on both front and back with a geometrical pattern of interlocking vases. The front of the tray is adorned with sprigs of flowers on a yellow ground; the back uses color to create a sense of volume, alternating pinks and purples with blues and greens. When viewers walk past the back of the tray, the vase-like shapes dynamically swell and recede, an optical illusion caused by the alternation of warm and cool colors. For viewers to experience this illusion, however, the tray has to be propped upright; the illusion is hidden when the tray is displayed horizontally in a manner consistent with its function. The hidden optical illusion at the base of the tray was likely a playful jest, a light-hearted expression of wit.

THE QING NOTION OF ILLUSION

In the Qianlong emperor's gardens in the Forbidden City, of which the Juanqinzhai is the centerpiece, there were nearly ten *tongjing hua*. Often they were hung in rooms directly next to spaces for Buddhist meditation, as is the case with two other structures in the gardens adjacent to the Juanqinzhai, the Yucui xuan and the Yanghe jingshe.[29] In the Yanghe jingshe, one first encountered a *tongjing hua* by the court painters Wang

FIGURE 6.4 Enameled tray of the Kangxi reign period. *Source*: National Palace Museum, Taipei.

Youxue and Yao Wenhan depicting boys with hobbyhorses, then another by Wang Youxue, which featured a scroll that wrapped around the ceiling at a 90-degree angle.[30] Through a door shaped like a lotus petal, one entered a tiny room with characters written above the door stating, "This religious site is for peaceful cultivation in the Western Paradise" (西方極樂世界安養道場). The placement of those paintings next to spaces for

Historicizing Recession 163

meditation suggests that trompe l'oeil was pressed into the service of exploration regarding the illusory nature of all material form.

The *tongjing hua* have been considered as triumphs of linear perspective, fooling and delighting viewers with pictorial illusion. Kristina Kleutghen writes, "As expected for most perspectival paintings, the space of each scenic illusion resolves only at a single vanishing point. It therefore has only one perfect viewing position, which also implies the presence of the imperial viewer at a particular position in the original space."[31] Kleutghen suggests that erased brushwork was combined with the use of monofocal perspectivalism "to visually replace walls with spaces and objects that appear to exist tangibly in three dimension," resulting in convincing trompe l'oeil effects.

> Seventeenth- and eighteenth-century comments, as well as the literary record, indicate that touch was often responsible for a viewer's recognition of what he saw as a painting: viewers did not understand a seemingly permeable space to be a wall-mounted illusionistic painting until they touched it, or even accidentally bumped into it. The same visual depth cues in the painting that drew viewers forward to touch the objects depicted, however, also moved them inexorably toward the discovery of the painting's materiality and the collapse of the illusion.[32]

The "accidental bump" that Kleutghen references recalls Grannie Liu. Kleutghen considers the *tongjing hua* in isolation from their architectural contexts; this allows her to construe them as illusory in the sense of successfully providing an experience of trompe l'oeil. In contrast, I suggest that they must be understood within their architectural contexts; the painted doors and partitions, for example, were mirror images of the actual partitions adjacent to them. The combination of actual and painted architectural elements (partitions, railings, lattices, and windows) was employed to engage a conception of "illusion" that was not so much affiliated with Western notions of trompe l'oeil as with the concern regarding the emptiness of form in the Madhyamaka school of thought central to Qianlong's Buddhist practice. This pairing of actual and depicted architectural elements was in the language of the Imperial Household workshops understood as the "pairing of true and false" (*zhenjia*). The point is not to simulate the actual with the painted but to pair the painted and actual; the viewer holds both in tension. The principles of Italian *quadratura* were used to effect a state of suspension between investment in illusion and disinvestment from it.

It is very unlikely that these paintings succeeded in fooling the eyes of viewers in the Forbidden City. The Qing emperors erected entire buildings along the models of earlier buildings, so that similar structures, with identical copies of *tongjing hua*, stood on the east and west sides of the Forbidden City. The Juanqinzhai on the west side was a to-scale copy of the earlier Jingshengzhai on the east side. The *tongjing hua* affixed to its walls were not unique, but were copies of paintings affixed to the walls of earlier buildings that the Qianlong emperor frequented.[33] Viewers at court may have marveled at the technical accomplishment of those paintings, but they could not possibly have been taken in by the trompe l'oeil, given that they viewed multiple iterations of the same paintings in different settings. The famed wisteria ceiling in the theater of the Juanqinzhai was not the emperor Qianlong's first wisteria ceiling, but the third or fourth that he had commissioned.[34] In this sense, Grannie Liu's experience of the painting in Baoyu's bedroom cannot in any way be considered analogous to the experience of viewers at court.

I suspect that the architectural pairing of "true and false doors" in the Forbidden City that I discussed in chapter 5 is a technique derived from seventeenth-century Italian *quadratura*. The paintings affixed to these doors were not always executed in Western style; they could be traditional Chinese landscapes or figures. Perhaps for that reason, their relationship to Italian *quadratura* is not widely acknowledged. I propose, however, that one set of distant ancestors of the paired "true and false doors" in the Fuwangge and Juanqinzhai are the pairs of actual and trompe l'oeil doors—all framed with painted faux marble—that oppose each other in the Alexander room of the Palazzo Pitti, which Gherardini's teacher Angelo Colonna and his partner Agostino Mitelli frescoed with illusionistic architecture during the 1630s for Ferdinando II de' Medici.

The pairing of painted and actual doors became a principle of design throughout the Qianlong gardens. As an example, consider the paired bamboo moon gates of the theater room of the Juanqinzhai, which form double apertures through which viewers first enter the actual space of

FIGURE 6.5 Juanqinzhai. Paired bamboo moon gates. *Source*: Provided by the Palace Museum.

the theater room and then approach the painted wall. The fence on either side of both moon gates is critical to the focus on the moon gates themselves; the fence fragments the surrounding space and directs our attention to the aperture (see figure 6.5). The apertures of the operational and painted moon gates organize the experience of the panoramic *tongjing hua*, encouraging spectators to hold both "true" and "false" in tension. With this pairing of true and false doors or gates, there is no notion that the operational door is a priori.

The notion of illusion suggested by the paired moon gates is neither restricted to the pictorial plane nor a matter of subjective deception. The door of the "actual" bamboo lattice is as illusory as the painted one. This conception of illusion is quite different from that of trompe l'oeil, for here illusion is not derivative but all-encompassing. The significance of the pairing of actual and illusionistic architectural elements in the Forbidden City is not to be found in a conversation about trompe l'oeil or verisimilitude, but rather in considering the role of illusionistic painting as it evokes the illusory quality of the everyday world.

CONCLUSION

In this chapter, I have provided a way of thinking about the relation between literary and historical objects that reverses the conventional thinking about the literary object as a reflection of a historical substrate. Literary objects enable us to better understand historical objects not by providing illustrative examples but by inculcating in us the habits of mind by which we can read historical artifacts according to the thinking of their time. Once we consider the perspectivalism of the painting of the Juanqinzhai in terms of the fluid volumetric illusion inherent in *The Story of the Stone*'s use of the term *aotu*, we realize that the recessed space behind the painted lady with the clock appears as we walk past the painting. The perspectivalism is not monofocal but polyfocal; it is devoted as much to the creation of illusionistic spaces of recession as to the delineation of three-dimensional forms.

This point has crucial ramifications for our thinking about the relation between perspectivalism and verisimilitude. When Grannie Liu bumps into the painting of the young girl and exclaims, "How can they paint a picture so that it sticks out like that?" the scholarly consensus has been that perspectival techniques render the young girl and the objects surrounding her lifelike. When we consider the painting of the lady with the clock in the second-story balcony of the Juanqinzhai, it becomes clear that perspectival techniques were not used in the depiction of the woman herself. Rather, Italian techniques of polyfocal perspectivalism produced the illusionistic appearance of recessed space in the wall behind the human figure.

Instead of tricking viewers into mistaking planar projection for volumetric form, the *tongjing hua* of the Qianlong gardens remind viewers to contemplate the possibility that any manifestations of the phenomenal world outside the paintings are themselves illusory. The use of Italian *quadratura* in the theater room of the Juanqinzhai to create a space in which actual and depicted architectural elements mirror each other across its vastness can serve as a metaphor for thinking about eighteenth-century Chinese notions of illusion. The point would not be to read the painted bamboo lattice in terms of the actual "bamboo" lattice, but rather to inhabit the space between them, to reside in the space created by the duality of the depicted and the actual. This was the emperor's perspective as he sat on the throne in the Juanqinzhai; he held the depicted and actual bamboo moon gates to his left and right in tension. Neither was privileged over the other, and the emperor incorporated both in his purview.

The *tongjing hua* of the theater room of the Juanqinzhai drew on Italian scenography to grant viewers an experience of the fluidity and dynamism of space, the metamorphosis of space in the anamorphosis of the painting of the lady with the clock a reminder of the elastic and instable quality of volumetric form and space itself. The *tongjing hua* of the Qianlong gardens ask us to consider the process by which the evanescent forms of the world beyond are endowed with solidity by our habitual mistaking of evanescence and insubstantiality for static form. It is not simply that the *tongjing hua* deceive viewers into mistaking their painted surfaces for reality. Rather, they serve as a reminder that the world beyond is neither solid nor enduring. Instead of believing Grannie Liu to be an ignorant rustic who has never encountered Western perspectival painting, then, we should realize that her sigh is reminiscent of Yao Yuanzhi's and Zhang Jingyun's sense of loss when they realized they were standing before a painted wall. As Pu Songling's story makes clear, the painted wall is synonymous with an operational conception of fictionality in which the text acts on the reader to make clear the illusory quality of the reader's everyday world. This was the eighteenth-century Chinese understanding of trompe l'oeil, and the ultimate significance of Grannie Liu's encounter with the painting of the young girl.

Conclusion
Literary Objects

One summer in Beijing, while I was engaged in research on the eighteenth-century plate-glass mirror, my apartment was burglarized and my iPhone and computer were stolen. I naïvely spent the next day at the local police station begging the police to recover my devices, which "Find My iPhone" showed to be at an address in Guangzhou. After many hours it became clear that my cell phone was fated to find another home in Guangzhou, just as the ingots of Ling Mengchu's story left the miser Jin when their destiny with him came to an end. At the end of a fruitless conversation, I left by way of the entrance that the policemen themselves used. By the door hung a large plate-glass mirror, some 10 feet tall by 12 feet wide. The mirror was meant to remind policemen of the necessity for an overarching perspective distinct from any subject position, the impartial "bird's-eye view" that the Qianlong emperor found he could achieve with the technological aid of silvered plate glass. Days later, I entered the main entrance of a local elementary school and spied a large plate-glass mirror in a double-sided screen frame at the foot of the stairs, placed to encourage not physical but mental self-reflection. The associations that the plate-glass mirror held in eighteenth-century Beijing are still in play, even if sometimes obscured by the bustle of contemporary life.

I began this book by asking how the representation of literary objects could help us understand the conception of fictionality in the late Ming and Qing. One reason for choosing the texts I did was that a secondary literature existed that was premised on the logic that the vernacular fiction of this period is undergirded by historical mimeticism. I have pressed forward with that assumption, asking how a better understanding of fictional objects in historical context might shift their interpretive weight. But the significance of such literary objects cannot be arrived at simply by considering external historical processes such as the global circulation of glass to heads of state. As we have seen, literary objects exceed the historical objects that scholars posit as potential analogues. The boxlike nature of metaphorical mapping that we explored in chapter 3, "Du Shiniang's Jewel Box," can perhaps serve as an analogy for the mapping of literary objects onto historical analogues; no equivalence is ever final.

In that sense, these fictional texts engage but do not fully support the expectation of verisimilitude that readers might bring. The assumption that historical objects exist prior to fictional representations (an assumption arguably set in motion in Plato's *Republic*) is one these texts do not fully share. Rather than thinking of the fictional objects of Ming and Qing China as mimetic, we could think of them as deictic. Their various representations point to a space of imaginative potential, to a space that is *xu* rather than *shi*. Their significance is always contextual.

Earlier, I noted that to think of the objects of vernacular fiction solely in terms of their relation to the historical record is to ignore their essential literariness. Fictionality in the Ming and Qing is anchored in the temporal process of reading. The portrayal of the plate-glass mirror of Baoyu's bedroom, inconsistently depicted as both a freestanding and a wall-mounted mirror, is a case in point; readers encounter incongruous representations of the fictional object over the course of the text. In that sense, the conception of fictionality in late-imperial China is operational as much as it is ontological. What these texts aspire to grant us instead of verisimilitude is the experience of a dizzying confusion of simultaneous yet incompatible points of view.

I treat the panoramic paintings of the Qianlong gardens in chapter 6 in part because those paintings, conventionally thought of as engaging mimetic notions of verisimilitude, offer an entry into an operational conception of fictionality. If we think about the architectural positioning of the trompe l'oeil paintings of the Qianlong gardens, and then consider the repetitive placement of copies of the same painting in multiple structures across the Forbidden City, we understand that the works are not meant to create persuasive illusions that deceive the viewer. Rather, the way in which the forms within the paintings shift as the viewer approaches suggests that the movement toward the painting is what is key; the viewer literally interacts with the painting to produce illusions. Moreover, the placement of those panoramic paintings next to sites of meditation suggests that the experience of the works is preparatory: the trompe l'oeil serves as a reminder that a similar experience of phenomenal form structures the illusions of the world around us.

As Qianlong's poem "On the Mirror" tells us, viewing reflections is not necessarily about appreciating mimeticism. Rather, it is about learning to move between presumably incompatible points of view to inhabit an impartial perspective free of a singular, subjective position. We are better poised to read the "reflection" in the trompe l'oeil paintings of the Qianlong gardens when we see that they are not about deceiving the eye with verisimilitude, but rather are about creating illusions that we momentarily inhabit and then exit as we progress past. The recognition of misperception is our cue to disinvestment. We are not fooled by the trompe l'oeil so much as alerted that we are engaged in a more complex process of investing in the fictional and disinvesting from it. "The Painted Wall" and the various anecdotes we considered in conjunction with it speak to a particular feature of the late-imperial conception of fictionality: the fictionality of the literary text leads us to consider the fictionality of all phenomenal experience.

In chapter 23 of *The Story of the Stone*, the protagonist Baoyu is sitting on a rock reading the thirteenth-century play *The Western Wing* (*Xixiang ji* 西廂記). He has just come to the line "Fallen flowers form battle arrays" (*luo hong cheng zhen* 落紅成陣) when a shower of petals falls over his copy of *The Western Wing*.[1] In a moment of happenstance, the line that Baoyu reads describes his immediate environment, suggesting that the world within the book and the world exterior to the book are co-temporaneous and mutually permeable. The text of *The Western Wing* enters the world of *The Story of the Stone* and becomes absorbed in it as the characters for "arrays" (*zhen* 陣) and "fall" (*luo* 落) from the play's line "Fallen flowers form battle arrays" surface in the novel's own description of the petals falling upon the book: "suddenly a little gust of wind blew over" (*zhi jian yi zhen feng guo* 只見一陣風過)—here the character translated as "battle arrays" (*zhen* 陣) is reused as "gust," the measure word for wind—and the petals "fell over his clothes, his book, and all the ground around him" (落得滿身滿書滿地皆是).[2]

For an expansive moment, the world within the book and the world outside the book are held in tension. Baoyu both holds the book in his hands and is enveloped by the world of the book, inhabiting both frames of reference. This porousness of boundaries is central to the idea of a contagion between the worlds within and without the book. It allows the immaterial circumstances of *The Western Wing* to incarnate suddenly in a material form within *The Story of the Stone*, and suggests, with an almost anticipatory referentiality, that the novel will emerge in the world of the reader.

This moment is even more suggestive: the petals that rain on Baoyu and the book suggest that desire is being awakened. As the petals alight on Baoyu's body, he is infused with desire for the forms of this world (we might recall the shower of petals that the Heavenly Maiden Scattering Flowers rains upon the monk Śāriputra in the Vimalakīrti Sutra).[3] The experience of fictional illusion itself sets in motion a desire for worldly experience. *The Story of the Stone* thus stages a scene of mindless reading to indicate that the reading of fiction could become a technique for inhabiting structures of attachment and detachment. In this view, fiction acts upon the reader, cultivating the capacity to hold the worlds within and without the book in tension. The reader crosses the boundary from one ontological realm to the other, inhabiting both simultaneously. Within the linear trajectory of the plots we have considered, fictional objects have the responsibility to show that the trajectory from investment to disinvestment over the course of a narrative is but a rehearsal for a deeper understanding of the inherent emptiness of the phenomenal forms of this world. The objects of late-imperial fiction encourage readers to engage with the sensual world of the text while being conscious of its illusory nature, opening the way to understanding not only the fictionality of literary texts, but also that of quotidian existence.

Like those who encounter the painted wall, readers of Ming and Qing fiction straddle two ways of knowing. When we experience the pleasure of finding historical analogues to literary objects, we are with licentiate Zhu inside the wall, in the realm of desire, seeking to attach ourselves to the material and sensual. When we consider the contribution of literary objects to the Ming and Qing conception of fictionality, we stand with the monk who strums the painted wall. It may seem that the stance of the monk is more sophisticated. Neither position, however, should be privileged over the other. Our perspective should be bifocal: the search for historical exemplars of literary objects that will allow us to imagine the context in which these novels and stories were written is just as important as our conception of the literary object as a textual effect, and indeed furnishes a necessary foundation for it. It is ultimately through an immersion in the scholarly desire for historical referents that we realize, in the words of the Heavenly Maiden Scattering Flowers, that "All things are like that—they do not exist, yet do not not exist."[4]

Notes

INTRODUCTION: THE SUBSTANCE OF FICTION

1. Feng Menglong, "Jiang Xingge chonghui zhenzhu shan," in Feng Menglong, *Yushi mingyan* (Hangzhou: Zhejiang guji chubanshe, 2015), 8.
2. Craig Clunas, *Superfluous Things: Material Culture and Social Status in Early Modern China* (Cambridge: Polity Press, 1991).
3. Wai-yee Li, "The Collector, the Connoisseur and Late-Ming Sensibility," *T'oung Pao*, 2nd series, 81, no. 4/5 (1995): 25–302; Wai-yee Li, "Shibian yu wanwu—lüe lun Qingchu wenren shenmei fengshang," *Bulletin of the Institute of Chinese Literature and Philosophy* 33 (2008): 35–76; Judith Zeitlin, "The Cultural Biography of a Musical Instrument: Little *Hulei* as Sounding Object, Antique, Prop and Relic," *Harvard Journal of Asiatic Studies* 69, no. 2 (2009): 395–441; S. E. Kile and Kristina Kleutgnen, "Seeing Through Pictures and Poetry: A History of Lenses (1681)," *Late Imperial China* 38, no. 1 (2017): 47–112; Kaijun Chen, "Transcultural Lenses: Wrapping the Foreignness for Sale in the History of Lenses," in *EurAsian Matters: China, Europe and the Transcultural Object*, ed. Anna Grasskamp and Monica Juneja (Heidelberg: Springer, 2018), 77–98; and "Craft in *Six Records of a Life Adrift*," in *Chinese Literature: Essays, Articles, Reviews* 39 (2017): 95–117.
4. On early twentieth-century readings of *The Story of the Stone* that viewed it as a roman à clef, see Haun Saussy, "Authorship and *The Story of the Stone*: Open Questions," in *Approaches to Teaching* The Story of the Stone (Dream of the Red Chamber), ed. Andrew Schonebaum and Tina Lu (New York: Modern Language Association of America, 2012), 70; and David Hawkes, "Introduction," in Cao

Xueqin, *The Story of the Stone*, vol. 1, trans. David Hawkes (London: Penguin Books, 1973), 46. On *Plum in the Golden Vase*, see Cheng Pei-kai, "Jiuse caiqi yu *Jin Ping Mei* cihua de kaitou—jianping *Jin Ping Mei* yanjiu de 'suoyin pai,'" *Chung-wai wen-hsüeh* 4, no. 20 (1983): 42–69.

5. For examples of this belletristic writing, see Meng Hui, *Pan Jinlian de fa xing* (Nanjing: Jiangsu renmin chubanshe, 2005); and Yang Zhishui, *Wu se: Jin Ping Mei du 'wu' ji* (Beijing: Zhonghua shuju, 2018). See also Yang Zhishui's review of writing in the *mingwu xue* vein in "Guanyu 'mingwu xinzheng,'" in *Nanfang wenwu*, no. 3 (2007): 79–80.

6. Shen Congwen, "'Banpaojia' he 'dianxiqiao': Guanyu *Honglou meng* zhushi yidian shangque," *Guangming ribao*, August 6, 1961, 4.

7. Hou Hui, *Honglou meng guizu shenghuo jiemi* (Beijing: Xinhua chubanshe, 2010), 69.

8. The most succinct definition of "vernacular fiction" opposes it to fiction written in classical Chinese, taking as a point of departure the European opposition between local languages and Latin, the written medium of the educated. Vernacular fiction was not composed in the language that its authors spoke at home or on the streets, but in *guanhua*, a lingua franca for officials. Patrick Hanan, *The Chinese Vernacular Story* (Cambridge, MA: Harvard University Press, 1981), 1. Moreover, vernacular fiction embeds many classical forms, from classical poetry to rhymeprose to legal documents. Shang Wei has argued that the term *vernacular* is not only a misnomer but also misleading with regard to Chinese writing, "as Chinese writing is almost always at variance with the spoken language." Shang Wei, "Writing and Speech: Rethinking the Issue of Vernaculars in Early Modern China," in *Rethinking East Asian Languages, Vernaculars, and Literacies, 1000–1919*, ed. Benjamin Elman (Leiden: Brill, 2014), 256.

9. Elaine Freedgood, *The Ideas in Things: Fugitive Meaning in the Victorian Novel* (Chicago: University of Chicago Press, 2006), 30–54.

10. Catherine Gallagher's thinking about literary characters may be relevant here. Drawing on Roland Barthes's observations in *S/Z* regarding the creation of character via the readers' repeated encounter of a proper name in a fictional text, Gallagher gives a complex account of the importance of the disjunctive experience of the reading of character. Roland Barthes, *S/Z: An Essay*, trans. Richard Miller (New York: Hill and Wang, 1974); Catherine Gallagher, "The Rise of Fictionality," in *The Novel*, ed. Franco Moretti, 2 vols. (Princeton, NJ: Princeton University Press, 2006), 1:359–60.

11. See Dorothy Ko, *The Social Life of Inkstones: Artisans and Scholars in Early Qing China* (Seattle: University of Washington Press, 2018); *Cinderella's Sisters: A Revisionist History of Footbinding* (Berkeley: University of California Press, 2005);

Every Step a Lotus: Shoes for Bound Feet (Berkeley: University of California Press, 2001); and Jonathan Hay, *Sensuous Surfaces: The Decorative Object in Early Modern China* (Honolulu: University of Hawai'i Press), 2010.

1. THE PYTHON ROBE OF *THE PLUM IN THE GOLDEN VASE*

1. David Rolston notes that scholars know more about the fictional household of Ximen Qing than any historical Ming household save that of the imperial family. Although the novel is superficially set in the time of the Song emperor Huizong, it is well established that the novel depicts the material culture of its time, and that it refers to events and figures of the sixteenth century. David Rolston, "Imagined (or Perhaps Not) Late Ming Music and Oral Performing Literature in an Imaginary Late Ming Household: The Production and Consumption of Music and Oral Performing Literature by and in the Ximen Family in the *Jin Ping Mei cihua* (*Plum in the Golden Vase*)," CHINOPERL 33, no. 1 (July 2014): 97–142.

2. Chen Zhao, Jin Ping Mei *xiaokao* (Shanghai: Shanghai shudian chubanshe, 1999), is an invaluable resource, listing hundreds of material objects found in *The Plum in the Golden Vase* (clothing, household utensils, sexual implements, food, and wine) with information about their provenance. Huang Lin also exhaustively lists the material objects found in the text, along with brief descriptions. Huang Lin, Jin Ping Mei *da cidian* (Chengdu: Bashu shushe, 1991), 865–969. See also Craig Clunas, *Superfluous Things: Material Culture and Social Status in Early Modern China* (Honolulu: University of Hawai'i Press, 2004 [1991]), 38; and "The Novel *Plum in the Golden Vase* as a Source for the Study of Ming Furniture," *Orientations* 23, no. 1 (January 1992): 60–68. In his later work, Clunas cautioned against the use of this novel as evidence of historical practice, pointing out that the decor of Ximen's study, for example, resembles a brothel more than it does a gentleman's study. Craig Clunas, "All in the Best Possible Taste: Ming Dynasty Material Culture in the Light of the Novel *Plum in the Golden Vase*," *Bulletin of the Oriental Ceramic Society of Hong Kong* 11 (1994–97): 9–19.

3. Naifei Ding has described the use of lists in *Plum in the Golden Vase* as semiophilic. Referring to Roland Barthes's notion of the superfluous detail that helps to foster a "reality effect," Ding suggests that, although the accumulation of such detail creates the semblance of a "reality effect," "that is perhaps more of an accidental and mistaken after-effect...what has been mistaken for an early 'realism' is actually an anti-object motivated celebration of conspicuous object consumption." Naifei Ding, *Obscene Things: Sexual Politics in* Jin Ping Mei (Durham, NC: Duke University Press, 2002), 189.

4. Ximen recycles an old saw that the accumulation of wealth and precious objects can only lead to calamity. These same sentiments appear in an essay by Lu Ji 陸楫 of Shanghai (fl. c. 1540), who advocated spending over frugality as a way of increasing the circulation of wealth in order to benefit the economy. The essay is translated by Lien-sheng Yang in "Economic Justification for Spending—An Uncommon Idea in Traditional China," *Harvard Journal of Asiatic Studies* 20, no. 1–2 (1957): 36–52.

5. Ximen's ridicule of the miser resonates with the satires of the miser in short stories such as Feng Menglong's "Song Sigong danao menghun Zhang" (*Gujin xiaoshuo*, no. 36); and the prologue story of Ling Mengchu's "*Zhuanyun han qiaoyu Dongting hong*" (*Chuke Pai'an jingqi*, no. 1). Although both texts were published within several decades of the appearance of *The Plum in the Golden Vase*, "Song Sigong" and the prologue story of "*Zhuanyun han*" were likely in circulation far earlier. On the dating of "Song Sigong," see Patrick Hanan, *The Chinese Short Story: Studies in Dating, Authorship, and Composition* (Cambridge, MA: Harvard University Press, 1973), 161–63.

6. *Jin Ping Mei cihua*, facsimile reprint (Hong Kong: Taiping shuju, 1993), 56.5a. The translation is my own. Martin Huang has read this passage as showing Ximen's blindness to the distinction between financial capital and his own sexual capital, which are both designated by the term *benqian*. He argues that although financial capital benefits from circulation, sexual capital is depleted with circulation and cannot be renewed; not understanding the difference, Ximen eventually dies of sexual exhaustion. Martin W. Huang, *Desire and Fictional Narrative in Late Imperial China* (Cambridge, MA: Harvard University Asia Center, 2001), 95–96.

7. Ximen's philosophical pronouncement is even more singular for being cast in poetic form. This is the only instance I can recall in the entire novel of Ximen Qing speaking in verse. Indeed, the idea of Ximen Qing reciting a poem seems so ludicrous that one wonders at this point if the narrator has unobtrusively taken over, but the words that follow the poem, "While he was speaking, they saw the servant-boy bringing in the meal" indicate that the poem is indeed in Ximen's voice. As Patrick Hanan has shown, in both the A and B editions, chapters 53 to 57 are by a different hand than the remainder of the novel, which may account for the idiosyncrasy in the portrayal of Ximen here. See Patrick D. Hanan, "The Text of the *Chin P'ing Mei*," *Asia Major* 9, no. 1 (1962): 14–33.

8. The debate regarding the degree to which the late Ming economy was protocapitalist is well-trodden territory; suffice it to say here that the concept of capital that gives return on investment is well established in the novel. For a comprehensive listing of episodes involving investment and speculation, including rates of interest, see Cai Guoliang, "*Jin Ping Mei* fanying de Ming houqi de chengshi

jingji shenghuo," in Jin Ping Mei *yanjiu* (Shanghai: Fudan daxue chubanshe, 1984), 327–37.

9. Yang Lin has done a careful investigation regarding the etymology of *dongxi* as a term for "thing." Yang negates claims that the term *dongxi* meant "thing" as early as the Han dynasty, stating that it is not until the Five Dynasties or Song dynasty that the term comes to designate material things. Yang Lin, "Wupin cheng 'dongxi' tanyuan," *Changjiang xueshu* 1 (2012): 99–109.

10. Ann Rosalind Jones and Peter Stallybrass explicitly link this dynamic to a capitalist conception of the object, observing that, for Marx, "The commodity comes to life through the death of the object, [for] only if one empties out the 'objectness' of the market can one make it readily exchangeable on the market." Ann Rosalind Jones and Peter Stallybrass, *Renaissance Clothing and the Materials of Memory* (Cambridge: Cambridge University Press, 2000), 8.

11. *Jin Ping Mei cihua*, 52.8b–9a; *The Plum in the Golden Vase or Chin P'ing Mei*, David Tod Roy. 5 vols. (Princeton, NJ: Princeton University Press, 1997–2015), vol. 3, 457. Throughout this chapter I primarily use David Tod Roy's translation, the one used most often in teaching, rather than my own so that readers can consult it to see the context of the quotations. I emend Wade-Giles to *pinyin* romanization within his translations, hence "Ximen Qing" instead of "Hsi-men Ch'ing." I use my own translation where a more literal one is needed. Although this analysis is based on the *cihua* edition of the novel (the A edition in Patrick Hanan's terminology), I have also consulted the B and C editions. For my present purposes, the differences among the texts do not matter substantially. On the differences between the A, B, and C editions, see Patrick Hanan, "The Text of the *Chin Ping Mei*," 1–57. For a reevaluation of the importance of the B edition, see Tian Xiaofei, *Qiushui tang lun* Jin Ping Mei (Tianjin: Tianjin renmin chubanshe, 2003), and "A Preliminary Comparison of the Two Recensions of *The Plum in the Golden Vase*," *Harvard Journal of Asiatic Studies* 62, no. 2 (2002): 347–89.

12. *Jin Ping Mei cihua*, 34.2b. Similarly, the summer bedstead of the inner study is described as "a bed with inlaid marble, black lacquer, and gold tracery, and blue gauze curtains hanging." I would add that these "semio-philic" lists ought to be viewed in the context of the noticeable presence of the list in late-imperial pleasure reading. In the drama miscellany *Zhaijin qiyin*, for example, the upper register (which occupies the top third of the page) consists exclusively of a list of geographical place-names for nearly a third of the text. See Gong Zhengwo, *Zhaijin qiyin*, ed. Wang Ch'iu-kuei, *Shanben xiqu congkan* edition (Taipei: Xuesheng shuju, 1984), 192–273.

13. Although we can read the profusion of nouns and adjectives in such passages as rhetorically motivated, we should remember that, given the degree of citation

of heterogeneous materials in *The Plum in the Golden Vase*, such lists might very well have been sutured in from notation books or manuals of style that described the materials to be used in making chairs in such a way.

14. When a matchmaker first introduces Ximen's fourth wife, Meng Yulou, to him, for example, Meng Yulou enters wearing a robe sporting the mythical *qilin*, even though her deceased husband was a mere cloth merchant. *Jin Ping Mei cihua* 7.6a–b; *The Plum in the Golden Vase*, vol. 1, 133.
15. *Jin Ping Mei cihua*, 8.1b; *The Plum in the Golden Vase*, vol. 1, 148.
16. *Jin Ping Mei cihua*, 8.8a–b; *The Plum in the Golden Vase*, vol. 1, 160.
17. *Jin Ping Mei cihua*, 34.2b; *The Plum in the Golden Vase*, vol. 2, 285. Importantly, the term here used for the lists of gifts, "account book" (*zhang bu*), is the same term that the late seventeenth-century commentator Zhang Zhupo (1670–1698) later used to describe *Jin Ping Mei cihua* itself. Zhang states that in its endless listing of things, the novel is nothing more than an accounts book for Ximen Qing's household, its authorship an act of notation rather than of exposition. Zhang Zhupo, *Di yi qi shu: Zhang Zhupo piping Jin Ping Mei* (Taipei: Liren shuju, 1982). Zhang Zhupo's revision of *The Plum in the Golden Vase* was in effect intended to render it less list-like, less inclusive, omitting randomness and superfluity from its narrative arc. His relentless excision of what he considered superfluous elements from the *cihua* version created a more structured narrative that has lost the hyper-inclusive, exhaustive quality with which the *cihua* version indexed a world.
18. *Jin Ping Mei cihua*, 34.3a; *The Plum in the Golden Vase*, vol. 2, 285.
19. *Jin Ping Mei cihua*, 34.5.b; *The Plum in the Golden Vase*, vol. 2, 289.
20. Ximen's ascent in status is echoed in that of his cronies and servants. As Ximen graduates from bribery to the exchange of favors, his servants rise to a point at which they can take bribes from others in return for interceding with him on their behalf. This becomes clear in the same chapter, when Ying Bojue and Ximen's servants accept bribes with regard to a different court case involving an adulterous affair between the wife of Ximen's manager, Han Daoguo, and his brother.
21. Recent scholarship on Ming-Qing fiction has drawn on Marcel Mauss's influential essay *The Gift* (1923) and Arjun Appadurai's edited volume *The Social Life of Things*. The vision of the gift in *The Plum in the Golden Vase* is far darker than that of Mauss, however, just as the novel's understanding of circulation is more jaundiced than that of Appadurai. Marcel Mauss, *The Gift: The Form and Reason for Exchange in Archaic Societies* (New York: W. W. Norton, 1990). Appadurai explores the importance of exchange in encoding the significance of objects; in turn he derives his emphasis on exchange from Georg Simmel's treatment of exchange as the source of economic value. See Georg Simmel,

The Conflict in Modern Culture and Other Essays, trans. K. Peter Etzkorn (New York: Teachers College Press, 1968), 47–63; Arjun Appadurai, "Introduction: Commodities and the Politics of Value," in *The Social Life of Things: Commodities in Cultural Perspective*, ed. Arjun Appadurai, 3–63 (Cambridge: Cambridge University Press, 1986).

22. *Jin Ping Mei cihua*, 34.5a; *The Plum in the Golden Vase*, vol. 2, 288.
23. Ying Bojue's explanation of his redistribution of the shad, followed by directions to his wife on marinating the shad, mimics the didactic tone of Ming encyclopedias of everyday life. These encyclopedias contain detailed instructions regarding gift-giving, including the occasions on which one should give gifts, what items should be given, and how the cards accompanying gifts should be addressed. For an example, see Yu Xiangdou, *Santai wanyong zheng zong* (Tokyo: Kyuko shoin, 2000), 15.102–25. See also Shang Wei, "*Jin Ping Mei* and Late Ming Print Culture," in *Writing and Materiality in China: Essays in Honor of Patrick Hanan*, ed. Judith T. Zeitlin and Lydia Liu (Cambridge: MA: Harvard University East Asia Center, 2003); and Shang Wei, "The Making of the Everyday World: *Jin Ping Mei cihua* and Encyclopedias for Daily Use," in *Dynastic Crisis and Cultural Innovation: From the Late Ming to the Late Qing and Beyond*, ed. David Der-wei Wang and Shang Wei, 63–92 (Cambridge, MA: Harvard University Press, 2005).
24. Julie Park describes how clothing has such a supplemental relation to interiority in the eighteenth-century English novel. Julie Park, *The Self and It: Novel Objects in Eighteenth-Century England* (Stanford, CA: Stanford University Press, 2010), xxiv.
25. The custom of giving python robes to the Grand Secretariat began in the fifteenth year of the Hongzhi reign period (1502), with gifts of red robes to Liu Jian (1433–1526), Grand Secretary from 1492 to 1513; Li Dongyang (1447–1516), Grand Secretary from 1494 to 1513; and Xie Qian (1450–1531), who served twice as Grand Secretary, from 1495 to 1506 and from 1527 to 1528. *Ming shi*, comp. Zhang Tingyu et al. (Beijing: Zhonghua shuju, 1974), 181.9b.
26. Only the emperor had the right to bestow a python robe, but the dowager empress could present one on his behalf. The Empress Dowager Li conferred a python robe on Zhang Juzheng after granting him the honorary post of tutor to the emperor in 1578.
27. In a particularly interesting case, in 1510, a woman surnamed Duan 段 from an old family of Nanjing asked to be clothed in her python robe when she realized that death was imminent and she needed to be dressed for her coffin. Li Dongyang, *Huailu tang ji, wen hou gao, juan* 30, 3b, rare manuscript, Harvard-Yenching Library.
28. Kong Shangren, *Taohua shan*, ed. Wang Jisi (Beijing: Renmin wenxue chubanshe, 1958), 185.

29. Cao Xueqin and Gao E, *Honglou meng*, vol. 2, ed. Yu Pingbo and Qi Gong (Beijing: Renmin wenxue chuubanshe, 2005), 1146.
30. Wu Jingzi, *Rulin waishi* (Hong Kong: Zhonghua shuju, 1991), 334.
31. Xi Zhou sheng (pseud.), *Xingshi yinyuan zhuan*, ed. Huang Xiaoqiu (Shanghai: Shanghai guji chubanshe), 611–25.
32. *Ming shi*, 67.10b.
33. The only sanctioned secondary transfer of the python robe was imperial reappropriation. *Da Ming hui dian*, in Shen Shixing et al., *Xuxiu Sikuquanshu* (Shanghai: Shanghai guji chubanshe, 2002), 165.18a.
34. Members of the Grand Secretariat received bonuses after having been in office for three, six, and nine years; officials of the first rank received bonuses after six and nine years. Bonuses granted after nine years of service to the Grand Secretariat typically included a python robe as well as fine cloth, wine, food, cash, and silver; the emperor might also mark special occasions, such as the retirement of the imperial tutor, with the gift of a python robe.
35. The Jiajing emperor presented python robes to prominent Daoist patriarchs on several occasions. In 1538 he presented a python robe and jade belt to the Daoist patriarch Shao Yuanjie (1459–1539). Wang Shizhen, *Yanshan tang bieji* (Beijing: Zhonghua shuju, 1985), 316.
36. *Ming shi, Sulu lie zhuan*, 325.11a (8420). See also Shen Defu, *Wanli yehuo bian* (Beijing: Zhonghua shuju, 1997), 830. On python robes being used as presentation gifts to tribes on the northern border, see also "Tulufan liezhuan" in *Ming shi*, 329.17a.
37. Zhang Xie, *Dong xiyang kao*, 44. See *Ming shi, juan* 134, 2200; *Ming Xianzong shilu, juan* 9, 1975; *Ming Xiaozong shilu, juan* 159, 2853; *Ming Shizong shilu, juan* 169, 3694. Also see Huang Weimin, "Mangyi yuzhi yu wan Ming xiaoshuo de min jian shu xie," *Sichuan shifan daxue xuebao* 39, no. 3 (May 2012): 115.
38. Inalienable possessions, writes Weiner, have "a subjective value that places them above exchange value"; authority arises from the possession's capacity to authenticate the owner's line of descent. Inalienable possessions thus confer upon those who own them an authority that is not transferred when such possessions are exchanged for goods or money (in the case of the python robe, possession authenticates the wearer's relation to the imperial family). When exchanged for goods or money, the inalienable possession loses its capacity to authenticate, instead providing only a link to the authority of the previous owner. Annette Weiner, *Inalienable Possessions: The Paradox of Keeping While Giving* (Berkeley: University of California Press, 1992), 6. The python robe may be compared to her example of a date palm bestowed upon a Trobriand islander by his matriline. The islander explains that when he dies, the relatives from his matriline will come to take the date palm back; it is not his to bequeath or gift

to anyone else (see Weiner, *Inalienable Possessions*, 25–26). The intended termination of transfer in the case of the python robe set it apart, however, from some of Weiner's other examples, such as genealogies, crowns, and ancestral portraits, which are meant to be transferred to descendants.

39. Perhaps for this reason, even the Ming emperors themselves would ignore the restrictions regarding the gifting of the python robe. Shen Defu, in his *Wanli yehuo bian*, criticized the Jiajing (1522–1567) emperor for giving four scarlet python robes to a favored minister to congratulate him on the acquisition of a concubine. The use of those presentation gifts to mark private occasions, he wrote, had spiraled out of control since the time of the Tianshun emperor (r. 1457–1465). Shen Defu, *Wanli yehuo bian*, vol. 1, 189.
40. *Jin Ping Mei cihua*, 25.12a; *The Plum in the Golden Vase*, vol. 2, 98.
41. The various items that Li Ping'er's adoptive father-in-law, the late Eunuch Director Hua, purloined from the palace furnish a further example of the instantiation of sociality via purloining, bribery, and graft. Besides the python robes, Li P'ing-er possessed an album of erotic pictures taken from the palace that she shared with Ximen early in their relationship, as well as hair pins made for imperial use that she passed out to Ximen's wives on her first visit to his compound. She tells Ximen early in their adulterous relationship that her husband knows nothing of these goods given to her by the Eunuch Director; the implication is that they were given in the context of an incestuous affair with her father-in-law. *Jin Ping Mei cihua*, 14.3b, 14.4a; *The Plum in the Golden Vase*, vol. 2, 78.
42. Michael Marmé, *Suzhou: Where the Goods of All Provinces Converge* (Stanford, CA: Stanford University Press, 2005), 140.
43. The bureau was disbanded in 1628, over concern that the eunuchs associated with it had grown too powerful. Marmé, *Suzhou*, 139–40.
44. Liu Xinglin and Fan Jinmin, *Changjiang sichou wenhua* (Wuhan: Hubei jiaoyu chubanshe, 2004), 262.
45. Liu Xinglin and Fan Jinmin, *Changjiang sichou wenhua*, 303. Also see Fan Jinmin and Jin Wen, *Jiangnan sichou shi yanjiu* (Beijing: Nongye chubanshe, 1993), 209.
46. *Ming Xizong shilu*, comp. Wen Tiren et al. (Taibei: Zhongyang yanjiuyuan lishi yuyan yanjiusuo, 1966), *juan* 30, 1506.
47. Marmé, *Suzhou*, 38.
48. Shen Defu, *Wanli yehuo bian*, vol. 1, 21.
49. *Ming shi*, 67.19a.
50. *Ming shi*, 67.19a.
51. A terse statute of 1527 in the *Da Ming huidian* (Collected statutes of the Ming) warns against recutting python robes into women's clothes. *Da Ming huidian* (Taipei: Dongnan chubanshe, 1964), 61.12a.

52. Shen Defu, *Wanli yehuo bian*, vol. 1, 20. See also Clunas, *Superfluous Things*, 152.
53. *Ming shi*, 67.19a. Shen Defu, *Wanli yehuo bian*, vol. 1, 20.
54. This detail regarding the *Erya* is in Shen Defu's account, but not in the account in the *Ming shi*. See *Ming shi*, 67.19a. Shen Defu, *Wanli yehuo bian*, vol. 1, 20.
55. *Dictionary of Ming Biography*, ed. L. Carrington Goodrich and Chaoying Fang, 2 vols. (New York: Columbia University Press, 1976), 1:941–45.
56. Gu Yingtai, ed., *Ming shi jishi benmo* (Beijing: Zhonghua shuju, 1977), 654.
57. Gu Yingtai, ed., *Ming shi jishi benmo*, 653–54.
58. *Ming shi*, 186.12a.
59. Liu Ruoyu, *Zhuozhong zhi*, in *Zhongguo yeshi jicheng* (Sichuan: Bashu shushe, 1993), 19.1a.
60. Liu Ruoyu, *Zhuozhong zhi*, in *Zhongguo yeshi jicheng*, 19.1a–b, 20.1a–2b. Roundels (*buzi*) were designs embroidered in gold or multicolored thread on the chest and back of a robe; the patterns indicated rank.
61. Liu Ruoyu, *Zhuozhong zhi*, 20.7b.
62. Liu Ruoyu, *Zhuozhong zhi*, 19.15b.
63. Liu Ruoyu intimates that such abuses would lead to personal catastrophe, quoting the *Zuo zhuan*, "Clothing that is inappropriate to one's status will bring a disaster upon one's person." *Zuo zhuan yi zhu*, ed. Li Mengsheng (Shanghai: Shanghai guji chubanshe, 1998), 279–80 and 19.4a. The phrase occurs in an anecdote about the liking Zheng Zizang had for a kind of cap made from sandpiper (*yu*) feathers. The use of such a cap was inappropriate to his status, and he fled toward Song, only to be killed by the Duke of Zheng at the border.
64. Gu Yingtai, ed., *Mingshi jishi benmo*, 670.
65. *Jin Ping Mei cihua*, 71.2a–2b; *The Plum in the Golden Vase*, vol. 3, 308.
66. Wang Shizhen, *Yanshan tang bieji*, 210.
67. *Ming shi*, 67.19a.
68. *Ming shi*, 67.9b. The two horns that the emperor refers to are the ones on the imperial dragon, which resemble deer antlers, and not the horns of the horned bull, which belong to an insignia of lower status than the flying fish. The ranks permitted to wear python and flying-fish robes shifted over time, and at one point reversed; during the Zhengde reign (1505–1521), flying-fish robes were permitted to officials of the second rank, and python robes to officials of the third rank.
69. *Xinke xiuxiang piping Jin Ping Mei*, ed. Qi Yan and Wang Rumei (Hong Kong: Joint Publishing Company, 1990), vol. 2, 976.
70. In chapter 71, Eunuch He speaks of giving a green robe to Ximen Qing, but in chapter 73, Ximen Qing sports a black robe. Clearly, the robe Ximen is wearing in chapter 73 is the same one that Eunuch He gave him in chapter 71. The translation smooths out the discrepancy, rendering the robe as green in both chapters. In this passage, the phrase "its golds and greens setting each other off"

(金碧掩映) refers to the thread of the flying-fish motif. The character 青 (*qing*), which describes the robe's fabric, is ordinarily translated as "green," but with regard to clothing designates a dark indigo that is nearly black. Thus the robe is dark blue or black with a flying-fish design in gold and green thread on the central roundel.

71. *Jin Ping Mei cihua*, 73.5b–6a; *The Plum in the Golden Vase*, vol. 4, 393–94; Wu Jingzi, *Rulin waishi* (Hongkong: Zhonghua shuju, 1991), 334.
72. *Da Ming lü, juan* 165, 32.
73. *Ming shi*, 67.9b.
74. *Ming Shizong shilu, juan* 54, 8737.
75. The title commissioner-in-chief (*dudu*) during the Ming and Qing referred to heads of the five chief military commissions in the central government (rank 1a). *Dudu* were usually granted noble status as high as duke. Charles O. Hucker, *A Dictionary of Official Titles in Imperial China* (Stanford, CA: Stanford University Press, 1985).
76. *Jin Ping Mei cihua*, 73.5b–6a; *The Plum in the Golden Vase*, vol. 4, 393–94. As the Chongzhen commentator remarks of Ying Bojue, "His flattery is marvelous in that it goes one level deeper; his showing off is smooth and unimpeded. All wealthy people need to have someone of his sort." *Xinke xiuxiang piping Jin Ping Mei*, 104.
77. Mary Douglas, "Primitive Rationing: A Study in Controlled Exchange," in *Themes in Economic Anthropology*, ed. Raymond Firth (London: Tavistock Publications, 1967), quoted in Appadurai, *The Social Life of Things*, 24–25.
78. Andrew Plaks, *The Four Masterworks of the Ming Novel: Ssu Ta Ch'i Shu* (Princeton, NJ: Princeton University Press, 1987). Xiaofei Tian supports this view, stating that "The *cihua* recension is clearly grounded in a social vision and ethic that we recognize in some way as 'Confucian,' whether or not we trace the values in the text to one particular school of Confucianism. The *xiuxiang* recension's divergences from the *cihua* often soften the strictness of moral judgment, leaving room for compassion, for mercy, and for a discovery of the emptiness of the passions." Xiaofei Tian, "A Preliminary Comparison of the Two Recensions of *Plum in the Golden Vase*," *Harvard Journal of Asiatic Studies* 62, no. 2 (2002): 347–89.
79. Zhang Zhupo, *Zhang Zhupo piping diyi qishu Jin Ping Mei, juan* 79, 21.
80. See Katharine Carlitz, *The Rhetoric of* Chin P'ing Mei (Bloomington: Indiana University Press, 1986), 28–44; and Andrew Plaks, *The Four Masterworks of the Ming Novel*, 157–59, 164–67. As Carlitz writes, "Never for a chapter are we away from [the] definition and violation" of the "canonical relations of ruler, subject and family in Confucian tradition." Katherine Carlitz, *The Rhetoric of* Chin P'ing Mei, 36.
81. On such juxtapositions in riddles and games, see Yuming He, *Home in the World: Editing the 'Glorious Ming' in Woodblock-Printed Books of the Sixteenth*

and *Seventeenth Centuries* (Cambridge, MA: Harvard University East Asia Center, 2013), 17–55. Shang Wei discusses the use of a well-known line from *The Analects*, "Is it not delightful?" in chapter 8 of *The Plum in the Golden Vase*, arguing that the vernacular context in which the line appears is characteristic of the use of that line in drinking games. Shang Wei, "Jin Ping Mei and Late Ming Print Culture," 199.

82. I would add that the comic juxtaposition of classical language and vernacular interpretation has a far wider reach than the *jiu ling*, and it is central to the southern drama (*chuanqi*). In this sense, these moments take place in a wider envisioning of the relation between classical and vernacular as registers.
83. Shang Wei writes, "A narrative work so composed challenges us to re-examine the concepts of author, fictional discourse, and literary unity.... There is no reason to adopt an interpretive approach that views the novel as a manifestation of a single, predominant consciousness using a unitary language, consistent rhetorical devices and patterns, and a coherent form of narrative discourse." Shang Wei, "Jin Ping Mei and Late Ming Print Culture," 195.
84. As Liao observes, "the quest for overall unity is a modern phenomenon." Chaoyang Liao, "Three Readings in the *Jin Ping Mei cihua*," CLEAR 6, no. 1/2 (1984): 83.

2. LING MENGCHU'S SHELL

1. Ling Mengchu, *Chuke Pai'an jingqi*, ed. Wang Gulu (Shanghai: Gudian wenxue chubanshe, 1957), 4. The story is translated without the prologue in Ling Mengchu, *Amazing Tales: First Series*, trans. Wen Jing'en (Beijing: Panda Books, 1998). Because at the time of writing there was no translation conventionally assigned to students, I translated the passages from the story. An excellent translation has since been published: Ling Mengchu, *Slapping the Table in Amazement: A Ming Dynasty Story Collection*, trans. Shuhui Yang and Yunqin Yang (Seattle: University of Washington Press, 2018), 9–36.
2. Ling Mengchu, *Chuke Pai'an jingqi*, 4.
3. Ling Mengchu, *Chuke Pai'an jingqi*, 4.
4. The contrast between the prologue tale and its classical antecedent is particularly instructive. Jin Weihou's attachment to the ingots is far more eroticized than in the original. In the classical anecdote, the miser Jin's place is taken by a couple surnamed Chen, who have worked all their lives to save 24 ingots of silver. They wrap and seal the ingots multiple times, then sew them into their pillow. One night they both share the same dream, that 24 licentiates (*xiucai*) wearing white clothes bow to them from the foot of the bed, saying "We are leaving you to go to the Ju family of Sanpai lou." The couple wakes with a start to find they have shared the same dream. They then open the pillow and

discover the silver gone; when the husband finds the Ju family, they confirm that the 24 ingots did arrive in their home. The prologue tale appeared in a collection of anecdotes roughly contemporary to Ling Mengchu's collection, Zhou Hui's 1610 *Jinling suoshi, juan* 3 (Beijing: Wenxue guji kanxingshe, 1955). See Tan Zhengbi, *Sanyan liangpai ziliao* (Shanghai: Shanghai guji chubanshe, 1980), 573.

5. The weight of an ingot of silver was different in various geographical regions, but this was known, and conversion rates were established. Moreover, all ingots were not of the same quality; the patterns of markings on the silver after it was cast indicated the purity of the silver. Thus Jin needs to save the best bits of silver to cast the ingots.

6. We might also view the animated ingots as transitional objects in the psychologist D. W. Winnicott's sense of the word; in this case we would say that Jin personifies the objects as a means of coping with the anxieties caused by a purely symbolic conception of capital. See D. W. Winnicott, *Playing and Reality* (London: Tavistock Publications, 1971), 1–25.

7. This adhesion of an older notion of fetishism within commodity fetishism itself could be read into Marx's paradigmatic example of the commodity fetish, his talking table, which "so soon as it steps forth as a commodity . . . is changed into something transcendent . . . in relation to all other commodities, it stands on its head, and evolves out of its wooden brain grotesque ideas, far more wonderful than 'table-turning' ever was." Karl Marx, "The Fetishism of the Commodity and Its Secret," in *Capital*, vol. 1, trans. Ben Fowkes (New York, 1976), 163–77. Peter Stallybrass has observed that the paradoxical relation of the two conceptions of fetishism is one of Marx's least understood, or least recognized, jokes. Peter Stallybrass, "Marx's Coat," in *Border Fetishisms*, ed. Patricia Spyer (London: Routledge, 1998), 184. For relevant readings of this passage in Marx, see Bill Brown, *A Sense of Things: The Object Matter of American Literature* (Chicago: University of Chicago Press, 2003), 29; and Barbara Johnson, *Persons and Things* (Cambridge: Harvard University Press, 2008), 141.

8. Richard von Glahn has written that at no point in Chinese history did money have a greater symbolic import than in the late Ming. Richard von Glahn, "The Enchantment of Wealth: The God Wutong in the Social History of Jiangnan," *Harvard Journal of Asiatic Studies* 51, no. 2 (December 1991): 651–714.

9. Eileen Freedgood makes a related point as she emphasizes that the mid-Victorian period is one in which "thing culture" does not give way to commodity culture "but persists within it, however vestigially or invisibly." Elaine Freedgood, *The Ideas in Things: Fugitive Meaning in the Victorian Novel* (Chicago: University of Chicago Press, 2006), 142.

10. See Wang Jide's (d. 1623) dramatic criticism. Wang wrote: "In choosing a subject one prizes *shi* [historical reference]; in treating it one prizes *xu* [the creative

additions of the author]." Wang Jide, *Qulü*, in *Zhongguo gudian xiqu lunzhu jicheng*, vol. 4 (Beijing: Zhongguo xiju chubanshe, 1959), 154.

11. David Rolston notes that events characterized as *xu* may also be factual in nature, but "are merely told indirectly; they happen offstage, as it were," and that in criticism of the essay, arguments classified as *shi* are presented directly, whereas arguments characterized as *xu* are presented indirectly. Similarly, in painting, detailed depiction is labeled *shi*; less detailed depiction is considered *xu*. David Rolston, *Traditional Chinese Fiction and Fiction Commentary: Reading and Writing Between the Lines* (Stanford, CA: Stanford University Press, 1997), 182.

12. A word is considered *xu* if its meaning cannot be fully defined or pinned down (the term *qing* is an excellent case in point), and for this reason words that have an emotive, subjective context are considered *xu*. As a linguistic term, "*xu* characters" (*xuzi*) are those that impart modality or indicate sentiment. See Stephen Owen, *Readings in Chinese Literary Thought* (Cambridge, MA: Harvard Council on East Asian Studies, 1996), 425.

13. Li Rihua, "Guang Xieshi xu" (*Preface to the Expanded Xieshi*), dated 1615, in *Zhongguo lidai xiaoshuo xuba xuanzhu*, ed. Zeng Zuyin et al. (Xianning: Changjiang wenyi, 1982), 76. See David Rolston, *Traditional Chinese Fiction and Fiction Commentary*, 183.

14. Chen Xizhong, Hou Zhongyi, and Lu Yuchuan, eds. *Shuihu zhuan huiping ben*. (Beijing: Beijing daxue, 1981), 510. See Rolston, *Traditional Fiction and Fiction Commentary*, 183. The third preface to Jin Shengtan's commentary on *The Water Margin* (*Shuihu zhuan*) is dated 1641. The commentary was printed in 1644.

15. Ye Xie, *Yuan shi*, cited in Owen, *Readings in Chinese Literary Thought*, 532.

16. Ling Mengchu, *Chuke Pai'an jingqi*, 7.

17. The *Ming History* refers to an area known as the country of Jiling (*Ming shi*, 325.23a–b). The character used for "ling" is different than the one used in the story, however. The name "Jiling" may refer to the eastern coast of India, the historical Kalinga. However, as Tina Lu observes in her reading of this story, Jiling is unmappable, and it is precisely the fictive, unmappable quality of Jiling that is key to Wen Shi's fabulous acquisition of wealth. Tina Lu, *Accidental Incest, Filial Cannibalism, and Other Peculiar Encounters in Late Imperial Chinese Literature* (Cambridge, MA: Harvard University Asia Center, 2008), 37.

18. Ling Mengchu based the episode of the oranges from Lake Dongting on a classical anecdote, and the contrast between the original version and his vernacular story illuminates Ling Mengchu's concern to illustrate the limitations of strategic thinking in business. In the original version, recorded in Zhou Yuanwei's (*jinshi* 1585) *Jinglin xu ji*, a merchant buys oranges in Fujian to sell abroad precisely because this requires little capital. When he reaches his foreign destination, he

deliberately displays the oranges on dozens of plates, in an attempt to attract the barbarians (*yi*) of this region. He haggles with the natives, ultimately reaping 1,000 taels. The classical anecdote contains none of the moralizing against strategic thinking that is the primary concern of Ling Mengchu's vernacular story; Ling Mengchu rewrote the anecdote to emphasize the fact that Wen reaps a windfall precisely because he is not interested in trade. See Tan Zhengbi, *Sanyan liangpai ziliao* (Shanghai: Shanghai guji chubanshe, 1980), 573. As Chen Yongzheng points out, Ling Mengchu also revises the original to praise the spirit of risk in engaging in overseas trade; Zhou Yuanwei had spoken of the merchants of Fujian and Guangdong who engaged in trade with the "barbarians" as "merchant traitors" (*jian shang*). Chen Yongzheng, *Shijing fengqing: Sanyan Erpai de shi jie* (Hong Kong: Zhonghua shuju, 1988), 29.
19. Patrick Hanan, *The Chinese Vernacular Story* (Cambridge, MA: Harvard University Press, 1981), 153.
20. Ling Mengchu, *Chuke Pai'an jingqi*, 12.
21. Ling Mengchu, *Chuke Pai'an jingqi*, 12.
22. Ling Mengchu, *Chuke Pai'an jingqi*, 14–15.
23. The brief anecdote ends by relaying that after some days at sea, the Persian's ship was about to sink. The sailors determined that the sea god (*haishen*) was demanding gems on board the ship. They searched everywhere on board for gems, and finding none to give the spirit, decided to drown the Persian. Finally the Persian cut open his armpit and took out the gem, which the sailors gave to the sea god; he stretched out a hairy arm, lifted up the gem, and departed. Li Fang, *Taiping guangji* (Beijing: Renmin wenxue chubanshe, 1957), 402.5b.
24. Ling Mengchu, *Chuke Pai'an jingqi*, 16.
25. A related phenomenon occurs in vernacular stories that feature crimes; key information is obscured, seemingly with the primary purpose of alerting the reader to the fact that he or she has partial information and does not understand the internal conditions operating inside the tale. Almost as if to tease the reader, the text will state "the magistrate told the jailers to do such and such." It is not that the literary approximation of the "real" is imperfect, but that the literary text will not divulge the information.

3. DU SHINIANG'S JEWEL BOX

1. Shen Guangren, "Mingdai xiaoshuo zhong zhutiwu de xiangzheng xing yu qingjie xing," *Shanghai Shifan daxue xuebao* 6 (2001): 53.
2. On the relation between the vernacular tale and its classical source text, see Patrick D. Hanan, "The Making of 'The Pearl-Sewn Shirt' and 'The Courtesan's

Jewel-Box,'" *Harvard Journal of Asiatic Studies* 33 (1973): 125. On Song Maocheng's *Jiuye ji*, see Lynn A. Struve, "Song Maocheng's Matrixes of Mourning and Regret," *NAN NÜ: Men, Women and Gender in China* 15, no. 1 (2013): 69–108. Allan H. Barr's study of Song Maocheng's *Jiuyue ji* suggests that the character of Du Shiniang was inspired by the historical courtesan Du Wei. Allan H. Barr, "The Wanli Context of the 'Courtesan's Jewel Box' Story," *Harvard Journal of Asiatic Studies* 57, no. 1 (June 1997): 107–41.

3. Feng Menglong, "Du Shiniang nüchen baibao xiang," in Feng Menglong, *Jingshi tongyan*, ed. Yan Dunyi (Beijing: Renmin wenxue chubanshe, 1995). Two translations of this story are often cited: Feng Menglong, "Du Tenth Sinks the Jewel Box in Anger," trans. Robert Ashmore, in *An Anthology of Chinese Literature: Beginnings to 1911*, ed. Stephen Owen (New York: Norton, 1996), 835–55; and "Du Shiniang Sinks Her Jewel Box in Anger," in *Stories to Caution the World: A Ming Dynasty Collection*, vol. 2, trans. Shuhui Yang and Yunqin Yang (Seattle: University of Washington Press, 2005), 547–65.

4. As Patrick D. Hanan noted, one of the primary changes that Feng Menglong made in revising the classical biography into a vernacular story was to render Du Shiniang more mysterious: "All the indications of her emotions given in 'The Faithless Lover' have been removed or moderated in 'The Courtesan's Jewel Box.' Where she has been described before as weeping or jubilant or moved or melancholy, she is now presented as impassive." Patrick D. Hanan, "The Making of 'The Pearl-Sewn Shirt' and 'The Courtesan's Jewel-Box,'" 152.

5. Feng Menglong, *Jingshi tongyan, juan* 32, 5a; Feng Menglong, "Du Shiniang," in *Stories to Caution the World*, vol. 2, 550.

6. For early precedents, we could look to the tale of Yu Rang in *Strategems of the Warring States* (*Zhanguo ce*) and Sima Qian's *Historical Records* (*Shiji*). See *Zhanguo ce*, ed. Liu Xiang (Shanghai: Shanghai guji chubanshe, 1998), 597; and Sima Qian, *Shiji, juan* 86, 2519. For late-imperial examples, see Judith Zeitlin, *The Historian of the Strange; Pu Songling and the Chinese Classical Tale* (Stanford, CA: Stanford University Press, 1993), 74–76.

7. Yang observes that Feng Menglong avoids the obvious choice among characters pronounced "mei," the character *mei* (美), meaning "beautiful"; the rarity of Du Shiniang's personal name dignifies her. See Shuhui Yang, *Appropriation and Representation: Feng Menglong and the Chinese Vernacular Story* (Ann Arbor: University of Michigan Center for Chinese Studies, 1998), 143.

8. Feng Menglong, *Jingshi tongyan, juan* 32, 11b. Feng Menglong, "Du Shiniang," *Stories to Caution the World*, vol. 2, 556.

9. Feng Menglong, *Jingshi tongyan, juan* 32, 12a–b; Feng Menglong, "Du Shiniang," in *Stories to Caution the World*, vol. 2, 556.

10. On the poet Gao Qi, see Frederick W. Mote, *The Poet Kao Ch'i: 1336–1374* (Princeton: Princeton University Press, 1962).
11. Feng Menglong, *Jingshi tongyan*, juan 32, 15b.
12. Feng Menglong, *Jingshi tongyan*, juan 32, 9a; Feng Menglong, "Du Shiniang," in *Stories to Caution the World*, vol. 2, 554.
13. Feng Menglong, *Jingshi tongyan*, juan 32, 13b; Feng Menglong, "Du Shiniang," in *Stories to Caution the World*, vol. 2, 558.
14. Feng Menglong, *Jingshi tongyan*, juan 32, 20b; Feng Menglong, "Du Shiniang," in *Stories to Caution the World*, vol. 2, 563.
15. Feng Menglong, *Jingshi tongyan*, juan 32, 21a; Feng Menglong, "Du Shiniang," in *Stories to Caution the World*, vol. 2, 564. The narrator describes the spectators on the riverbank as "a wall" speaking with one voice; they speak in chorus, registering astonishment and asking for explanation. These spectators are not important in and of themselves; rather, as Patrick Hanan has noted, they signal that Feng Menglong here employs a dramatic convention, in which the protagonist unveils her thoughts in the final scene in a cataclysmic outpouring of withheld emotion. Patrick Hanan, "The Making of the 'Courtesan's Jewel-Box' and 'The Pearl-Sewn Shirt,'" 147–48.
16. *Lunyu*, in *Shisan jing zhushu*, ed. Ruan Yuan (Beijing: Zhonghua shuju, 1980), juan 16, 2520.
17. *Han Feizi jijie*, ed. Wang Xianshen (Beijing: Zhonghua shuju, 1998), 266.
18. I am indebted here and in the discussion that follows to Chana Kronfeld's thinking regarding metaphorical mapping. See Chana Kronfeld, *The Full Severity of Compassion: The Poetry of Yehuda Amichai* (Stanford, CA: Stanford University Press, 2015), 250–65.
19. Purple gold was a metallic substance with an inner radiance whose composition is still unknown, used to cast statues of the Buddha because its radiance lent the impression that light emanated from the interior of the statues. See Luo Wenhua, "Qing gong zijin lima zaoxiang kaoshu," in *Gugong bowuyuan yuankan*, no. 6 (2004): 49–59.
20. Feng Menglong, *Jingshi tongyan*, juan 32, 21b; Feng Menglong, "Du Shiniang," in *Stories to Caution the World*, vol. 2, 563.
21. Feng Menglong, *Jingshi tongyan*, juan 32, 20b; Feng Menglong, "Du Shiniang," in *Stories to Caution the World*, vol. 2, 563.
22. Zhou Mi, *Guixin zashi*, vol. 2, 25b, rare manuscript, Harvard-Yenching Library. Also see the discussion of this passage in Craig Clunas, *Chinese Furniture* (London: Bamboo Publishing, 1988), 81.
23. Gao Lian, *Zunsheng bajian* (Hangzhou: Zhejiang guji chubanshe, 2019), 617.
24. Wen Zhenheng, *Zhangwu zhi* (Shanghai: Shangwu yinshu guan, 1936), 61.

25. Song Maocheng, "Fuqing nong zhuan," in *Jiu yue ji*, ed. Wang Liqi (Beijing: Zhongguo shehui kexue chubanshe, 1984), 117–18. Here I use Patrick Hanan's translation of "Fuqing nong zhuan," in Patrick D. Hanan, "The Making of 'The Courtesan's Jewel-Box' and 'The Pearl-Sewn Shirt,'" 146.
26. Rania Huntington, "Ghosts Seeking Substitutes: Female Suicide and Repetition," *Late Imperial China* 28, no. 1 (June 2005): 8–9.
27. Song Maocheng, "Ji nünu zhuishuiwen," *Jiuyue ji*, 194.
28. Song Maocheng, "Huanghe ji wangnüwen," *Jiuyue ji*, 195.
29. As Shen Guangren has written, "the box gradually surpasses its materiality." Shen Guangren, "Mingdai xiaoshuo zhong zhutiwu de xiangzheng xing yu qingjie xing," *Shanghai Shifan daxue xuebao shehui kexue bao* (*zhexue shehui kexueban*) 6 (2001): 53.

4. LI YU'S TELESCOPE

1. *Hangzhou fuzhi*, ed. Chen Shan et al. (Taipei: Chengwen chubanshe, 1983), *juan* 150, 8b–9a. See also Sun Chengsheng, "Ming Qing zhi ji xifang guangxue zhishi," *Ziran kexueshi yanjiu* 26, no. 3 (2007): 363–76, especially 364.
2. Jonathan Crary's discussion of Goethe's observation of the after-image of color produced on white paper by the camera obscura similarly suggests that subjective experience is physiologically produced: "The human body, in all its contingency and specificity, generates 'the spectrum of another colour', and thus becomes the active producer of optical experience." Jonathan Crary, *Techniques of the Observer: On Vision and Modernity in the Nineteenth Century* (Cambridge, MA: MIT Press, 1990), 69.
3. See Joseph McDermott, "Chinese Lenses and Chinese Art," *Kaikodo Journal* 19 (Spring 2001); Jennifer Purtle, "Scopic Frames: Devices for Seeing China c. 1640," *Art History* 33, no. 1 (February 2010): 54–73; Richard Vinograd, "Hiding in Plane Sight," in *Comparative Early Modernities*, ed. David Porter (Basingstoke: Palgrave Macmillan, 2012), 144; Kristina Kleutghen, "Peepboxes, Society and Visuality in Early Modern China," *Art History* 38, no. 4 (September 2015): 763–77.
4. Purtle writes of single-point perspective as an "artefact of monocular vision," adding that "in China the vestigial (or imperfectly understood) elements of single-point perspective constitute the incursion of that representational system into an indigenous mode of representing previously driven solely by binocular experience." Jennifer Purtle, "Scopic Frames: Devices for Seeing China c. 1640," *Art History* 33, no. 1 (February 2010): 58–59. I would argue that single-point perspective is a form of notation that is dependent on binocular vision. There is no evidence that a knowledge of lenses influenced painterly practice. Li Yu's acquaintance Zhu Sheng, for example, was the premier maker of lenses in Hangzhou and

also a specialist in traditionally rendered bamboo and orchids recruited by Li Yu's son-in-law to furnish examples for *The Mustard Seed Garden Manual of Painting*. For more on Zhu Sheng, see Yang Xin, "Zhu Sheng sheng nian de ding zheng," *Gugong bowuyuan yuankan*, no. 6 (2001): 27–29.

5. See Hsu Hui-Lin, "Jing yu qianzhi: Shilun Zhongguo xushi wenlei zhong xiandai shixue jingyan de qiyuan," *T'ai-ta Chung-wen Hsueh-pao* 48 (March 2015): 133–34.

6. Adam Schall von Bell (Tang Ruowang) was recruited to serve the Jesuit mission in China by Nicholas Trigault. He arrived in China in July 1619. He was named director of the Imperial Bureau of Astronomy in 1645. Other texts mentioning the telescope written in China during the first decades of the seventeenth century include Manuel Dias's (Yang Manuo) 1615 *Tian wen lüe* (Summary of Astronomy).

7. Tang Ruowang (Adam Schall von Bell) and Li Zubai, *Yuanjing shuo*, in *Ming Qing zhi ji xixue wen ben*, ed. Huang Xingtao and Wang Guorong, vol. 3 (Beijing: Zhonghua shuju, 2013), 12b. The text also describes the discoveries of Galileo, the optics of the telescope, and reflections and refraction. Schall is indebted throughout to Galileo's *Sidereus Nuncius* of 1610, the first text to describe observations made with a telescope, and he reprints the illustrations of the phases of the moon in *Sidereus Nuncius* without attribution to Galileo.

8. Tang Ruowang (Adam Schall von Bell) and Li Zubai, *Yuanjing shuo*, 15a.

9. Tang Ruowang (Adam Schall von Bell) and Li Zubai, *Yuanjing shuo*, 7a.

10. Joseph Needham and Lu Gwei-djen introduced the work of Bo Jue to Western sinology in "The Optick Artists of Chiang-su," *Proceedings of the Royal Microscopical Society* 2, no. 1 (1967): 113–38. The characters 珏 and 子珏, romanized by Needham and Lu as "Yu" and "Ziyu," should be romanized as "Jue" and "Zijue."

11. We can infer from the passage that Bo Jue was able to calculate the parabolic trajectory of the cannonball as well as calculate the optics of the lenses. Zou Yi, *Qizhen yesheng* (Beijing: Beiping gugong bowuyuan tushuguan, 1936), *juan* 6, 15a–15b.

12. Qu Dajun, *Guangdong xinyu* (Beijing: Zhonghua shuju, 2006), 419. Canton was, with Hangzhou and Suzhou, a provincial center in the making of lenses, but it developed later. See Wang Jinguang, "Qing chu guangxue yiqi zhizaojia: Sun Yunqiu," *Kexueshi jikan*, no. 5 (1963): 58–62.

13. Zou Yi, *Qizhen yesheng*, *juan* 6, 15a.

14. S. E. Kile and Kristina Kleutgen argue that lens makers in Ming and Qing China were craftsmen and that lenses were "decidedly non-literary products." They view Bo Jue's reluctance to speak as evidence of the "distinctly manual, non-literary quality of Bo's talent," citing him as an example of the artisan as lens maker. S. E. Kile and Kristina Kleutgen, "Seeing Through Pictures and Poetry: *A History of Lenses* (1681)," *Late Imperial China* 38, no. 1 (June 2017):

47–112. If we look at the text of his biography in the *Qizhen yesheng*, however, that clearly is not the case. I have found no evidence that lens makers such as Bo Jue were thought of as craftsmen.

15. Eileen Reeves has written that in the early seventeenth century the telescope was associated with foresight, "as if the spatial component could be exchanged for a temporal one, such that he who saw distant things was somehow viewing his future." Reeves, *Evening News: Optics, Astronomy and Journalism in Early Modern Europe* (Philadelphia: University of Pennsylvania Press, 2014), 63.

16. The Jesuit mission in Hangzhou was established in 1611. See Liam Brockey, *Journey to the East: The Jesuit Mission to China, 1579–1724* (Cambridge, MA: Belknap Press of Harvard University Press, 2007), 89.

17. Li Yu is thought to have lived in Hangzhou for a period of about ten years, perhaps ending in the late 1650s. He relocated to Hangzhou at a later, unspecified date. See Patrick D. Hanan, *The Invention of Li Yu* (Cambridge, MA: Harvard University Press, 1988), 216, n. 37, for an extensive discussion of the available evidence regarding Li Yu's dates of residence in Hangzhou.

18. The Yingxiu tang and the Baoning tang editions of the story are identical. The undated Xiaoxianju edition has a long disquisition on lenses at the beginning of the second chapter that does not appear in the other editions. As Sun Chengsheng has shown, the Xiaoxianju edition quotes from Sun Yunqiu's *A History of Lenses* (*Jingshi*, preface 1681), which Li Yu likely saw in draft. Hence the Xiaoxianju edition likely dates to the period just before Li Yu's death in 1680.

19. Albert van Helden's "The Invention of the Telescope" is still the most thorough account of the various claims to discovery of the magnifying power of a combination of convex and concave lenses in the Netherlands in 1608 (the word *telescopium* was not coined until 1611). Albert van Helden, "The Invention of the Telescope," *Transactions of the American Philosophical Society* 6, no. 4 (June 1977): 3–67. Although 1608 is universally taken as the date of the invention of the telescope, van Helden observes that the Neapolitan polymath Giambattista della Porta (1535–1615) had written of such an invention in the second edition of his *Magia naturalis* (1589), and that the Florentine Rafael Gaulterotti (1548–1639) claimed to have made such an instrument at the end of the sixteenth century to aid with the joust but had not found it worthy of note. Both inventors thought it a trivial discovery. Gaulterotti wrote to Galileo, "as it seemed to me a feeble thing, I neglected it." Albert van Helden, "The Invention of the Telescope," 19.

20. The surnames of Qu Jiren and Zhan Xianxian serve as homonyms for words that describe various forms of sight. The character *qu*, when read as *ju*, means to regard someone in fear or surprise. The surname Zhan is a homonym for the character *zhan* 瞻 with an "eye" radical, meaning to look from afar. While we

would not want to make too much of Li Yu's play on words, the surnames suggest that his protagonists are in some way defined by the act of looking.

21. The anonymous novel *The Carnal Prayer Mat* (*Rou putuan*), now attributed to Li Yu, clearly plays with the same theme; there the voyeur is a thief able to sneak into the homes of the gentry to spy on their women. The novel was written in 1657 and published in 1693.
22. Li Yu, *Li Yu quan ji*, vol. 4, 75; Li Yu, *A Tower for the Summer Heat*, trans. Patrick Hanan (New York: Ballantine Books, 1992), 5.
23. Li Yu, *Li Yu quan ji*, vol. 4, 74; Li Yu, *A Tower for the Summer Heat*, 4.
24. Jing Zhang suggests that "Master Thievish Eyes" (*zeiyan guanren*), the term used at the end of "A Tower for the Summer Heat" to describe its protagonist, "most likely derives from the emergence of the voyeur as a character type in late Ming novels and most prominently in *Plum in the Golden Vase* (Jin Ping Mei)." Jing Zhang, "In His Thievish Eyes: The Voyeur/Reader in Li Yu's 'The Summer Pavilion,'" *Southeast Review of Asian Studies* 34 (2012): 27.
25. As the introduction continues, we find that the poems have introduced not only the topic of voyeurism, but also that of Li Yu's own talent. Li Yu tells us that he composed the poems in his youth; originally there were ten but four were lost. Interspersed with the poems are comments thought to have been furnished by Li Yu's friend Du Jun (1611–1687): "Marvelous!" and "A man of talent!"
26. As Patrick Hanan has remarked, "He took the voice of the traditional narrator, which vaguely suggests an oral storyteller addressing his audience, and personalized it, so that it sounds not unlike Li Yu's voice as we hear it in his essays." Hanan, "Preface," in Li Yu, *A Tower for the Summer Heat*, viii.
27. Li Yu, *Li Yu quanji*, vol. 4, 75; Li Yu, *A Tower for the Summer Heat*, 6.
28. In an article on point of view in late-imperial Chinese fiction, David Rolston notes a number of terms that traditional commentary uses to remark upon point of view. Those terms note moments when the text temporarily conveys information to the reader "through the sight, hearing/speech, or general consciousness of one character rather than the narrator." Rolston, "Traditional Chinese Fiction, Traditional Fiction Criticism, and Point of View," *Chinese Literature: Essays, Articles, Reviews* 15 (1993): 118–42. The difference between those moments and Li Yu's experiment is a matter of duration; Li Yu plays with an extended period of focalization.
29. Li Yu, *Li Yu quanji*, vol. 4, 81; Li Yu, *A Tower for the Summer Heat*, 11.
30. Li Yu, *Li Yu quanji*, vol. 4, 79; Li Yu, *A Tower for the Summer Heat*, 11–12.
31. Li Yu, *Li Yu quanji*, vol. 4, 79–80; Li Yu, *A Tower for the Summer Heat*, 12.
32. Li Yu, *Li Yu quanji*, vol. 4, 80–81; Li Yu, *A Tower for the Summer Heat*, 14.
33. Li Yu, *Li Yu quanji*, vol. 4, 82; Li Yu, *A Tower for the Summer Heat*, 15.
34. Li Yu, *Li Yu quan ji*, vol. 4, 82; Li Yu, *A Tower for the Summer Heat*, 15.

35. Li Yu, *Li Yu quanji*, vol. 4, 82. Here I use my own translation, which is less felicitous but more literal than that of Hanan.
36. Lu Ban, also known as Gongshu Ban, was an inventor and carpenter of the Spring and Autumn period and is believed to have lived approximately from 507 to 444 BCE. Lu Ban is said to have invented a wooden bird that could stay in the air for three days, a weighted ladder for use during sieges, and a kind of battering ram. According to the Zhao Qi commentary on the *Mencius*, Lilou, also known as Lizhu, was capable of seeing new autumn feathers from a hundred feet away. See *Mengzi zhengyi*, vol. 1, ed. Jiao Xun (Beijing: Zhonghua shuju, 1987), 475; and *Zhuangzi jishi*, vol. 2, ed. Guo Qingfan (Beijing: Zhonghua shuju, 1961), 353.
37. See Hanan, *The Invention of Li Yu*, especially 45–59.
38. This is the second of Wang Qi's two collections of letters; the first was published in 1663.
39. Wang Qi, ed., *Fenlei chidu xinyu*, juan 22, 410. Zhu Sheng is mentioned in the Xiaoxianju edition of the story but his personal name is omitted. Li Yu describes him as a "famed literatus of Zhejiang." Patrick Hanan deduced his identity. See Li Yu, *A Tower for the Summer Heat*, 19, n. 8. Zhu Sheng, who mentored Sun Yunqiu, was a noted painter of bamboo whose biographical details are unclear. The art historian Yang Xin speculates that he may have been a professional artist. See Yang Xin, "Zhu Sheng shengnian de ding zheng," *Gugong bowu yuan yuankan* 6 (2001): 27–29.
40. Since the letter is undated, we know only that it was composed before 1667, when the anthology was published.
41. The telescope was also used in astronomical observation. The Yongzheng emperor (r. 1723–1735) reminisced that his father, Kangxi, once led him with his brothers to view an eclipse through a telescope: "Once long ago when an eclipse was nearly halfway in progress . . . the light from the sun became dazzling and it became hard to look at the sky. The Emperor thought to lead me and all my brothers personally to experience and observe the eclipse in the Qianqing palace. In all four directions he used white paper to shut out the sun's rays, and then we saw by how much the prediction was mistaken. This was an experiment that I personally took part in." Quoted in *Shizong Xianhuangdi shengxun*, juan 8, 20, in *Wenyuange siku quanshu*, comp. Zhang Yushu. (Taipei: Taiwan shangwu yinshuguan, 1983). Yongzheng was born in 1678, so we can guess that the event he speaks of took place in the late 1680s or 1690s. This passage conveys the breathless wonder that Yongzheng must have felt. Indigenously made telescopes were already available in Hangzhou, Suzhou, and Canton at this time. It is unlikely that the imperial privilege described here is that of using a telescope. Rather, the sense of excitement and entitlement relates to the fact

that Yongzheng was allowed to use a telescope as a boy in order to observe an eclipse as a means to verify the predictions of the Board of Astronomy, a privileged act.

42. *Shengzu Renhuangdi yuzhi wenji*, vol. 2, *juan* 37, 4, in *Wenyuange siku quanshu*.
43. Dorothy Berinstein, "Hunts, Processions, and Telescopes: A Painting of an Imperial Hunt by Lang Shining (Giuseppe Castiglione)," *RES* 35 (Spring 1999): 180–81. See also Mei Mei Rado, "Encountering Magnificence: European Silks at the Qing Court during the Eighteenth Century," in *Qing Encounters: Artistic Exchanges Between China and the West*, ed. Petra Chu and Ding Ning (Los Angeles: Getty Research Institute, 2015), 58–75.
44. Li Yu, *Li Yu quanji*, vol. 4, 84–85; Li Yu, "A Tower for the Summer Heat," 21.
45. Li Yu, *Li Yu quanji*, vol. 4, 85; Li Yu, "A Tower for the Summer Heat," 22.
46. Patrick Hanan uses the term *glass* rather than *lens* to translate *jing*, which is particularly appropriate because it blurs the distinction between the two meanings of *jing* (lens and mirror), and because the term *glass* is used in seventeenth-century English sources for both lenses and mirrors.
47. Li Yu, *Li Yu quanji*, vol. 4, 88; Li Yu, *A Tower for the Summer Heat*, 26.
48. Li Yu, *Li Yu quanji*, vol. 4, 97; Li Yu, *A Tower for the Summer Heat*, 38.
49. The pairing of "A Tower for the Summer Heat" with the next story in the collection, "Return to Right Hall" (whose protagonist is a swindler), suggests that Li Yu saw Jiren as a confidence man.
50. Sun Chengsheng, "Ming Qing zhi ji xifang guangxue zhishi," 368.
51. Zhu Sheng, "Jingshi xiaoyin," in Sun Yunqiu, *Jingshi*. Rare manuscript, Shanghai Municipal Library. See also Sun Chengsheng, "Ming Qing zhi ji xifang guangxue zhishi," 372.
52. Zhu Sheng, "Jingshi xiaoyin," in Sun Yunqiu, *Jingshi*. See also Sun Chengsheng, "Ming Qing zhi ji xifang guangxue zhishi," 372.
53. *Hufu zhi*, comp. Lu Zhaoyu and Ren Zhaolin, rare manuscript, 6.10a, 1792. Princeton, NJ: Princeton University Library.
54. *Wu xianzhi*, ed. Wu Xiuzhi et al., comp. Cao Yunyuan, 1933 edition (Taipei: Chengwen chubanshe, 1970), 75.5a.
55. Local products were not necessarily artisanal. In his *Account of a Tour of Macao and Fujian* (*Yue Min xunshi jilüe*), Du Zhen wrote that the people of Macao brought out a number of local products (*fang wu*) as tribute—among them a telescope—when he engaged in a tour of inspection there (presumably in 1684). It is likely, given the nature of the gifts, that he refers to the Jesuit mission, which had its most stable base in Macao. In addition to a glass screen and three self-chiming clocks, there was a telescope of four or five draws inlaid with engraved gold tracery and precious stones. Du Zhen wrote of the telescope that if one focused on the object to be observed and slowly extended the tubes, one

could spy the slightest object from dozens of leagues away. Du Zhen, *Yue Min xunshi jilüe*, in *Jindai Zhongguo shiliao congkan xubian*, vol. 98 (Taipei: Wenhai chubanshe, 1983), 2.26a.

56. Sun Yunqiu, *Jingshi*, 7b. Sun Yunqiu's text here incorporates Schall's exact wording regarding those "whose eyes do not leave their books and histories and whose vision is unused to leaping beyond their table and mat," though he implicitly takes issue with Schall's analysis. Whereas Schall wrote that the habit of not looking up from one's desk can gradually affect one's nature (*xing*) and thereby permanently affect one's sight, Sun Yunqiu disagrees: "This does not derive from habit but is because one's heavenly endowment of blood and vital energy (*qi*) is insufficient." Sun Yunqiu, *Jingshi*, 2a.

57. Sun Yunqiu, *Jingshi*, 2b. Similarly, the text regarding lenses to preserve the eyesight of children speaks of lenses that can be used to prevent their eyes from being harmed. Those lenses, which "Western literati" call lenses to preserve the eyes, were to be worn in childhood; if worn for about ten years, one's eyesight would not fail later in life. Sun Yunqiu, *Jingshi*, 3a.

58. Kile and Kleutghen note that the cross-hatching "is here replicated in simplified form to accommodate the material qualities of the woodblock" and "has created forms with enhanced three-dimensionality." See S. E. Kile and Kristina Kleutghen, "Seeing Through Pictures and Poetry: *A History of Lenses* (1681)," 76–77.

59. Sun Yunqiu, *Jingshi*, 4a–4b. See also Sun Chengsheng, "Ming Qing zhi ji xifang guangxue zhishi," 373.

60. Sun Yunqiu, *Jingshi*, 4b–5a. See also Sun Chengsheng, "Ming Qing zhi ji xifang guangxue zhishi," 363–76.

61. Chen Kaijun has emphasized this quality of the text in his analysis of Sun Yunqiu's *History of Lenses*. Chen Kaijun, "Transcultural Lenses: Wrapping the Foreignness for Sale in the *History of Lenses*," 77–100.

62. Li Yu, *Li Yu quanji*, vol. 4, 82; Li Yu, *A Tower for the Summer Heat*, 16.

63. Li Yu, *Li Yu quanji*, vol. 4, 84; Li Yu, *A Tower for the Summer Heat*, 19.

64. Li Yu, *Li Yu quanji*, vol. 4, 82; Li Yu, *A Tower for the Summer Heat*, 17.

65. Robert Hooke, *Micrographia*, rare manuscript, University of Michigan Library, 211. The claim that early lenses easily permitted the viewer to see the infinitesimally small or far away created an exaggerated sense of empiricism. Lynn Festa examines the difficulties that Hooke described as he attempted to view a louse through the microscope, noting that "magnification was actually accompanied by a loss of resolution." Lynn M. Festa, *Fiction Without Humanity: Person, Animal, Thing in Early Enlightenment Literature and Culture* (Philadelphia: University of Pennsylvania Press, 2019), 109.

66. Li Yu, *Li Yu quanji*, vol. 4, 83; Li Yu, *A Tower for the Summer Heat*, 15.

67. Li Yu, *Li Yu quanji*, vol. 4, 84; Li Yu, *A Tower for the Summer Heat*, 18–19. Li Yu claims that the "Western scholars" of whom he speaks, presumably Jesuits, "knew how to manufacture these glasses and gave them to people as presents." Adam Schall von Bell presented the Chongzhen emperor with a telescope in the first month of 1634, and he presented a telescope and other astronomical instruments to the Shunzhi emperor in the second month of 1644. It seems unlikely that, as Li Yu claims, telescopes of Western manufacture found their way from the Jesuits into the hands of collectors of curios. Historians know of only two telescopes that may have accompanied the Jesuit missions. The first was the telescope donated by Cardinal Borromeo to the Jesuit mission of 1618; it may have been offered by Schall and Jacobus Rho to the Chongzhen emperor in the first month of 1634. The second was brought to Fujian by the Lithuanian Jesuit Andrew Rudomina (1594–1632). After Rudomina's death, the telescope fell into the possession of his fellow Jesuit Jules Aleni, who eventually presented it to a Korean emissary in China, from whence it went to Korea. Wang Chuan, "Xiyang wangyuanjing yu Ruan Yuan wangyuege," *Shuxue yanjiu* (April 2000): 83.

68. As I mentioned in note 39 above, here Patrick Hanan as translator has supplied Zhu's personal name. Hanan deduced on the basis of the letter from Lu Jun to Zhu Sheng that Zhu Xi'an (the maker of optical devices) and Zhu Sheng (the artist renowned for his paintings of bamboo in snow) were identical. See Patrick Hanan's translation in Li Yu, *A Tower for the Summer Heat*, 19.

69. Li Yu, *Li Yu quanji*, vol. 4, 84; Li Yu, *A Tower for the Summer Heat*, 19.

70. When the historian of science Sun Chengsheng discovered the correspondence between the two texts, he noted that Li Yu borrowed from Sun Yunqiu's *History of Lenses*, taking its more classical phrasing and rendering it more vernacular. Sun Yunqiu's register was much closer to that of Adam Schall von Bell (or rather, that of his amanuensis Li Zubai), to whom Sun was indebted for specific phrasing. Sun Chengsheng compares Sun Yunqiu's text with that of Schall, identifying a number of passages that are identical. Sun Chengsheng, "Ming Qing zhi ji xifang guangxue zhishi," 368. For example, Sun Yunqiu writes of the telescope: "This lens is suited to using from a high place; one can see mountains and rivers and seas, forests and villages, all are as before your eyes. If the objects are at a distance between several dozen *li* and several thousand paces away, you can use the telescope to look at people and distinguish things, and it's even clearer than if you were face to face." Adam Schall von Bell had written: "When you use it in a tower or platform in a high place, then you can see mountains and rivers in the distance, forests and villages, and although people and objects are moving about, they are as if before your eyes." Li Yu's text in turn reads: "If you use it for looking at people or things at a distance of several hundred yards

to a few *li*, you'll find them more distinct than if they are sitting opposite you." Tang Ruowang (Adam Schall von Bell) and Li Zubai, "Yuanjing shuo," vol. 1, 7a; Li Yu, *Li Yu quanji*, vol. 4, 82–84; Li Yu, *A Tower for the Summer Heat*, 16–18.

71. Sun Yunqiu, *Jingshi,* 4a–5a; Sun Chengsheng, "Ming Qing zhi ji xifang guangxue zhishi," 374.
72. Li Yu, *Li Yu quanji*, vol. 4, 83; Li Yu, *A Tower for the Summer Heat*, 17.
73. Zhu Riru, "Jingshi xiaoyin," in Sun Yunqiu, *Jingshi*, 1a. See also Sun Chengsheng, "Ming Qing zhi ji xifang guangxue zhishi," 372.
74. Although one might expect that Sun Yunqiu, as Li Yu's junior, copied Li Yu's text, it seems unlikely in that the expertise in lenses was Sun Yunqiu's, and Sun Yunqiu's treatment was more extensive. Sun's *History of Lenses* includes full entries in a similar vein on eleven different kinds of lenses, whereas Li Yu's story has only five. Those lenses might well have been Sun Yunqiu's specialties. The grouping of types of lenses is identical in both texts and quite idiosyncratic.

5. THE PLATE-GLASS MIRROR IN *THE STORY OF THE STONE*

1. See Tina Lu, *Accidental Incest, Filial Cannibalism, and Other Peculiar Encounters* (Cambridge, MA: Harvard University Asia Center, 2008), 237; Shang Wei, "Truth Becomes Fiction When Fiction Is True: *The Story of the Stone* and the Visual Culture of the Manchu Court," *Journal of Chinese Literature and Culture* 2, no. 1 (April 2015): 207–48; Anthony C. Yu, *Rereading the Stone: Desire and the Making of Fiction in* Dream of the Red Chamber (Princeton, NJ: Princeton University Press, 1997), 145–51.
2. "Daguan yuan" is variously translated as "Grand View Garden" or "Prospect Garden." Andrew Plaks has explored the various resonances of the term *daguan*, from its association with the contemplation of the ruler in hexagram 20 of the *Book of Changes* (*Yi jing*) to its significance in the *Zhuangzi* and in Han rhyme prose. Andrew Plaks, *Archetype and Allegory in* The Dream of the Red Chamber (Princeton, NJ: Princeton University Press, 1976), 179–81.
3. This is a particularly difficult line to translate; another possibility is that the mountains and their reflections are uneven, not quite matching each other.
4. Here Qianlong refers to the palace of the moon goddess, Chang'e.
5. The city of the Ghandarvas is similar to a mirage in the desert. It is one of eight analogies for illusion in Buddhist thought, the others being the moon reflected in water, echoes, rainbows, dreams, mirages, the illusions of magicians, and, most important, mirrors.
6. "Jing yu," *Qing Gaozong yuzhi shiwen quanji* (Beijing: Zhongguo renmin daxue chubanshe, 1993), vol. 3, *juan* 34.5b–6a.

7. In 1746, Qianlong had the windows of the Chonghua palace completely changed to full glass panes. The original glass installed in the Chonghua palace during the Qianlong reign is still there—the only truly old glass still preserved in the Forbidden City. Yuan Hongqi, "Chonghua gong de zhuangxiu yu chenshe," in *Zhongguo Zijincheng xuehui di sanci xueshu taolun hui*, vol. 3 (Beijing: Zijin cheng chubanshe, 2004), 132–38.
8. Here Qianlong uses two different terms for mirror, *jing* 鏡 and *jian* 鑑. The first term, which also is used for "lens" during this period, was conventionally associated with the glass mirror. There are many examples to the contrary, however, and this was by no means a hard and fast distinction.
9. In his various inscriptions, Qianlong many times employed the phrase "is it one or two?" (*shi yi shi er*) or "it is not one or two" (*fei yi fei er*). This structure of thought is elucidated in the scholarship on the famous series of paintings "One or Two" (*Shi yi shi er*) commissioned by Qianlong. See Patricia Berger, *Empire of Emptiness: Buddhist Art and Political Authority in Qing China* (Honolulu: University of Hawai'i Press, 2003), 51–52, and Wu Hung, *The Double Screen: Medium and Representation in Chinese Painting* (Chicago: University of Chicago Press, 1996), 231–36.
10. The scholar Wu Hsiao-yun writes that Qianlong enjoyed the interplay of *xu* and *shi* in plate glass. Wu Hsiao-yun, "Qianlong huangdi de jingzi—guanyu jianshang, diancang yu shiyong de xuanze," in *Huangdi de jingzi: Qing gong jing jian wen hua yu dian cang*, ed. Wu Hsiao-yun (Taipei: National Palace Museum, 2015).
11. This screen and throne originally were housed in the Ningshou gong at the northeast side of the Forbidden City, which Qianlong built in the 1770s. As Nancy Berliner observes, the throne is typical of Qianlong's taste in that it displays the most contemporary materials in a very traditional design. Nancy Berliner, *The Emperor's Private Paradise: Treasures from the Forbidden City* (Salem, MA: Peabody Essex Museum, 2010), 141.
12. Nancy Berliner, *The Emperor's Private Paradise*, 141.
13. See Jonathan Hay, *Sensuous Surfaces: The Decorative Object in Early Modern China* (Honolulu: University of Hawai'i Press, 2010), 225–38; Claudia Brown and Donald Rabiner, *The Robert H. Clague Collection: Chinese Glass of the Qing Dynasty, 1644–1911* (Phoenix, AZ: Phoenix Art Museum, 1987); Emily Byrne Curtis, *Glass Exchange Between Europe and China, 1550–1800* (Farnham, UK: Ashgate, 2009), 61; Shang Wei, "Truth Becomes Fiction When Fiction Is True," 207–48; Wu Meifeng, "Jia zuo zhen shi zhen yi jia: Cong Yangxindian zaobanchu huojidang kan sheng Qing shiqi Qinggong yongwu zhi 'zaojia,'" in *Shi xue yü shi shi: Wang Ermin jiaoshou bazhi songshou rongqing xueshu lunwen ji* (Taibei: Guangwen shuju, 2009), 215–70; and Kristina Kleutgehn, *Imperial*

Illusions: Crossing Pictorial Boundaries in the Qing Palaces (Seattle: University of Washington Press, 2015), 240–41.

14. For an example of glass as a pseudo-porcelain, see two eighteenth-century wine cups in the Sir Percival David collection of the British Museum (catalogue numbers 850 and 851).

15. Various scholars have discussed glass used as imitation gemstone. See Claudia Brown and Donald Rabiner, *The Robert H. Clague Collection: Chinese Glass of the Qing Dynasty: 1644–1911*; Emily Byrne Curtis, *Glass Exchange Between Europe and China, 1550–1800: Diplomatic, Mercantile and Technological Interactions* (Farnham, UK: Ashgate, 2009), 61; and Wu Meifeng, "Jia zuo zhen shi zhen yi jia," 215–70.

16. Wu Meifeng casts the interest of the imperial workshops in substituting one medium for another as a kind of forgery or fakery; hence her use of the term *jia*. Wu Meifeng, "Jia zuo zhen shi zhen yi jia," 215–70. I would argue that a sanctioned intermedial substitution of substance should be distinguished from forgery. During the Yongzheng reign, glass substituted for gems in court regalia: officers of the third rank would have hat toppers of blue glass rather than sapphire; of the fourth rank, blue glass rather than lapis; of the fifth rank, clear glass rather than rock crystal, and of the sixth rank, white glass rather than mother of pearl. This was not a matter of fakery or forgery so much as a sanctioned substitution of substances. The aesthetic substitution of substance I discuss above similarly should not be considered a form of fakery or forgery.

17. Kangxi brought Stumpf to Beijing from Guangzhou because of his skill in glassmaking. To provide Stumpf with skilled laborers, Chinese artisans from areas of domestic glass production with long histories, Guangzhou as well as Boshan in Shandong, were summoned to the capital. Many of the raw materials for the glassworks were likely imported to Beijing from Boshan. On the establishment of the imperial glassworks under Stumpf, see Emily Byrne Curtis, "Complete Plan of the Glass Workshop," in *Pure Brightness Shines Everywhere: The Glass of China*, ed. Emily Byrne Curtis (Aldershot, UK: Ashgate, 2004), 49–57. Also see Claudia Brown, Donald Rabiner, and Clarence F. Shangraw, *A Chorus of Colors: Chinese Glass from Three American Collections* (San Francisco: Asian Art Museum of San Francisco, 1995), 18; and Yang Boda, "Qing Dynasty Glass," in Claudia Brown and Donald Rabiner, *The Robert H. Clague Collection: Chinese Glass of the Qing Dynasty, 1644–1911*, 75.

18. Gao Shiqi, a noted painter whose gardens in Hangzhou the Kangxi emperor had admired, served the Kangxi emperor as private secretary for twenty years. He was given residence in the Imperial City and attended the emperor daily. Arthur W.

Hummel, *Eminent Chinese of the Ching Period* (Washington, DC: Government Printing Office, 1943), 413–14. See also Susan Naquin, *Peking: Temples and City Life, 1400–1900* (Berkeley: University of California Press, 2000), 320.

19. Gao Shiqi, *Pengshan miji*, in *Congshu ji cheng xu bian* (Shanghai: Shanghai shudian, 1994), *juan* 3, 1a. Previous translations have read this passage to describe an enclosed theater with glass windows and interior frescoed walls. See William Watson and Chumei Ho, *The Arts of China, 1600–1900* (New Haven, CT: Yale University Press, 2007), 141; Catherine Jami, *The Emperor's New Mathematics: Western Learning and Imperial Authority During the Kangxi Reign (1662–1722)* (Oxford: Oxford University Press, 2012), 244. I think it more likely, however, that the passage describes an external stage surrounded on each side by buildings with glass windows, and that artists had painted on the glass in Western style. This would be in keeping with records of Western painting done on glass windows in the Yuanming yuan under the Yongzheng emperor. Gao Shiqi wrote in 1703; these paintings must have been done by Giovanni Gherardini, the first Western painter to serve a Chinese emperor, whom I discuss in chapter 6.

20. Gao Shiqi, *Pengshan miji*, *juan* 3, 2a. See also Catherine Jami, *The Emperor's New Mathematics*, 244. Gao Shiqi notes the size of the mirror in part because it is a mark of the emperor's favor. Gao Shiqi's record from 1703 is the earliest record I know of that mentions an imperial presentation of a Western mirror in recognition of distinguished service. The most recent instance I know of was the Empress Dowager Cixi's presentation of a floor-to-ceiling mirror that was originally a gift from the Netherlands to the family of the Emperor Pu Yi's wife, Wanrong (1906–1946). Easily eight feet high and twelve feet wide, it was installed in the study of the courtyard house inhabited by Wan Rong's family in Mao'er hutong in the Houhai district of Beijing, where it stands today.

21. Yang Boda, "Qing Dynasty Glass," 74.

22. In 1721, on learning that the papal legate Carlo Ambrogio Mezzabarba planned to return to Rome via Portugal, the Kangxi emperor entrusted him with two cases of glassware, three pairs of glass lanterns, and two cases each of porcelain, enamelware, and lacquerware gifts to be presented to the king of Portugal and the pope. Kangxi then appointed the Jesuit Antonio de Magalhaes as a Mandarin of the third order, so that he would hold the proper rank at court to serve as Kangxi's envoy. The ship carrying the glassware sank in Brazil, but detailed lists of the pieces survive. Emily Byrne Curtis, "The Rainha dos Anjos: Her Precious Cargo," in *Pure Brightness Shines Everywhere*, 59. Kangxi also sent glass-blown objects made in the imperial workshops to the czar, as Georg Johann Unverzagt noted in 1725. Emily Byrne Curtis, "Chinese Glass: A Present to His Czarish Majesty," *Journal of Glass Studies* 51 (2009): 139.

23. *Da Qing yi tong zhi*, comp. Jiang Tingxi (Shanghai: Shanghai guji chubanshe, 1995–1999), *juan* 423.4. In 1688, a mission of French Jesuits presented to Kangxi a number of glass objects as well as an English telescope. Emily Byrne Curtis, *Glass Exchange between Europe and China, 1530–1800*, 69, citing the Archives des Missions Etrangères, Paris, vol. 0479, *Chine: Jésuites*, 89, September 30, 1688. For gifts to the court from European countries, see *Huangchao wenxian tongkao*, comp. Zhang Tingyu, revised Ji Huang, Liu Yong et al., in *Shitong, juan* 298 (Hangzhou: Zhejiang guji chubanshe, 2000). For information on gifts of glass objects from European countries, see *Huangchao tongdian*, comp. Ji Huang and Liu Yong, in *Shitong, juan* 60.
24. See Emily Byrne Curtis, "Cristalli: Four Cases of Precious Glass," in *Glass Exchange Between Europe and China, 1550–1800*, 81–99.
25. Two French Jesuits, Pierre d'Incarville (Tang Zhizhong) and Gabriel-Leonard de Brossard (Ji Wen), who had gained the skills to make plate glass in Rouen, the location of the French royal glassworks, arrived in Beijing in 1740 to work in the imperial glassworks. Emily Byrne Curtis, *Glass Exchange Between Europe and China, 1550–1800*, 47. The Compagnie de la Chine established a French glassworks in Canton in the early eighteenth century; although it was short-lived, its influence had a long reach. Yang Boda believes that the glassworkers employed at the imperial workshops were almost entirely artisans from Guangzhou who helped to introduce French techniques to the palace workshops. Two Guangzhou artisans, Cheng Xianggui and Zhou Jin, were summoned to Beijing in 1709, where they used an eclectic combination of Chinese and European techniques. One of the French glassworkers in Canton, surnamed d'Andigné, was presented to Kangxi by the French Jesuit mission; he was later joined by another, surnamed Villette, who might have brought to Beijing techniques of making sheet glass. Emily Byrne Curtis, *Glass Exchange Between Europe and China, 1550–1800*, 44. It was not necessary for the Qianlong emperor to fashion his own sheet glass, though; in 1786, the Jesuit missionary Bourgeois reported in a letter to Louis-François de la Tour, librarian and secretary to the king of France, that Qianlong had so much Venetian and French glass that he had a quantity broken up to fashion the windows for the European palaces of the Yuanming yuan. Emily Byrne Curtis, *Glass Exchange Between Europe and China, 1550–1800*, 47, 54.
26. In 1771, the viceroy of Canton sent the Qianlong emperor, as part of the tribute from Guangdong province, four sheets of foreign glass (one of a length of about 2.3 meters, and one of a width of about 1.3 meters) as well as a *zitan* tripartite screen with glass panels and a dressing mirror with a *zitan* frame. Yang Boda, *Tributes from Guangdong to the Qing Court* (Hong Kong: Art Gallery, The Chinese University of Hong Kong, 1987), 61.

27. In 1729, Hao Yulin, the viceroy of Guangdong, presented two glass mirrors and two sets of bookshelves with glass doors to the Yongzheng emperor. In 1731, the Provincial Governor of Guangdong, Yang Yongbin, presented Yongzheng with a longevity screen containing a mirrored panel that must have been fashioned in Guangdong using European glass. In 1737, the third year of Qianlong, Zheng Wusai, the Deputy Superintendent of Guangdong maritime customs, presented Qianlong with a glass screen for the *kang*. Yang Boda, *Tributes from Guangdong to the Qing Court*, 11, 40–42, 60.
28. The first presentation list (*jindan*) sent to the court from Canton that lists mirrors is dated to the 26th day of the 11th month of 1722 (the 61st year of Kangxi's reign) and is attributed to an official named Suozi, likely a maritime customs superintendent. Yang Boda, *Tributes from Guangdong to the Qing Court*, 40, 41.
29. Yang Boda, *Tributes from Guangdong to the Qing Court*, 11, 40.
30. Cao Xueqin and Gao E, *Honglou meng*, vol. 1, ed. Yu Pingbo and Qi Gong (Beijing: Renmin wenxue chubanshe, 2005), 360, 654; Cao Xueqin, *The Story of the Stone: A Chinese Novel by Cao Xueqin in Five Volumes*, vol. 2, trans. David Hawkes (New York: Penguin, 1973), 162; vol. 3, 161. Western items owned by the Jias in the novel include a grandfather clock (chapter 6), crepe, gauze, the wool rug on Lady Wang's *kang* (chapter 3), napkins and spoons (chapters 40 and 59), grape wine (chapter 60), and the snuff that Baoyu recommends to Qingwen when she has a cold (chapter 52). Many of those items entered China as tribute; Portugal, for example, sent red and white wine to the Yongzheng court in the fifth year of his reign. The tribute items that enter the Jia family's purview also testify that tribute gifts could be regifted multiple times. For example, in chapter 26, Xifeng gives to Baoyu's cousin Daiyu some tea leaves originally from Siam.
31. It is thought to date to Ji Yun's time, and therefore is likely to be the oldest such mirror in a private residence in Beijing. See Bruce Doar, "A Non-Princely Mansion from Qing-Dynasty Beijing," *China Heritage Quarterly*, no. 12 (December 2007).
32. *Yangxindian zaobanchu shiliao jilan*, ed. Zhu Jiajin (Beijing: Zijincheng chubanshe, 2003), 259.
33. *Yangxindian zaobanchu shiliao jilan*, ed. Zhu Jiajin, 218. Yang Boda notes that Zu Binggui also presented Yongzheng with a number of glass items, such as bowls and snuff bottles, made locally in Guangzhou. Yang Boda, *Tributes from Guangdong to the Qing Court*, 53.
34. Wu Hung, *Wu, hua, ying: Chuan yi jing quan qiu xiao shi* (Shanghai: Shanghai renmin chubanshe, 2021), 31.
35. This double-sidedness has been ignored in the criticism of *The Story of the Stone* but was established by Zhang Shuxian, a researcher at Beijing's Palace Museum, in an article on the architecture and furnishing of Baoyu's chambers. Zhang

Shuxian, "Yihong yuan shinei kongjian tanmi," *Cao Xueqin yanjiu*, no. 2 (2018): 48.

36. For the term "total vision," see Andrew Plaks, *Archetype and Allegory in* The Dream of the Red Chamber (Princeton, NJ: Princeton University Press, 1976), 214.
37. The figure of the mirror as a corrective for one's own misapprehension appeared in Han narrative art. Eugene Y. Wang, "Mirror, Death and Rhetoric: Reading Later Han Chinese Bronze Artifacts," *Art Bulletin* 76, no. 3 (September 1994): 511–34. The Tang-dynasty official Zhang Jiuling (678–740) submitted a remonstration to the Tang emperor Xuanzong in 736 titled "Record of the Thousand-Autumn Bronze Mirror" to protest the emperor's having made his birthday into a holiday called the "Thousand-Autumn Festival"; Zhang drew on the ancient trope of the mirror of history in asking the emperor to reflect on the reasons for the decline of previous dynasties. Eugene Y. Wang, "Mirror, Moon and Memory in Eighth-Century China: From Dragon Pond to Lunar Palace," in *Clarity and Luster: New Light on Bronze Mirrors in Tang and Post-Tang Dynasty China, 600–1300*, ed. Claudia Brown and Ju-hsi Chou (Cleveland, OH: The Cleveland Museum of Art in association with Brepols), 46.
38. Mencius wrote that the mirror of Yin, that is, the example of the Shang dynasty, was not remote. *Mengzi yi zhu*, ed. Yang Bojun (Beijing: Zhonghua shuju, 1988), 165. Drawing on this association with remonstrance, Sima Guang (1019–1086) titled his sweeping history of China from 403 BCE to 959 CE *The Comprehensive Mirror in Aid of Governance* (*Zizhi tongjian*). For more on the significance of the mirror in early and medieval China, see Michael Nylan, "Beliefs About Seeing: Optics and Moral Technologies in Early China," *Asia Major* (3rd series) 21, no. 1 (2008): 89–132, and Paula Varsano, "Disappearing Objects/Elusive Subjects: Writing Mirrors in Early Medieval China," *Representations* 124 (Fall 2013): 96–124.
39. The bronze "Mirror for the Romantic" may superimpose a "contemplation of impurity" or "reflection on repulsiveness" (*bu jing guan*)—a type of Buddhist meditation that asks the viewer to contemplate the vile nature of the body to curb his lusts—on the Confucian associations of the mirror with self-reflection and self-examination. The figure of the mirror in both Chan and Tantric Buddhism is also relevant, as Anthony Yu has observed. Yu quotes Alex Wayman to state that there are three elements tied to the image of the mirror: the image of the mirror as mind, the mirror as simile for the theory of dharmas, and the use of the mirror for divinatory purposes. Alex Wayman, "The Mirror as a Pan-Buddhist Metaphor-Simile," *History of Religions* 13, no. 4 (May 1974): 252; Anthony C. Yu, *Rereading the Stone*, 145.
40. Cao Xueqin, *The Story of the Stone*, vol. 1, 252. As Anthony Yu has remarked, in Buddhist texts the wet dream signals the mutual permeability of waking and dreaming worlds and furnishes convincing proof that the presumed illusion of

dream has as much claim to truth status as the waking world. Anthony C. Yu, *Rereading the Stone*, 143.

41. In the Madhyamaka thought so important to the Qianlong emperor, the figure of the mirror exemplified the lack of intrinsic character to the self. Nāgārjuna (ca. 150–ca. 250 CE), the founder of the Madhyamaka school, stated, "With recourse to a mirror, one sees the reflected image of one's face, but in reality this (reflection) is nothing at all. In the same way, with recourse to the personality aggregates, the idea of self (*ahamkara*) is conceived, but in reality it is nothing at all, like the reflection of one's face." Alexander Wayman, "The Mirror as Pan-Buddhist Metaphor-Simile," *History of Religions* 13, no. 4 (May 1974): 260.

42. In the thought of Six Dynasties literary elites such as Shen Yue, the philosophy of Laozi and Zhuangzi combined with classical Buddhist thought. Shen Yue forges a connection between the non-self (*fei wo*) of Mahayana Buddhism and the classical Daoist term "having no self" or "forgetting the self." Shen Yue distinguished between an ordinary person's ability to temporarily forget the self and the sage's ability to achieve a non-self of constant duration, remarking, "But an ordinary person's nonbeing is only temporary, and the moment is fleeting; the sage's nonbeing lasts long and indeed reaches very far." Xiaofei Tian, *Beacon Fire and Shooting Star* (Cambridge, MA: Harvard University East Asia Center for the Harvard-Yenching Institute, 2007), 231.

43. *Zhuangzi jishi*, ed. Guo Qingfan (Beijing: Zhonghua shuju, 1961), 307; Burton Watson, trans., *The Complete Works of Chuang-tzu* (New York: Columbia University Press, 2013), 97.

44. *Zhuangzi jishi*, 197; Watson, *The Complete Works of Chuang-tzu*, 70. See also Paul Demiéville, "The Mirror of the Mind," in *Sudden and Gradual: Approaches to Enlightenment in Chinese Thought*, ed. Peter N. Gregory (Honolulu: University of Hawai'i, Kuroda Institute, 1987), 18.

45. For a critical reevaluation of the relation between the two poems, see Luis O. Gomez, "Purifying Gold: The Metaphor of Effort and Intuition in Buddhist Thought and Practice," in *Sudden and Gradual: Approaches to Enlightenment in Chinese Thought*, ed. Peter Gregory, 67–168.

46. Paul Demiéville, "The Mirror of the Mind," in *Sudden and Gradual*.

47. *Chongjiao bajia pingpi Honglou meng*, ed. Feng Qiyong (Nanchang: Jiangxi jiaoyu chubanshe, 2000), 346. Cao Xueqin, *The Story of the Stone*, vol. 1, 346.

48. The English word *partition* is used to translate a number of Chinese terms for spatial dividers that stop short of being actual walls, such as partitions formed by extended door frames that act as partial walls, and full-length floor-to-ceiling partitions (*bisha chu*).

49. For more on the Fuwangge, see *Fuwangge: Qianlong huayuan yanjiu yu baohu*, 2 vols. (Beijing: The Forbidden City Publishing House, 2014); and *Juanqinzhai:*

Qianlong huayuan huangjia wenhua xilie, ed. Gugong bowuyuan gujian bu (Tianjin: Tianjin daxue chubanshe, 2012).

50. *Fuwangge: Qianlong huayuan yanjiu yu baohu*, 38.
51. Qiancheng Li observes that in "Baoyu's sojourn in the human realm he is considered as wandering in a state of *mi* or *wuming*, an unenlightened state of loss and disorientation, lacking knowledge of his original nature." Qiancheng Li, *Fictions of Enlightenment: Journey to the West, Tower of Myriad Mirrors, and Dream of the Red Chamber* (Honolulu: University of Hawai'i Press, 2004), 148. From this point of view, the disorienting quality of Baoyu's chambers reflects the elemental disorientation of Baoyu himself.
52. *Chongjiao bajia pingpi Honglou meng*, 346.
53. Cao Xueqin and Gao E, *Honglou meng*, 180; Cao Xueqin, *The Story of the Stone*, vol. 1, 346–47.
54. The articulation of space in Baoyu's quarters is so difficult to map mentally that it is worth considering how eighteenth- and nineteenth-century dramatists who wrote sequels to *The Story of the Stone* envisioned this scene. In Wu Lanzheng's *Jiang Heng Qiu*, published posthumously in 1806, the mirror is curtained by transparent gauze. The *fu jing* role type says, "How is it that right before us, the path ends in a bookshelf?" The *chou* (clown) role type replies, "Look, when you look back at this transparent gauze curtain, there is a bright world that faces you. If you look at it from the side, you will see that it is actually a mirror." The clown goes on to say that even though they often stroll in the imperial gardens, here it is easy to lose one's way. Wu Lanzheng, *Jiang Heng Qiu*, in *Honglou meng xiqu ji*, vol. 2, ed. A Ying (Beijing: Zhonghua shuju, 1978), 267.
55. Qiancheng Li also observes that not only do Jia Zheng, Baoyu, and Grannie Liu lose their way in this part of the garden, but Miaoyu describes the paths of the garden as confusing. Qiancheng Li, *Fictions of Enlightenment*, 150.
56. When Jia Zheng does not recognize himself in the mirror, his blankness mirrors that of his own mirror image, which, having no capacity for thought, does not recognize him. In the Astasāhasrikā Prajñāpāramitā this absence of mentation of any kind is related to an impartiality that is immediately evident in a lack of concern regarding spatial positioning. Alexander Wayman, "The Mirror as a Pan-Buddhist Metaphor-Simile," 259.
57. Cao Xueqin and Gao E, *Honglou meng*, 442–43. Here I use the translation of Yang Xianyi and Gladys Yang, since it is more faithful to the original text. Cao Xueqin, *A Dream of Red Mansions*, ed. Yu Pingbo and Qi Gong, vol. 2, trans. Yang Xianyi and Gladys Yang (Beijing: Renmin wenxue chubanshe, 2005), 834–35.
58. Cao Xueqin and Gao E, *Honglou meng*, 443; Cao Xueqin, *A Dream of Red Mansions*, vol. 2, 834–35. The Yangs' translation here again is more literal,

capturing the phrase *qing jia mu* as "son-in-law's mother." Hawkes's translation describes the son's mother-in-law as "another old woman, whom she took to be her old gossip from the village." Cao Xueqin, *The Story of the Stone*, vol. 2, 319.

59. Cao Xueqin and Gao E, *Honglou meng*, 443; Cao Xueqin, *A Dream of Red Mansions*, vol. 2, 835.
60. Cao Xueqin, *The Story of the Stone*, vol. 2, 319–20.
61. The mirror becomes an emblem of Baoyu's fate at the end of chapter 22, when Baoyu writes a lantern riddle on the mirror. Each of Baoyu's cousins has submitted a riddle concerning an object that proleptically comes to emblematize their fate. Jia Zheng becomes subdued after he discerns that the answer to Baoyu's lantern riddle is "a mirror." For Baoyu's father, the implied equation between Baoyu and the mirror is a threatening omen. Baoyu's riddle reads: "Southward you stare. He'll northward glare. Grieve, and he's sad. Laugh, and he's glad" (南面而坐, 北面而朝。象憂亦憂, 象喜亦喜). The *Qixu* and *Gengchen* editions do not include Baoyu's riddle about the mirror at the end of chapter 22; the *Jiachen* edition does. *Chongjiao bajia pingpi Honglou meng*, vol. 1, 470; Cao Xueqin, *The Story of the Stone*, vol. 1, 449.
62. Cao Xueqin and Gao E, *Honglou meng*, 612–13; Cao Xueqin, *The Story of the Stone*, vol. 3, 85.
63. Cao Xueqin and Gao E, *Honglou meng*, 613, Cao Xueqin, *The Story of the Stone*, vol. 3, 85.
64. On the trope of the shared dream and its relevance here, see Shang Wei, "Truth Becomes Fiction When Fiction Is True," 236.
65. Cao Xueqin and Gao E, *Honglou meng*, 614. I have translated this passage myself to offer a more literal translation; the relevant passage can be found in Cao Xueqin, *The Story of the Stone*, vol. 3, 86.
66. *Chongjiao bajia pingpi Honglou meng*, 1267. Shang Wei rightly notes that this passage "deviates from that of Zhuangzi's butterfly dream in that it does not involve the motif of metamorphosis." Shang Wei, "Truth Becomes Fiction When Fiction is True," 235–36.
67. Michael Nylan, "Vital Matters," in *Having a Word with Angus Graham: At Twenty-Five Years into His Immortality*, ed. Roger T. Ames and Carine DeFoort (Albany: State University of New York Press, 2018), 85.
68. *Zhuangzi jishi*, ed. Guo Qingfan, vol. 1, 112. See also Watson, *The Complete Works of Chuang Tzu*, 49.
69. The term *sack of skin* is used in the Daoist deliverance play "Lan Caihe." Anonymous, *Han Zhongli dutuo Lan Caihe*, in *Yuanqu xuan waibian*, vol. 3, ed. Sui Shusen (Beijing: Zhonghua shuju, 1959), 975. It also appears in the Sutra of Forty-Two Chapters (*Sishi er zhang jing*) to describe the physical body in meditation.

70. Jia Zheng's initial mistaking of the mirror for a door recalls the description of the partition that surrounds the mirror as containing mysterious portals (*youhu*). The term refers obliquely to the inscription Baoyu had suggested for the mirrorlike stone at the entrance to the garden in chapter 17, "pathway to mysteries," which in turn references a poem by the Tang poet Chang Jian in which the poet follows a winding path to a secluded and mysterious space for Chan meditation. "Ti Poshan si hou Chanyuan," in Chang Jian, *Chang Jian shige jiaozhu*, ed. Wang Xijiu (Beijing: Zhonghua shuju, 2017), 209. The reference to Baoyu's quotation of Chang Jian suggests that as Jia Zheng loses his way in the maze of dazzling inlays and hidden apertures, he potentially treads a path to a meditative quality of perception—a path that he, with characteristic self-confidence, will fail to follow.
71. Here the novel might draw on the venerable Yogācāra trope of mirror as the voidness gate to liberation. Alexander Wayman, "The Mirror as a Pan-Buddhist Metaphor-Simile," 254. Wayman notes that in the Prajñāpāramitā scriptures, mirrorlike knowledge can be a metaphor for infinite consciousness and for consciousness that reflects without being changed. The emphasis in these scriptures on the understanding of voidness helped bolster the importance of the mirror as metaphor for the mind, even though the Prajñāpāramitā scriptures did not employ the metaphor itself.
72. I have translated these phrases instead of using Hawkes's translation to emphasize that the character *mi* here speaks to disorientation. *Chongjiao bajia pingpi Honglou meng*, vol. 2, 1268.
73. *Chongjiao bajia pingpi Honglou meng*, vol. 2, 1268.
74. *Chongjiao bajia pingpi Honglou meng*, vol. 2, 1268; Cao Xueqin, *The Story of the Stone*, vol. 3, 87.
75. Zhang Shuxian, "Yihong yuan shinei kongjian tanmi," in *Cao Xueqin yanjiu*, no. 2 (2018): 48. Wu Hung, "Beyond Stereotypes: The Twelve Beauties in Qing Court Art and *The Dream of the Red Chamber*," in *Writing Women in Late-Imperial China*, ed. Kang-I Sun Chang and Ellen Widmer, 306–65. Shang Wei, "Truth Becomes Fiction When Fiction Is True," 229; and "*The Story of the Stone* and Its Visual Representations, 1791–1919," in *Approaches to Teaching* The Story of the Stone (Dream of the Red Chamber), ed. Andrew Schonebaum and Tina Lu (New York: The Modern Language Association of America, 2012), 346–81.
76. Zhang Shuxian, "Yihong yuan shinei kongjian tanmi," *Cao Xueqin yanjiu*, no. 2 (2018): 49.
77. As Nancy Berliner has written, this mirrored door that opens to the trompe l'oeil murals of the theater room is "a metaphor perhaps of the ability to walk through a mirror into an imaginary world." Nancy Berliner, *The Emperor's Private*

Paradise, 175. The anteroom of the famed theater of the Juanqinzhai has been described in recent scholarship as a bedchamber because it currently contains a bed. It is uncertain what function the room was originally meant to serve. There is no way of knowing whether it contained a bed during Qianlong's time, since the earliest recording of the furnishings of Juanqinzhai dates to the Jiaqing period.

78. False doors had genuine architectural frames that were filled in with wooden boards. The wood was covered with white silk or wallpaper. In the unrestored Yanghe jingshe of the Forbidden City, one can see such a door with the traces of silk still affixed. The records of the imperial workshops show that "true and false" doors were designed not only for the Ningshou gong and other palaces within the Forbidden City, but also for the summer palaces in Yuanming yuan and Chengde as well as the traveling palace Panshan. In some cases, the paper or silk affixed to the false doors was painted with bookcases, landscapes, speckled bamboo, or portraits of beautiful women (perhaps drawing on the old trope of a woman stepping down from the painting). The paintings on false doors could be done in Western oils, but it is likely that traditional Chinese painting techniques were used more often. Wu Meifeng notes that all the artists of the Ruyi guan, the imperial painting workshop, painted the false doors; such doors were not the province of the artists who specialized in Western painting. Wu Meifeng, "Jia zuo zhen shi zhen yi jia," in *Shi xue yü shi shi*, 121.

79. Yuan Mei, *Yuan Mei quanji*, ed. Wang Yingzhi (Nanjing: Jiangsu guji chubanshe, 1993), 854–55. Also see Arthur Waley, *Yuan Mei: Eighteenth Century Chinese Poet* (London: G. Allen and Unwin, 1956), 187.

80. According to the Tang-dynasty *Xijing zaji*, the first emperor of the Qin had a rectangular mirror 5 *chi* and 9 *cun* (1.83 m) tall and 4 *chi* (1.25 m) wide, luminous inside and out, that he shone on his courtiers to reflect their true characters. When people approached it, they would appear upside down in it. It could reveal a person's internal organs without obstruction. The first emperor used it to see the internal organs of his palace women, and if their livers were enlarged and hearts palpitated, he would kill them. *Xijing zaji*, rare manuscript, the Chinese University of Hong Kong Library, *juan* 3, 4a–4b. Eugene Wang notes that eighth-century bronze mirrors reference this trope. A long inscription by a mirror-maker dated 722, for example, states that "It is often said that the bright mirror of the King of Qin illuminates the gall and the heart. It possesses the efficacy unobtainable even by good craftsmen." Eugene Y. Wang, "Mirror, Moon and Memory in Eighth-Century China," 42–67.

81. The term I have translated as "mica" (*yun mu*) refers to substances, such as glass or ice, that have the translucence of mica, as well as to mica itself.

82. *Liuli* has a wide range of significances, from lapis lazuli to yellow and green glazes to substances that are translucent like crystal. It was also used to refer to Western glass.
83. Yuan Mei compares Zhang Chaojin to the tortoise holding up the three immortal isles to show that he appreciates the weighty burdens of Zhao's office.
84. Yuan Mei, *Yuan Mei quan ji*, 854–55.
85. Yuan Mei, *Piben Suiyuan shihua*, ed. Mao Guangsheng (Beijing: Shangwu yinshu guan, 1926), *juan* 2, 5b.
86. The *Hanyu dacidian* gives *The Story of the Stone* as the locus classicus of the term *liuli shijie*. In the Tang-dynasty *Sutra on the Merits of the Fundamental Vows of the Master of Healing, the Lapis Lazuli Radiance*, Tathāgata describes the realm of the Healing Buddha (Bhaiṣajya-guru) as a realm without temptation, suffering, or "woeful paths of existence," where the ground itself is made of *liuli*, a purifying, transformative, glass-like substance. The term *liuli* also has a long literary history as a clear, jewel-like substance. In Yuan Mei's usage, these multiple threads conflate to create the notion of an otherworldly realm composed of glass. Raoul Birnbaum has extensively discussed the translation of the term *liuli* in the context of the Bhaiṣajya-guru Sutra. See Raoul Birnbaum, *The Healing Buddha* (Boulder, CO: Shambhala Books, 1979), 65ff.
87. Cao Xueqin and Gao E, *Honglou meng*, 57; Cao Xueqin, *The Story of the Stone*, vol. 1, 140.

6. HISTORICIZING RECESSION VIA *THE STORY OF THE STONE* AND THE JUANQINZHAI

1. Wu Hung first advanced the notion of a shared spatial imaginary between the Juanqinzhai and *The Story of the Stone* in 1997: Wu Hung, "Beyond Stereotypes: The Twelve Beauties in Qing Court Art and the *Dream of the Red Chamber*," in *Writing Women in Late-Imperial China*, ed. Kang-I Sun Chang and Ellen Widmer (Stanford, CA: Stanford University Press, 1997), 306–65. Shang Wei has furthered the pairing by suggesting, "The painting that Grannie Liu bumps into resembles illusionistic paintings exemplified by the one on the upper story of the theater hall inside the Lodge of Retirement," that is, the Juanqinzhai. Shang Wei, "Truth Becomes Fiction When the Fiction Is True," *Journal of Chinese Literature and Culture* 2, no. 1 (April 2015): 222. Many art historians have explored the scene in *The Story of the Stone*. See, for example, the discussion in James Cahill, *Pictures for Use and Pleasure: Vernacular Painting in High Qing China* (Berkeley: University of California Press, 2010), 161–65. Cahill notes that the painting expanded the room, "opening the depicted space to imagined entry,"

an insight that I develop here. See also Kristina Kleutghen, *Imperial Illusions: Crossing Pictorial Boundaries in the Qing Palaces* (Seattle: University of Washington Press, 2015), 240.
2. *Chongjiao bajia pingpi Honglou meng*, vol. 2, 929; *The Story of the Stone: A Chinese Novel by Cao Xueqin in Five Volumes*, vol. 2, trans. David Hawkes (New York: Penguin, 1973), 318–19.
3. *Chongjiao bajia pingpi Honglou meng*, vol. 2, 929; *The Story of the Stone*, vol. 2, 318–19.
4. Cao Xueqin, *Honglou meng*, 436–37; *The Story of the Stone*, vol. 2, 309.
5. *Donglin lianshe shiba gaoxian zhuan*, rare manuscript, Harvard-Yenching Library, Cambridge, MA, 12a.
6. Here Cao Xueqin draws on the old trope of the girl who steps down from the painting. For an example, see Feng Menglong, comp., *Qingshi leilüe*, rare manuscript, Shanghai Municipal Library. Reprint, Zhang Zugao et al. (Shenyang: Chunfeng wenyi chubanshe, 1986), *juan* 9, 40a.
7. For a definition of *tongjing hua*, see Kristina Kleutghen, *Imperial Illusions*, 5–6. Kleutghen's definition works well for our purposes: "massive wall- and ceiling-mounted paintings in full color on silk, produced collaboratively by the best Chinese and Western painters serving the emperor." This use of the term is narrow, however. The term *tongjing hua* also encompassed small paintings set into screens and large paintings painted in traditional Chinese ink that revealed no Western influence. Marco Musillo, describing the relation between *quadratura* and *tongjing hua*, notes that although *tongjing hua* employs techniques of *quadratura*, *quadratura* takes a more coherent approach to creating scenographic spaces. Marco Musillo, *The Shining Inheritance: Italian Painters at the Qing Court, 1699–1812* (Los Angeles: The Getty Research Institute, 2016), 117.
8. Marco Musillo, *The Shining Inheritance*, 101.
9. Carlo Cesare Malvasia, *Felsina pittrice: Vite de pittori bolognesi* (1769), vol. 3 (Whitefish, MT: Kessinger Library Reprints, 2010), 51–57.
10. Ebria Feinblatt, "Angelo Michele Colonna: A Profile," *The Burlington Magazine* 121, no. 919 (October 1979): 621.
11. See Matteo Ripa, *Storia della Fondazione della Congregazione e del Collegio dei Cinesi*, vol. 1, 386, as cited in Marco Musillo, *The Shining Inheritance*, 33.
12. Marco Musillo, *The Shining Inheritance*, 101.
13. Ferdinando Galli Bibiena, *L'architettura civile: Preparata sú la geometria e ridotta alle prospettive: considerazioni pratiche* (Parma: Per Paolo Monti, 1711), rare manuscript, Getty Research Institute, Los Angeles. *L'architettura civile* was reprinted as *Direzioni della prospettiva teorica corrispondenti a quelle dell'architettura* (Lelio dalla Volpe, 1753–64) in Bologna. See Marco Musillo's

treatment of Bibiena's *veduta per angolo* and of this woodcut illustration in *The Shining Inheritance*, 92–93.

14. Pierre Jartoux, Letter from Beijing, 1704. The English translation comes from Marco Musillo, *The Shining Inheritance*, 102. The original French is found in Jean-Baptiste Du Halde, *Description géographique, historique, chronologique, politique et physique de l'empire de la Chine et de la Tartarie chinoise* (Paris: P. G. Lemercier 1735), vol. 3, 140–41.

15. Mikinosuke Ishida, "A Biographical Study of Giuseppe Castiglione (Lang Shihning), a Jesuit Painter in the Court of Peking under the Ch'ing Dynasty," *Memoirs of the Research Department of the Toyo Bunko* 19 (1960): 102–3.

16. Zhang Jingyun, *Qiuping xinyu*, rare manuscript, Keio University, 5.38.

17. See Judith Zeitlin, *The Historian of the Strange: Pu Songling and the Chinese Classical Tale* (Stanford, CA: Stanford University Press, 1993), 183–99 (analysis), 216–18 (translation); and Wai-yee Li, *Enchantment and Disenchantment: Love and Illusion in Chinese Literature* (Princeton, NJ: Princeton University Press, 1993), 110–14, 138.

18. Pu Songling, *Liaozhai zhiyi*, ed. Zhang Youhe (Shanghai: Shanghai guji chubanshe, 1997), vol. 1, 14–17.

19 As Judith Zeitlin notes, Zhu misses five chances at sudden enlightenment, choosing instead to dally inside the wall with the figure of an apsara described as the Heavenly Maiden Scattering Flowers. Judith Zeitlin, *The Historian of the Strange*, 192.

20. Guo Qingfan, ed., *Zhuangzi jishi*, comp. Wang Xiaoyu (Beijing: Zhonghua shuju, 1961), 43; Burton Watson, trans., *The Complete Works of Chuang-Tzu* (New York: Columbia University Press, 2013), 185.

21. Pu Songling, *Liaozhai zhiyi*, vol. 1, 14.

22. In an anecdote in Ji Yun's collection *Yuewei caotang biji*, for example, a figure of the Heavenly Maiden Scattering Flowers painted with Western perspectivalism is discovered to be a succubus. "A literatus spent the night in a monk's cell in a temple. On the wall hung a scroll of a beautiful woman whose eyes and brows were as alive, and whose clothing seemed to ripple as though in movement. When the literatus asked the monk, 'Are you not afraid of disturbing your Zen mind?' the monk replied, 'This is a painting of the Heavenly Maiden Scattering Flowers done by Du Fenmu. It's been in the temple for over a hundred years, but I have never had the leisure to examine it closely.' One night, they stared at the painting in the lamplight, and as they watched, the person in the painting seemed to protrude from it by one or two inches. The literatus said, 'This is a European painting, so when you look at it, it seems to have depths and protrusions. How can this be by Du Fenmu?' Suddenly a voice from the painting said, 'I would

like to descend, please don't be surprised, sir.'" The literatus scolded the woman in the painting, asking what manner of succubus she might be, and walked toward the lamp with the intention of burning the scroll. From the painting came a sobbing voice begging for mercy, saying that her body was almost complete and, should she be consigned to the fire, her labors would be lost. The monk then exclaimed that he had a disciple who, while living in this cell, sickened and died, and asked the painting whether this was not on account of her. The girl in the painting pleaded for compassion, but the literatus threw the painting into the flames of the stove—whereupon the stench of flesh filled the room. Ji Yun, *Yuewei caotang biji*, ed. Wang Xiandu (Shanghai: Shanghai guji chubanshe, 1998), 539.

23. Burton Watson, trans., *The Vimalakirti Sutra* (New York: Columbia University Press, 1997), 91.
24. Pu Songling, *Liaozhai zhiyi*, vol. 1, 15.
25. David Hawkes's translation is not literal here; he simply translates these as "Convex Pavilion" and "Concave Pavilion." Cao Xueqin, *The Story of the Stone*, vol. 3, 514.
26. Cao Xueqin, *Honglou meng*, 845; Cao Xueqin, *The Story of the Stone*, vol. 3, 514.
27. Neither the term *aotu* nor this scene has received consideration in the writing on Western perspectivalism and *The Story of the Stone*. But scholars have puzzled over this particular exchange and wondered how Cao Xueqin might have come to underscore the terms *ao* and *tu* in this passage. The scholar Zhang Yimin suggests that Lin Daiyu and Shi Xiangyun's debate over the vulgarity of the terms as well as the brief history of the terms that Lin Daiyu proposes originated in volume 64 of the Ming poet Yang Shen's (1488–1599) collection *Collected Writings of the Sheng Studio* (*Sheng'an ji*). See also Yang Shen, *Yang Sheng'an congshu*, ed. Wang Wencai and Wan Guangzhi (Chengdu: Tiandi chubanshe, 2002), 481; and *Jingyin wenyuange siku quanshu* (Taipei: Taiwan shangwu yinshuguan, 1983), *juan* 64, 6b–7a. Cao Xueqin indeed seems to have reworked Yang Shen's text to produce this conversation between Shi Xiangyun and Lin Daiyu; Yang Shen similarly defends the characters *ao* and *tu* against the charge of vulgarity, and most crucially cites the same sources: Dong Fangshuo (154–93 BCE), *Classic of Divine Marvels* (*Shenyi jing*); and Zhang Yanyuan's Tang-dynasty *Records of Painting* (*Huaji*) in support. Zhang Yimin, "Guanyu aotu zhi yi de chuchu," *Honglou meng xuekan* 1 (2000): 68–70.
28. Gu Qiyuan and Lu Can, *Gengsibian kezuo zhuiyu*, ed. Tan Dihua and Chen Jiahe (Beijing: Zhonghua shuju, 1987), 153. This anecdote appears in a number of texts, most notably Yang Shen's *Sheng'an ji*. At the time of Gu Qiyuan's writing, the understanding of both Italian and Buddhist techniques of volumetric shading

appears to have been lost. By Cao Xueqin's time, however, the knowledge of European techniques of perspective and rendering volume, both Italian and Dutch, were well known not only in Beijing, but also in the Jiangnan region and in Guangzhou.

29. As Nancy Berliner has written, the Qianlong garden contained no less than six sites for Buddhist devotional practices. The very first grotto contained the Yizhai, decorated with Buddhas, bodhisattvas, and luohans; a small Buddhist hermitage followed. The Cuishang lou contains a portrait of the Qianlong emperor as the Bodhisattva Mañjuśrī. Nancy Berliner, "The Qianlong Garden in the Palace of Tranquility and Longevity," in Nancy Berliner, ed., *The Emperor's Private Paradise: Treasures from the Forbidden City* (Salem, MA: Peabody Essex Museum, 2010), 149–50.
30. See Kristina Kleutghen, *Imperial Illusions*, 114–23, for readings of these paintings. *Imperial Illusions* attributes the painting in the east bay of the Yanghe jingshe to Yao Wenhan, but in fact it is by Wang Youxue.
31. Kristina Kleutghen, *Imperial Illusions*, 17.
32. Kristina Kleutghen, *Imperial Illusions*, 14.
33. Nie Chongzheng, "Architectural Decoration in the Forbidden City: Trompe-l'oeil Murals in the Lodge of Retiring from Hard Work," *Orientations* 7 (August 1995): 51–55.
34. See Nie Chongzheng, "Gugong Juanqinzhai tianding hua, quanjing hua santi," *Juangshi* 3 (2009): 68.

CONCLUSION: LITERARY OBJECTS

1. Cao Xueqin and Gao E, *Honglou meng* (Beijing: Renmin wenxue chubanshe, 2000), 241; Cao Xueqin, *The Story of the Stone: A Chinese Novel by Cao Xueqin in Five Volumes*, vol. 1, trans. David Hawkes (New York: Penguin Books, 1980), 463. I have modified Hawkes's translation slightly, in part drawing on Stephen H. West and Wilt L. Idema's translation of *The Western Wing*. In *The Western Wing*, the phrase that Hawkes translates as "the red flowers in their hosts are falling" (*luo hong cheng zhen* 落紅成陣) occurs at the opening of Book 2, where the lovelorn Yingying uses the phrase to convey the sense that her youth is passing as she pines for student Zhang. West and Idema translate this line as "Fallen flowers form battle arrays." The phrasing may also recall that at the moment Yingying speaks, the temple in which she resides is surrounded by battle troops. See Wang Shifu, *Jiping jiaozhu Xixiang ji*, annot. Wang Jisi and Zhang Renhe (Shanghai: Shanghai guji chubanshe, 1987), 47; Wang Shifu, *The Moon and the Zither: The Story of the Western Wing*, trans. Stephen H. West and Wilt L. Idema (Berkeley: University of California Press, 1991), 219.

2. The phrasing here also anticipates the first line of Daiyu's poem on burying flowers in chapter 27, "The blossoms fade and falling fill the air" (花謝花飛花滿天). Cao Xueqin and Gao E, *Honglou meng* (Beijing: Renmin wenxue chubanshe, 2000), 290–91; Cao Xueqin, *The Story of the Stone*, vol. 2, trans. David Hawkes (New York: Penguin Books, 1980), 38–39.
3. Burton Watson, trans., *The Vimalakirti Sutra* (New York: Columbia University Press, 1997), 91.
4. Watson, *The Vimalakirti Sutra*, 91.

Bibliography

CHINESE-LANGUAGE SOURCES

Anonymous. *Han Zhongli dutuo Lan Caihe* 漢鐘離度脫藍采和. In *Yuanqu xuan waibian* 元曲選外編, vol. 3, ed. Sui Shusen 隋樹森. Beijing: Zhonghua shuju, 1959.

Cai Guoliang 蔡國梁. "Jin Ping Mei fanying de Ming houqi de chengshi jingji shenghuo" 金瓶梅反映的明後期的城市經濟生活. In *Jin Ping Mei yanjiu* 金瓶梅研究, ed. Fudan xuebao shehui kexuebao bianjibu 復旦學報社會科學報編輯部. Shanghai: Fudan daxue chubanshe, 1984.

Cao Xueqin 曹雪芹 and Gao E 高鶚. *Honglou meng* 紅樓夢, ed. Yu Pingbo 俞平伯 and Qi Gong 啟功. Beijing: Renmin wenxue chubanshe, 2005.

——. *Chongjiao bajia pingpi Honglou meng* 重校八家評批紅樓夢, ed. Feng Qiyong 馮其庸. Nanchang: Jiangxi jiaoyu chubanshe, 2000.

Chang Jian 常建. *Chang Jian shige jiaozhu* 常建詩歌校註, ed. Wang Xijiu 王錫九. *Zhongguo gudian wenxue jiben congshu* 中國古典文學基本叢書. Beijing: Zhonghua shuju, 2017.

Chen Yongzheng 陳永正. *Shijing fengqing: Sanyan Erpai de shi jie*. 市井風情：三言二拍的世界. Hong Kong: Zhonghua shuju, 1988.

Chen Xizhong 陳曦鐘, Hou Zhongyi 侯忠義, and Lu Yuchuan 魯玉川, eds., *Shuihu zhuan huiping ben* 水滸傳會評本. Beijing: Beijing daxue, 1981.

Chen Zhao 陳詔. *Jin Ping Mei xiaokao* 金瓶梅小考. Shanghai: Shanghai shudian chubanshe, 1999.

Cheng Pei-kai 鄭培凱. "Jiuse caiqi yu *Jin Ping Mei* cihua de kaitou – jianping *Jin Ping Mei* yanjiu de 'suoyin pai'" 酒色財氣與金瓶梅詞話的開頭-簡評金瓶梅研究的索隱派. *Chung-wai wen-hsüeh* 4, no. 20 (September 1983): 42–69.

Da Ming hui dian 大明會典, comp. Xu Pu 徐溥 and Liu Jian 劉健, rev. Li Dongyang 李東陽, ed. Shen Shixing 申時行. Taipei: Dongnan chubanshe, 1964.

Da Qing yi tong zhi 大清一統志, comp. Jiang Tingxi 蔣廷錫. 1744. Shanghai: Shanghai guji chubanshe, 1995-1999.

Donglin lianshe shiba gaoxianzhuan 東林蓮社十八高賢傳. Rare Manuscript, Harvard-Yenching Library, Cambridge, MA.

Du Zhen 杜臻. *Yue Min xunshi jilüe* 粵閩巡視紀略. In *Jindai Zhongguo shiliao congkan xubian* 近代中國史料叢刊續編, vol. 98. Taipei: Wenhai chubanshe, 1983.

Fan Jinmin 范金民 and Liu Xinglin 劉興林. *Changjiang sichou wenhua* 長江絲綢文化. Wuhan: Hubei jiaoyu chubanshe, 2004.

——. *Jiangnan sichou shi yanjiu* 江南絲綢史研究. Beijing: Nongye chubanshe, 1993.

Feng Menglong 馮夢龍. *Jingshi tongyan* 警世通言. Shanghai: Shanghai guji chubanshe, 1987.

——. *Qingshi leilüe* 情史類略. Rare manuscript, Shanghai Municipal Library. Reprint, Zhang Fugao 張福高 et al. Shenyang: Chunfeng wenyi chubanshe, 1986.

——. *Yushi mingyan* 喻世明言. Hangzhou: Zhejiang guji chubanshe, 2015.

Fuwangge: Qianlong huayuan yanjiu yu baohu 符望閣—乾隆花園研究與保護. 2 vols. Beijing: The Forbidden City Publishing House, 2014.

Gao Lian 高濂. *Zunsheng bajian* 遵生八箋. Hangzhou: Zhejiang guji chubanshe, 2019.

Gao Shiqi 高士奇. *Pengshan miji* 蓬山密記. Shanghai: Shanghai shudian, 1994.

Ge Hong 葛洪 and Liu Xin 劉歆. *Xijing zaji* 西京雜記, ed. Cheng Rong 程榮 (1590–1599). Rare manuscript, Chinese University of Hong Kong Library, Hong Kong.

Gong Zhengwo 龔正我. *Zhaijin qiyin* 摘錦奇音. In *Shanben xiqu congkan* 善本戲曲叢刊, ed. Wang Ch'iu-kuei 王秋桂. Taipei: Xuesheng shuju, 1984.

Gu Qiyuan 顧起元 and Lu Can 陸粲. *Gengsibian kezuo zhuiyu* 庚巳編客座贅語, ed. Tan Dihua 譚棣華 and Chen Jiahe 陳稼禾. Beijing: Zhonghua shuju, 1987.

Gu Yingtai 谷應泰, ed. *Mingshi jishi benmo* 明史紀事本末. Beijing: Zhonghua shuju, 1977.

Han Feizi jijie 韓非子集解, ed. Wang Xianshen 王先慎. Beijing: Zhonghua shuju, 1998.

Hangzhou fuzhi 杭州府志, ed. Chen Shan 陳善 et al. [1922 edition]. Reprint, Taipei: Chengwen chubanshe, 1983.

Hou Hui 侯會. *Honglou meng guizu shenghuo jiemi* 紅樓夢貴族生活揭秘. Beijing: Xinhua chubanshe, 2010.

Hsu, Hui-lin 許暉林. "Jing yu qianzhi: Shilun Zhongguo xushi wenlei zhong xiandai shijue jingyan de qiyuan" 鏡與前知: 試論中國敘事文類中現代視覺經驗的起源. *Tai-ta Chung-wen Hsueh-pao* 臺大中文學報 48 (March 2015).

Huangchao tongdian 皇朝通典, comp. Ji Huang 嵇璜 and Liu Yong 劉墉. In *Shitong* 十通. Hangzhou: Zhejiang guji chubanshe, 2000.

Huangchao wenxian tongkao 皇朝文獻通考, comp. Zhang Tingyu 張廷玉 et al., rev. Ji Huang 嵇璜, Liu Yong 劉墉 et al. In *Shitong* 十通. Hangzhou: Zhejiang guji chubanshe, 2000.

Huang Lin 黃霖. *Jin Ping Mei da cidian* 金瓶梅大辭典. Chengdu: Bashu shushe, 1991.

Huang Weimin 黃維敏. "Mangyi yuzhi yu wan Ming xiaoshuo de minjian shuxie" 蟒衣逾制與晚明小說的民間書寫. *Sichuan shifan daxue xuebao* 39, no. 3 (May 2012): 115.

Hufu zhi 虎阜志, comp. Lu Zhaoyu 陸肇域 and Ren Zhaolin 任兆麟. 1792. Rare manuscript, Princeton University Library, Princeton, NJ.

Ji Yun 紀昀. *Yuewei caotang biji* 閱微草堂筆記, ed. Wang Xiandu 汪賢度. Shanghai: Shanghai guji chubanshe, 1998.

Jiaqing chongxiu Da Qing yi tong zhi 嘉慶重修大清一統志, ed. Mu Zhang'a 穆彰阿 and Pan Xi'en 潘錫恩. Shanghai: Shanghai guji chubanshe, 2008.

Jin Ping Mei cihua 金瓶梅詞話. Facsimile reprint, Hong Kong: Taiping shuju, 1993.

Jin Ping Mei cihua 金瓶梅詞話, ed. Tao Muning 陶慕寧. Beijing: Renmin wenxue chubanshe, 1991. Rev. ed. 2011.

Juanqinzhai: Qianlong huayuan huangjia wenhua xilie 倦勤齋: 乾隆花園皇家文化系列, ed. Gugong bowuyuan gujian bu. Tianjin: Tianjin daxue chubanshe, 2012.

Li Dongyang 李東陽. *Huailu tang ji* 懷麓堂集. 1681. Rare manuscript, Harvard-Yenching Library, Cambridge, MA.

Li Dou 李斗. *Yangzhou huafang lu*. 揚州畫舫錄, ed. Wang Bei 汪北. 1795. Beijing: Zhonghua shuju, 2007.

Li Fang 李昉. *Taiping guangji* 太平廣記. Beijing: Renmin wenxue chubanshe, 1957.

Li Rihua, 李日華. "Guang Xieshi xu" 廣諧史序. In *Zhongguo lidai xiaoshuo xuba xuanzhu* 中國歷代小說序跋選注, ed. Zeng Zuyin 曾祖蔭 et al. Xianning: Changjiang wenyi, 1982.

Li Wai-yee 李惠儀. "Shibian yu wanwu: lüe lun Qingchu wenren shenmei fengshang" 世變與玩物: 略論清初文人審美風尚. *Bulletin of the Institute of Chinese Literature and Philosophy*, no. 33 (September 2008): 35–76.

Li Yu 李漁. *Li Yu quan ji* 李漁全集, ed. Wang Yiqi 王翼奇. Hangzhou: Zhejiang guji chubanshe, 1998.

Ling Mengchu 凌濛初. *Chuke Pai'an jingqi* 初刻拍案驚奇, ed. Wang Gulu 王古魯. Shanghai: Gudian wenxue chubanshe, 1957.

Liu Ruoyu 劉若愚. *Zhuozhong zhi* 酌中志. In *Zhongguo yeshi jicheng* 中國野史集成. Sichuan: Bashu shushe, 1993.

Liu Tong 劉侗 and Yu Yizheng 于奕正. *Dijing jingwulüe* 帝京景物略, ed. Zhou Sun 周損. Shanghai: Shanghai guji chubanshe, 2001.

Lunyu 論語. In *Shisan jing zhushu* 十三經註疏, ed. Ruan Yuan 阮元. Beijing: Zhonghua shuju, 1980.

Luo Wenhua 羅文華. "Qing gong zijin lima zaoxiang kaoshu" 清宮紫金琍瑪造像考述. *Gugong bowuyuan yuankan*, no. 6 (2004): 49–59.

Meng Hui 孟暉. *Pan Jinlian de faxing* 潘金蓮的髮型. Nanjing: Jiangsu renmin chubanshe, 2005.

Mengzi yi zhu 孟子譯注, ed. Yang Bojun 楊伯峻. Beijing: Zhonghua shuju, 1988.

Ming shi 明史. Zhang Tingyu 張廷玉 et al., comps. Beijing: Zhonghua shuju, 1974.

Ming Xizong shilu 明熹宗實錄. Wen Tiren 溫體仁 et al., comps. Taibei: Zhongyang yanjiuyuan lishi yuyan yanjiusuo, 1966.

Nie Chongzheng 聶崇正. "Gugong Juanqinzhai tiandinghua, quanjinghua santi" 故宮倦勤齋天頂畫、全景畫三題. *Zhuangshi* 裝飾 3 (2009): 68.

Pu Songling 蒲松齡. *Liaozhai zhiyi* 聊齋誌異, ed. Ren Duxing 任篤行. Jinan: Qilu shushe, 2000.

———. *Liaozhai zhiyi huijiao huizhu huiping ben* 聊齋誌異: 會校會注會評本, ed. Zhang Youhe 張友鶴. Rev. ed., 1978. Reprint, Shanghai: Shanghai guji chubanshe, 1997.

Pu tongshi yan jie, Lao Qida yan jie 樸通事諺解, 老乞大諺解, ed. Cui Shizhen 崔世珍. Taipei: Lianjing chuban shiye gongsi, 1978.

Qi Yan 齊煙 and Wang Rumei 王汝梅, eds. *Xinke xiuxiang piping Jin Ping Mei* 新刻繡像批評金瓶梅. Hong Kong: Joint Publishing Company, 1990.

Qing Gaozong yuzhi shiwen quanji 清高宗御制詩文全集. Beijing: Zhongguo renmin daxue chubanshe, 2013.

Qu Dajun 屈大均. *Guangdong xinyu* 廣東新語. Beijing: Zhonghua shuju, 2006.

Shen Congwen 沈從文. "'Banpaojia' he 'dianxiqiao': Guanyu *Honglou meng* zhushi yidian shangque" "'瓟觡斝'和'点犀盉': 關於〈紅樓夢〉註釋一點商榷. *Guangming ribao* 光明日報, August 6, 1961.

Shen Defu 沈德符. *Wanli yehuo bian* 萬曆野獲編. Beijing: Zhonghua shuju, 1997.

Shen Guangren 沈廣仁. "Mingdai xiaoshuo zhong zhutiwu de xiangzheng xing yu qingjie xing" 明代小說中主題物的象征性與情節性. *Shanghai Shifan daxue xuebao shehui kexue bao (zhexue shehui kexueban)* 上海師範大學學報(哲學社會科學版) 6 (2001): 49–54.

Shengzu Renhuangdi yuzhi wenji 聖祖仁皇帝御製文集. In *Wenyuange siku quanshu* 文淵閣四庫全書, comp. Zhang Yushu 張玉書. Taibei: Taiwan shangwu yinshuguan, 1983.

Shizong Xianhuangdi shengxun 世宗憲皇帝聖訓. In *Wenyuange siku quanshu* 文淵閣四庫全書. Taibei: Taiwan shangwu yinshuguan, 1983.

Song Junhua 宋俊華. "Mangyi kaoyuan jiantan Ming gongting yanju de wujiang daban" 蟒衣考源兼談明宮廷演劇的武將打扮. *Zhongshan daxue xuebao* 中山大學學報, no. 4 (2001): 56–62.

Song Maocheng 宋懋澄. *Jiuyue ji* 九籥集, ed. Wang Liqi 王利器. Beijing: Shehui kexue chubanshe, 1984.

Sun Chengsheng 孫承晟. "Ming Qing zhi ji xifang guangxue zhishi zai Zhongguo de chuanbo ji qi yingxiang: Sun Yunqiu 'Jingshi' yanjiu" 明清之際西方光學知識在中國

的傳播及其影響: 孫雲球'鏡史'研究. *Ziran kexue shi yanjiu* 自然科學史研究 26, no. 3 (2007): 363–76.

Sun Yunqiu 孫雲球. *Jingshi* 鏡史 [1681]. Rare manuscript, Shanghai Municipal Library, Shanghai.

Tan Zhengbi 譚正璧. *Sanyan liangpai yuanliu kao* 三言兩拍源流考, ed. Chang Derong 常德榮. Shanghai: Shanghai guji chubanshe, 2012.

———. *Sanyan liangpai ziliao* 三言兩拍資料. Shanghai: Shanghai guji chubanshe, 1980.

Tang Ruowang 湯若望 (Adam Schall von Bell). *Yuanjing shuo* 遠鏡說, 1626. In *Ming Qing zhi ji xixue wen ben* 明清之際西學文本, vol. 3, ed. Huang Xingtao 黃興濤 and Wang Guorong 王國榮. Beijing: Zhonghua shuju, 2013.

Tian Xiaofei 田曉菲. *Qiushui tang lun* Jin Ping Mei 秋水堂論金瓶梅. Tianjin: Tianjin renmin chubanshe, 2005.

Wang Chuan 王川. "Xiyang wangyuanjing yu Ruan Yuan wangyuege" 西洋望遠鏡與阮元望月歌. *Xueshu yanjiu* 4 (2000): 82–88.

Wang Jide 王驥德. *Qulü* 曲律. In *Zhongguo gudian xiqu lunzhu jicheng* 中國古典戲曲論著集成. Vol. 4:154. Beijing: Zhongguo xiju chubanshe, 1959.

Wang Jinguang 王錦光. "Qing chu guangxue yiqi zhizaojia: Sun Yunqiu" 清初光學儀器製造家孫雲球. *Kexueshi jikan* 5 (1963): 58–62.

Wang Qi 汪淇, ed. *Fenlei chidu xinyu* 分類尺牘新語. Taipei: Guangwen shuju, 1971.

Wang Shifu 王實甫. *Jiping jiaozhu* Xixiang ji 集評校注西廂記, annot. Wang Jisi 王季思 and Zhang Renhe 張人和. Shanghai: Shanghai guji chubanshe, 1987.

Wang Shizhen 王士禎. *Chibei outan* 池北偶談. Beijing: Zhonghua shuju, 1982.

Wang Shizhen 王世貞. *Yanshan tang bieji* 弇山堂別集, Beijing: Zhonghua shuju, 1985.

———. *Yanzhou sibu gao* 弇州四部稿, Jingyin wenyuange Siku quanshu edition 景印文淵閣四庫全書. Taipei: Taiwan shangwu yinshuguan, 1983.

Wen Zhenheng 文震亨. *Zhangwu zhi* 長物誌. Shanghai: Shangwu yinshu guan, 1936.

Wu Hsiao-yun 吳曉筠. "Qianlong huangdi de jingzi—guanyu jianshang, diancang yu shiyong de xuanze" 乾隆皇帝的鏡子—關於鑑賞、典藏與使用的選擇. In *Qing gong jing jian wen hua yu dian cang* 清宮鏡鑑文化與典藏, ed. Wu Hsiao-yun 吳曉筠. Taipei: National Palace Museum, 2015.

Wu Hung 巫鴻. *Wu, hua, ying: chuan yi jing quan qiu xiao shi.* 物畫影:穿衣鏡全球小史. Shanghai: Shanghai renmin chubanshe, 2021.

Wu Jingzi 吳敬梓. *Rulin waishi* 儒林外史. Hong Kong: Zhonghua shuju, 1991.

Wu Lanzheng 吳蘭徵. *Jiang Heng Qiu* 絳蘅秋. In A Ying 阿英, ed. *Honglou meng xiqu ji* 紅樓夢戲曲集, vol. 2. Beijing: Zhonghua shuju, 1978.

Wu Meifeng 吳美鳳. "Jia zuo zhen shi zhen yi jia: Cong Yangxindian zaobanchu huojidang kan sheng Qing shiqi Qinggong yongwu zhi 'zaojia'" 假作真時真亦假: 從養心殿造辦處活計檔看盛清時期清宮用物之造假. In *Shi xue yu shi shi: Wang Ermin jiaoshou bazhi songshou rongqing xueshu lunwen ji* 史學與史識: 王爾敏教授八秩嵩壽榮慶學術論文集, 215–70. Taibei: Guangwen shuju, 2009.

Wu xianzhi 吳縣志, ed. Cao Yunyuan 曹允源 and Wu Xiuzhi 吳秀之 et al. [1933 edition]. Reprint, Taipei: Chengwen chubanshe, 1970.

Xi Zhousheng 西周生. *Xingshi yinyuan zhuan* 醒世姻緣傳. Shanghai: Shanghai guji chubanshe, 1981.

Xu Song 許嵩. *Jiankang shilu* 建康實錄. Beijing: Zhonghua shuju, 1986.

Yang Lin 楊琳. "Wupin cheng 'dongxi' tanyuan" 物品稱'東西'探源. *Changjiang xuebao* 長江學報 1 (2012): 99–109.

Yang Manuo 陽瑪諾 (Manuel Dias). *Tian wen lüe* 天問略. In *Mingqing zhiji xixue wenben* 明清之際西學文本, ed. Huang Xingtao 黃興濤 and Wang Guorong 王國榮. Beijing: Zhonghua shuju, 2013.

Yang Shen 楊慎. *Yang Sheng'an congshu* 楊升庵叢書, ed. Wang Wencai 王文才 and Wan Guangzhi 萬光治. Chengdu: Tiandi chubanshe, 2002.

Yang Xin 楊新. "Zhu Sheng shengnian de dingzheng." 諸升生年的訂正. *Gugong bowuyuan yuankan*, no. 6 (2001): 27–29.

Yang Zhishui 揚之水. "Guanyu mingwu xinzheng" 關於名物新証. In *Nanfang wenwu* 南方文物, no. 3 (August 2007): 79–80.

———. *Wu se: Jin Ping Mei du 'wu' ji* 物色: 金瓶梅讀'物'記. Beijing: Zhonghua shuju, 2018.

Ye Mengzhu 葉夢珠. *Yue shibian* 閱世編. Shanghai: Shanghai guji chubanshe, 1981.

Yi Su 一粟, ed. *Honglou meng ziliao huibian* 紅樓夢資料彙編. Beijing: Zhonghua shuju, 1964.

Yuan Hongqi 苑洪琪. "Chonghua gong de zhuangxiu yu chenshe" 重華宮的裝修與陳設. *Zhongguo Zijincheng xuehui lunwen ji* 中國紫禁城學會論文集, vol. 3. Beijing: Zijincheng chubanshe, 2004.

Yuan Mei 袁枚. *Piben Suiyuan shi hua* 批本隨園詩話, ed. Mao Guangsheng 冒廣生. Beijing: Shangwu yinshu guan, 1926.

———. *Yuan Mei quan ji* 袁枚全集, ed. Wang Yingzhi 王英志. Nanjing: Jiangsu guji chubanshe, 1993.

Yu Sanle 余三樂. *Wangyuanjing yu xifeng dongjian* 望遠鏡與西風東漸. Beijing: Shehui kexue wenxian chubanshe, 2013.

Yu Xiangdou 余象斗. *Santai wanyong zhengzong* 三台萬用正宗. Tokyo: Kyuko shoin, 2000.

Zhang Chenghua 張橙華. "Wudi keji jianshi" 吳地科技簡史. In *Wu wenhua shicong* 吳文化史從, ed. Wang Yousan 王友三. Nanjing: Jiangsu renmin chubanshe, 1993.

Zhang Jingyun 張景運. *Qiu ping xin yu* 秋坪新語. Rare manuscript, Harvard-Yenching Library, Cambridge, MA.

Zhang Shuxian 張淑嫻. "Yihongyuan shinei kongjian tanmi" 怡紅院室內空間探秘. *Cao Xueqin yanjiu* 曹雪芹研究 2 (2018): 49.

Zhang Yimin 張一民. "Guanyu ao tu zhi yi de chuchu" 關於凹凸之議的出處. *Honglou meng xuekan* 紅樓夢學刊 1 (2000): 68–70.

Zhang Zhupo 張竹坡. *Di yi qi shu: Zhang Zhupo piping Jin Ping Mei* 第一奇書: 張竹坡批評金瓶梅. Taipei: Liren shuju, 1982.
Zhanguo ce 戰國策, ed. Liu Xiang 劉向. Shanghai: Shanghai guji chubanshe, 1998.
Zhou Hui 周暉. *Jinling suoshi* 金陵瑣事 [1610]. Beijing: Wenxue guji kanxingshe, 1955. Reprint, Intercontinental Press, 2006.
Zhou Mi 周密. *Guixin zashi* 癸辛雜識. Rare manuscript, Harvard-Yenching Library, Cambridge, MA.
Zhou Yuanwei 周元暐. *Jinglin xu ji* 涇林續記. Rare manuscript, Peking University Library.
Zhuangzi jishi 莊子集釋, ed. Guo Qingfan 郭慶藩, comp. Wang Xiaoyu 王孝魚. Beijing: Zhonghua shuju, 1961.
Zhu Jiajin 朱家溍, ed. *Yangxindian zaobanchu shiliao jilan* 養心殿造辦處史料輯覽, 1st series. Beijing: Zijincheng chuban she, 2003.
Zou Yi 鄒漪. *Qizhen yesheng* 啟禎野乘. Beijing: Beiping gugong bowuyuan tushuguan, 1936.
Zuo zhuan yi zhu 左傳譯注, ed. Li Mengsheng 李夢生. Shanghai: Shanghai guji chubanshe, 1998.

EUROPEAN-LANGUAGE SOURCES

Appadurai, Arjun. "Introduction: Commodities and the Social Life of Value." In *The Social Life of Things: Commodities in Cultural Perspective*, ed. Arjun Appadurai, 3–63. Cambridge: Cambridge University Press, 1986.
Archives des Missions Etrangères, Paris, vol. 0479, *Chine*: Jésuites, 39–40, 1687.
Barthes, Roland. *S/Z: An Essay*, trans. Richard Miller. New York: Hill and Wang, 1974.
——. "The Reality Effect." In *French Literary Theory Today*, ed. Tzvetan Todorov, trans. R. Carter. Cambridge: Cambridge University Press, 1982.
Berger, Patricia. *Empire of Emptiness: Buddhist Art and Political Authority in Qing China*. Honolulu: University of Hawai'i Press, 2003.
Berinstein, Dorothy. "Hunts, Processions, and Telescopes: A Painting of an Imperial Hunt by Lang Shining (Giuseppe Castiglione)." *RES* 35 (Spring 1999): 180–81.
Berliner, Nancy, ed. *The Emperor's Private Paradise: Treasures from the Forbidden City*. Salem, MA: Peabody Essex Museum, 2010.
Berliner, Nancy, et al., eds. *Juanqinzhai in the Qianlong Garden: The Forbidden City*. London: Scala Publishers and the World Monuments Fund, 2009.
Birnbaum, Raoul. *The Healing Buddha*. Boulder, CO: Shambhala Books, 1979.
Brockey, Liam. *Journey to the East: The Jesuit Mission to China, 1579–1724*. Cambridge, MA: Belknap Press of Harvard University Press, 2007.
Brown, Bill. *A Sense of Things: The Object Matter of American Literature*. Chicago: University of Chicago Press, 2003.

Brown, Claudia, and Donald Rabiner. *The Robert H. Clague Collection: Chinese Glass of the Qing Dynasty, 1644–1911*. Phoenix, AZ: Phoenix Art Museum, 1987.

———. *Clear as Crystal, Red as Flame: Later Chinese Glass*. New York: China House Gallery, China Institute in America, 1990.

Brown, Claudia, Clarence F. Shangraw, and Donald Rabiner. *A Chorus of Colors: Chinese Glass from Three American Collections*. San Francisco: Asian Art Museum of San Francisco, 1995.

Cahill, James. *The Compelling Image: Nature and Style in Seventeenth-Century Chinese Painting*. Cambridge, MA: Harvard University Press, 1982.

———. *Pictures for Use and Pleasure: Vernacular Painting in High Qing China*. Berkeley: University of California Press, 2010.

Cao Xueqin, and Gao E. *A Dream of Red Mansions*, vols. 1–4, trans. Xianyi Yang and Gladys Yang. Beijing: Foreign Languages Press, 2001.

———. *The Story of the Stone: A Chinese Novel by Cao Xueqin in Five Volumes*, trans. David Hawkes and John Minford. New York: Penguin, 1973.

Carlitz, Katharine. *The Rhetoric of Chin P'ing Mei*. Bloomington: Indiana University Press, 1986.

Chen Kaijun. "Transcultural Lenses: Wrapping the Foreignness for Sale in the History of Lenses." In *EurAsian Matters: China, Europe and the Transcultural Object*, ed. Anna Grasskamp and Monica Juneja, 77–100. Heidelberg: Springer, 2018.

Chou, Ju-hsi, and Claudia Brown. *The Elegant Brush: Chinese Painting Under the Qianlong Emperor, 1735–1795*. Phoenix, AZ: Phoenix Art Museum, 1985.

Clunas, Craig. "All in the Best Possible Taste: Ming Dynasty Material Culture in the Light of the Novel *Jin Ping Mei*." *Bulletin of the Oriental Ceramic Society of Hong Kong* 11 (1994–97): 13.

———. *Superfluous Things: Material Culture and Social Status in Early Modern China*. Urbana: University of Illinois Press, 1991.

Clunas, Craig, and Ian Thomas. *Chinese Furniture*. London: Bamboo Publishing, 1988.

Curtis, Emily Byrne. "Chinese Glass: A Present to His Czarish Majesty." *Journal of Glass Studies* 51 (2009): 139.

———. "Complete Plan of the Glass Workshop." In *Pure Brightness Shines Everywhere*, ed. Emily Byrne Curtis et al. Aldershot, UK: Ashgate, 2004.

———. *Glass Exchange Between Europe and China, 1550–1800: Diplomatic, Mercantile and Technological Interactions*. Farnham, UK: Ashgate, 2009.

———. "The Rainha dos Anjos: Her Precious Cargo." In *Pure Brightness Shines Everywhere: The Glass of China*, ed. Emily Byrne Curtis et al. Aldershot, UK: Ashgate, 2004.

Demiéville, Paul. "The Mirror and the Mind." In *Sudden and Gradual: Approaches to Enlightenment in Chinese Thought*, ed. Peter N. Gregory. Honolulu: University of

Hawai'i, Kuroda Institute, 1987. Originally published as "Le miroir spirituel," *Sinologica* 1, no. 2 (1947): 112–37.

Ding Naifei. *Obscene Things: Sexual Politics in Jin Ping Mei*. Durham, NC: Duke University Press, 2002.

Doar, Bruce. "A Non-Princely Mansion from Qing Dynasty Beijing." *China Heritage Quarterly*, no. 12 (December 2007).

Douglas, Mary. "Primitive Rationing: A Study in Controlled Exchange." In *Themes in Economic Anthropology*, ed. Raymond Firth. London: Tavistock Publications, 1967.

Du Halde, Jean-Baptiste. *Description géographique, historique, chronologique, politique et physique de l'empire de la Chine et de la Tartarie chinoise*. Paris: P. G. Lemercier, 1735.

Feinblatt, Ebria. "Angelo Michele Colonna: A Profile." *Burlington Magazine* 121, no. 919 (October 1979): 612–38.

Feng Menglong. *Stories to Caution the World: A Ming Dynasty Collection*, vol. 2, trans. Shuhui Yang and Yunqin Yang. Seattle: University of Washington Press, 2005.

Festa, Lynn M. *Fiction Without Humanity: Person, Animal, Thing in Early Enlightenment Literature and Culture*. Philadelphia: University of Pennsylvania Press, 2019.

Freedgood, Elaine. *The Ideas in Things: Fugitive Meaning in the Victorian Novel*. Chicago: University of Chicago Press, 2006.

Gallagher, Catherine. "The Rise of Fictionality." In *The Novel*, ed. Franco Moretti, vol. 1, 336–63. Princeton, NJ: Princeton University Press, 2006.

Galli Bibiena, Ferdinando. *L'Architettura civile: Preparata sú la geometria e ridotta alle prospettive*. Parma: Paolo Monti, 1711. Rare manuscript, Getty Research Institute, Los Angeles.

Galli Bibiena, Ferdinando. *Architect's Sourcebook and Sketchbook (1700–1743)*. New York: Metropolitan Museum of Art, acc. no. 49.5.

Garrett, Valery M. *Chinese Clothing: An Illustrated Guide*. New York: Oxford University Press, 1987.

Gomez, Luis O. "Purifying Gold: The Metaphor of Effort and Intuition in Buddhist Thought and Practice." In *Sudden and Gradual: Approaches to Enlightenment in Chinese Thought*, ed. Peter Gregory. Honolulu: University of Hawai'i, Kuroda Institute, 1987.

Goodrich, L. Carrington, and Chaoying Fang, eds. *Dictionary of Ming Biography*, 2 vols. New York: Columbia University Press, 1976.

Hanan, Patrick D. *The Chinese Short Story; Studies in Dating, Authorship, and Composition*. Cambridge, MA: Harvard University Press, 1973.

———. *The Chinese Vernacular Story*. Cambridge, MA: Harvard University Press, 1981.

———. *The Invention of Li Yu*. Cambridge, MA: Harvard University Press, 1988.
———. "The Making of The Pearl-Sewn Shirt and the Courtesan's Jewel-Box." *Harvard Journal of Asiatic Studies* 33 (1973): 124–53.
———. "The Text of the *Chin P'ing Mei*." *Asia Major* 9, no. 1 (1962): 1–57.
Hay, Jonathan. *Sensuous Surfaces: The Decorative Object in Early Modern China*. Honolulu: University of Hawai'i Press, 2010.
He, Yuming. *Home and the World: Editing the "Glorious Ming" in Woodblock-Printed Books of the Sixteenth and Seventeenth Centuries*. Cambridge, MA: Harvard University Asia Center, 2013.
Huang, Martin W. *Desire and Fictional Narrative in Late Imperial China*. Cambridge, MA: Harvard University Asia Center, 2001.
Hummel, Arthur W. *Eminent Chinese of the Ching Period*. Washington, DC: Government Printing Office, 1943.
Huntington, Rania. "Ghosts Seeking Substitutes: Female Suicide and Repetition." *Late Imperial China* 28, no. 1 (June 2005): 1–40.
Ishida, Mikinosuke. "A Biographical Study of Giuseppe Castiglione (Lang Shih-ning), a Jesuit Painter in the Court of Peking under the Ch'ing Dynasty." *Memoirs of the Research Department of the Toyo Bunko* (The Oriental Library), no. 19 (1960): 79–121.
Jami, Catherine. *The Emperor's New Mathematics: Western Learning and Imperial Authority During the Kangxi Reign (1662–1722)*. Oxford: Oxford University Press, 2012.
Johnson, Barbara. *Persons and Things*. Cambridge, MA: Harvard University Press, 2008.
Jones, Ann Rosalind, and Peter Stallybrass. *Renaissance Clothing and the Materials of Memory*. Cambridge: Cambridge University Press, 2000.
Kile, S. E., and Kristina Kleutghen. "Seeing Through Pictures and Poetry: *A History of Lenses* (1681)." *Late Imperial China* 38, no. 1 (June 2017): 47–112.
Kleutghen, Kristina. *Imperial Illusions: Crossing Pictorial Boundaries in the Qing Palaces*. Seattle: University of Washington Press, 2015.
———. "Peepboxes, Society, and Visuality in Early Modern China." *Art History* 38, no. 4 (September 2015): 763–77.
Ko, Dorothy Y. *Cinderella's Sisters: A Revisionist History of Footbinding*. Berkeley: University of California Press, 2005.
———. *Every Step a Lotus: Shoes for Bound Feet*. Berkeley: University of California Press, 2001.
———. *The Social Life of Inkstones: Artisans and Scholars in Early Qing China*. Seattle: University of Washington Press, 2017.
Li, Qiancheng. *Fictions of Enlightenment:* Journey to the West, Tower of Myriad Mirrors, *and* Dream of the Red Chamber. Honolulu: University of Hawai'i Press, 2004.

Li, Wai-yee. *Enchantment and Disenchantment: Love and Illusion in Chinese Literature*. Princeton, NJ: Princeton University Press, 1993.

———. "The Collector, The Connoisseur, and Late-Ming Sensibility." *T'oung Pao*, 2nd series, 81, no. 4/5 (January 1995): 265–302.

Li, Yu. *A Tower for the Summer Heat*, trans. Patrick Hanan. New York: Ballantine Books, 1992.

Liao, Chaoyang. "Three Readings in the *Jin Ping Mei cihua*." *CLEAR* 6, no. 1/2 (1984): 77–99.

Ling Mengchu. *Slapping the Table in Amazement: A Ming Dynasty Story Collection*, trans. Shuhui Yang and Yunqin Yang. Seattle: University of Washington Press, 2018.

Lu, Tina. *Accidental Incest, Filial Cannibalism, & Other Peculiar Encounters in Late Imperial Chinese Literature*. Cambridge, MA: Harvard University Asia Center, 2008.

Malvasia, Carlo Cesare. *Felsina pittrice: Vita de pittori bolognesi*, vol. 3 (1769). Whitefish, MT: Kessinger Library Reprints, 2010.

Marmé, Michael. *Suzhou: Where the Goods of All Provinces Converge*. Stanford, CA: Stanford University Press, 2005.

Marx, Karl. "The Fetishism of the Commodity and Its Secret." In *Capital: A Critique of Political Economy*, vol. 1, trans. Ben Fowkes. London: Pelican Books, 1976.

Mauss, Marcel. *The Gift: The Form and Reason for Exchange in Archaic Societies*, trans. W. D. Halls, with an afterword by Mary Douglas. New York: W. W. Norton, 1990.

McDermott, Joseph. "Chinese Lenses and Chinese Art." *Kaikodo Journal* 19 (Spring 2001): 9–29.

Mote, Frederick W. *The Poet Kao Ch'i: 1336–1374*. Princeton, NJ: Princeton University Press, 1962.

Musillo, Marco. *The Shining Inheritance: Italian Painters at the Qing Court, 1699–1812*. Los Angeles, CA: Getty Research Institute, 2016.

Naquin, Susan. *Peking: Temples and City Life, 1400–1900*. Berkeley: University of California Press, 2000.

Needham, Joseph, and Ling Wang. *Science and Civilisation in China*, vol. 4, part 2. Cambridge: Cambridge University Press, 1965.

Needham, Joseph, and Lu Gwei-djen. "The Optick Artists of Chiangsu." *Proceedings of the Royal Microscopical Society* 2, no. 1 (1967): 113–38.

Nie Chongzheng. "Architectural Decoration in the Forbidden City: Trompe-l'oeil Murals in the Lodge of Retiring from Hard Work." *Orientations* 26, 7 (July–August 1995).

Nylan, Michael. "Beliefs about Seeing: Optics and Moral Technologies in Early China." *Asia Major* (3rd series) 21, no. 1 (2008): 89–132.

———. "Vital Matters." In *Having a Word with Angus Graham: At Twenty-Five Years into His Immortality*, ed. Roger T. Ames and Carine DeFoort. Albany: State University of New York Press, 2018.

Ogden, Dunbar. *The Italian Baroque Stage: Documents by Giulio Troili, Andrea Pozzo, Ferdinando Galli-Bibiena, Baldassare Orsini*. Berkeley: University of California Press, 1978.

Owen, Stephen. *Readings in Chinese Literary Thought*. Cambridge, MA: Harvard Council on East Asian Studies.

Park, Julie. *The Self and It: Novel Objects in Eighteenth-Century England*. Stanford, CA: Stanford University Press, 2010.

Pietz, William. "The Problem of the Fetish, IIIa, Bosman's Guinea and the Enlightenment Theory of Fetishism." *RES: Anthropology and Aesthetics* 16 (Autumn, 1988): 105–24.

Plaks, Andrew H. *Archetype and Allegory in the* Dream of the Red Chamber. Princeton, NJ: Princeton University Press, 1987.

———. *The Four Masterworks of the Ming Novel*. Princeton, NJ: Princeton University Press, 1987.

Porter, David. *Comparative Early Modernities, 1100–1800*. New York: Palgrave Macmillan, 2012.

Purtle, Jennifer. "Scopic Frames: Devices for Seeing China c. 1640." *Art History* 33, no. 1 (February 2010): 54–73.

Rabiner, Donald. "Chinese Glass and the West." In Claudia Brown, Clarence F. Shangraw, and Donald Rabiner, *A Chorus of Colors: Chinese Glass from Three American Collections*. San Francisco: Asian Art Museum of San Francisco, 1995.

Rado, Mei Mei. "Encountering Magnificence: European Silks at the Qing Court during the Eighteenth Century." In *Qing Encounters: Artistic Exchanges Between China and the West*, ed. Petra Chu and Ding Ning, 58–75. Los Angeles: Getty Research Institute, 2015.

Reeves, Eileen. *Evening News: Optics, Astronomy and Journalism in Early Modern Europe*. Philadelphia: University of Pennsylvania Press, 2014.

———. *Galileo's Glassworks: The Telescope and the Mirror*. Cambridge, MA: Harvard University Press, 2008.

Rolston, David L. "Imagined (or Perhaps Not) Late Ming Music in an Imaginary Late Ming Household: The Production and Consumption of Music in the Ximen Family in the *Jin Ping Mei cihua*." *CHINOPERL* 33, no. 1 (July 2014): 92–142.

———. *Traditional Chinese Fiction and Fiction Commentary: Reading and Writing Between the Lines*. Stanford, CA: Stanford University Press, 1997.

———. "Traditional Chinese Fiction, Traditional Fiction Criticism, and Point of View" in *Chinese Literature: Essays, Articles, Reviews* 15 (1993): 118–142.

Rolston, David L., ed. *How to Read the Chinese Novel*. Princeton, NJ: Princeton University Press, 1990.
Shang Wei. "*Jin Ping Mei* and Late Print Culture." In *Writing and Materiality in China: Essays in Honor of Patrick Hanan*, ed. Judith T. Zeitlin and Lydia Liu. Cambridge, MA: Harvard University East Asia Center, 2003.
——. "*Jin Ping Mei* and the Making of Encyclopedias for Everyday Life." In *Dynastic Crisis and Cultural Innovation: From the Late Ming to the Late Qing and Beyond*, ed. David Wang and Wei Shang. Cambridge, MA: Harvard East Asian Monographs, 2006.
——. "*The Story of the Stone* and Its Visual Representations, 1791–1919." In *Approaches to Teaching* The Story of the Stone (Dream of the Red Chamber), ed. Andrew Schonebaum and Tina Lu. New York: Modern Language Association of America, 2012.
——. "Truth Becomes Fiction When the Fiction Is True: *The Story of the Stone* and the Visual Culture of the Manchu Court." *Journal of Chinese Literature and Culture* 2, no. 1 (April 2015): 207–48.
——. "Writing and Speech: Rethinking the Issue of Vernaculars in Early Modern China." In *Rethinking East Asian Languages, Vernaculars, and Literacies, 1000–1919*, ed. Benjamin Elman. Leiden: Brill, 2014.
Simmel, Georg. *The Conflict in Modern Culture and Other Essays*, trans. K. Peter Etzkorn. New York: Teachers College Press, 1968.
Spence, Jonathan D. *Tsao Yin and the Kang-hsi Emperor: Bondservant and Master*. New Haven, CT: Yale University Press, 1966.
Stallybrass, Peter. "Marx's Coat." In *Border Fetishisms*, ed. Patricia Spyer. London: Routledge, 1998.
Tian, Xiaofei. *Beacon Fire and Shooting Star: The Literary Culture of the Liang (502–557)*. Cambridge, MA: Harvard University Asia Center, 2007.
——. "A Preliminary Comparison of the Two Recensions of the *Jin Ping Mei*." *Harvard Journal of Asiatic Studies* 62, no. 2 (2002): 347–89.
Varsano, Paula. "Disappearing Objects/Elusive Subjects: Writing Mirrors in Early and Medieval China." *Representations* 124, no. 1 (Fall 2013): 96–124.
Vinograd, Richard. "Hiding in Plane Sight." In *Comparative Early Modernities*, ed. David Porter. Basingstoke, UK: Palgrave Macmillan, 2012.
Von Glahn, Richard. "The Enchantment of Wealth: The God Wutong in the Social History of Jiangnan." *Harvard Journal of Asiatic Studies* 51, no. 2 (December 1991): 651–714.
Waley, Arthur. *Yuan Mei: Eighteenth-Century Chinese Poet*. London: G. Allen and Unwin, 1956.
Wang, Eugene Yuejin. "Mirror, Death and Rhetoric: Reading Later Han Chinese Bronze Artifacts." *Art Bulletin* 71, no. 3 (1994): 511–34.

———. "Mirror, Moon, and Memory in Eighth Century China: From Coiling Dragon to Lunar Landscape." In *Clarity and Luster: New Light on Bronze Mirrors in Tang and Post-Tang Dynasty China, 600–1300*, ed. Claudia Brown and Ju-hsi Chou, 42–67. Cleveland, OH: Cleveland Museum of Art in Association with Brepols.

Wang, Shifu. *The Moon and the Zither: The Story of the Western Wing*. Trans. Stephen H. West and Wilt L. Idema. Berkeley: University of California Press, 1991.

Watson, Burton, trans. *The Complete Works of Chuang-tzu*. New York: Columbia University Press, 2013.

———. *The Vimalakirti Sutra*. New York: Columbia University Press, 1997.

Watson, William, and Chumei Ho. *The Arts of China, 1600–1900*. New Haven, CT: Yale University Press, 2007.

Wayman, Alexander. "The Mirror as a Pan-Buddhist Metaphor-Simile." *Journal of the History of Religions* 13, no. 4 (1974): 251–70.

Weiner, Annette. *Inalienable Possessions: The Paradox of Keeping While Giving*. Berkeley: University of California Press, 1992.

Winnicott, D. W. *Playing and Reality*. London: Tavistock Publications, 1971.

Wu Hung. *The Double Screen: Medium and Representation in Chinese Painting*. Chicago: University of Chicago Press, 1996.

———. "Beyond Stereotypes: The Twelve Beauties in Qing Court Art and *The Dream of the Red Chamber*." In *Writing Women in Late Imperial China*, ed. Kang-I Sun Chang and Ellen Widmer, 306–65. Stanford, CA: Stanford University Press, 1997.

Yang Boda. "Qing Dynasty Glass." In *the Robert H. Clague Collection: Chinese Glass of the Qing Dynasty, 1644–1911*, ed. Claudia Brown and Donald Rabiner. Phoenix, AZ: Phoenix Art Museum, 1987.

———. *Tributes from Guangdong to the Qing Court [Qingdai Guangdong gongpin]*. Hong Kong: Art Gallery, The Chinese University of Hong Kong, 1987.

Yang Lien-sheng. "Economic Justification for Spending—An Uncommon Idea in Traditional China." *Harvard Journal of Asiatic Studies* 20, no. 1–2 (1957): 36–52.

Yang, Shuhui. *Appropriation and Representation: Feng Menglong and the Chinese Vernacular Story*. Ann Arbor, MI: Center for Chinese Studies, University of Michigan, 1998.

Yu, Anthony C. *Rereading the Stone: Desire and the Making of Fiction in Dream of the Red Chamber*. Princeton, NJ: Princeton University Press, 1997.

Zeitlin, Judith T. "The Cultural Biography of a Musical Instrument: Little *Hulei* as Sounding Object, Antique, Prop, and Relic." *Harvard Journal of Asiatic Studies* 69, no. 2 (2009): 395–441.

———. *Historian of the Strange: Pu Songling and the Chinese Classical Tale*. Stanford, CA: Stanford University Press, 1993.

Index

Analects (Confucius), 64, 186n81
aotu, 160–61, 167, 215n27
Appadurai, Arjun, 180n21
architecture, 3, 114, 127, 164–67, 205n35, 211n78; Bibiena treatise on, 152; paintings and, 151, 152, 154, 156, 171
Aroma (Xiren), 135–36

bamboo lattice, 151, 166, 167–68
Baoyu. *See* Jia Baoyu; Zhen Baoyu
Barr, Allan H., 190n2
Barthes, Roland, 176n10, 177n3
Beijing: Buddhist temple story set in, 157–59; churches in, 155–57, 160; Changchun yuan (Summer Palace) in, 118; Forbidden City, 10, 91, 114, 138, 149, 162, 165, 171, 211n78; imperial glassworks in, 119, 202n17, 204n25; Italian *quadratura* in, 10, 145, 149; mirrors in, 109, 120, 121, 169, 203n20, 205n31; paintings or painting techniques in, 149, 151, 155–56, 216n28; palaces in, 205n35, 211n78; telescopes in, 83; Wen Shi in, 39, 44; Yonghe Temple in, 137
Berliner, Nancy, 116, 201n11, 210n77, 216n29
Bibiena, Ferdinando Galli, 152–53
Birnbaum, Raoul, 212n86
bodies: female, 160; impermanent or transient, 132, 135; impure, 206n39; of lice, 103, 198n65; "like wood," 158–59; as "sack of skin," 135, 209n69; spatial positioning of, 127–28; subjective experience and, 192n5
Bo Jue (Bo Zijue), 80–82, 95, 101, 193nn10–11, 193–94n14
Bologna, 10, 116, 149, 151
box or boxes, 1, 100, 192n29; Du Shiniang's, 1, 5, 7, 54–59, 64–67, 70–73, 76–77; empty, 65, 77; in "Faithless Lover," 56; *Han Feizi* anecdote of, 65; seventeenth-century, 67–73; terms for, 56, 64, 67, 70–73. *See also* courtesans: containers and

bribes, 21, 180n20, 183n41
Broad Account of the Strange (Guang yi ji), A,48
Buddhists or Buddhism: character *mi* "lost" in, 129; Chan/Zen, 125, 206n39, 210n70, 214n22; Daoism and, 207n42; emptiness or illusion in, 164, 200n5, 206–7n40; ephemerality of objects in, 12; mirror as metaphor in, 125, 200n5, 206n39, 207n41, 208n56, 210n71; painting techniques in, 161–62, 215n28; Tantric, 206n39; Qianlong-era, 164, 207n41, 216n29. *See also* Madhyamaka; Mañjuśrī; meditation; Prajñāpāramitā; Śāriputra; sutras; temples; Vimalakīrti

Cai Jing, 19, 26, 30
calligraphy, 38, 44, 50, 52, 92
cannons, 80–81
Canton, 119, 121, 193n12, 204n26; French glassworks in, 204n25; telescopes in, 196n41
Cao Xueqin, 2, 109, 123, 134–35, 142–43, 145, 213n6, 215n27; background or family of, 120
capital, 13–14, 178n6, 178n8, 179n10, 188n18
Carlitz, Katharine, 185n80
Castiglione, Giuseppe, 92, 116, 152; church paintings by, 155, 157, 160; painters taught by, 150; *quadratura* introduced to China by, 145; training of, 150, 151
Chang Jian, 210n70
Chen Kaijun, 2, 198n61
Chen Yongzheng, 189n18
Chen Zhao, 177n2
Chuke Pai'an jingqi, 7, 186n1

churches, 155–57, 160
circulation: animacy via, 13–14, 88; of capital or wealth, 13, 178n4, 178n6; illegitimate, 6, 25, 34–35; of gifts, 20, 21, 22, 25, 119; of glass, 119, 170; of objects, 6, 15, 22, 26, 62–63, 170; in *Plum in the Golden Vase*, 6, 180n21; of poems, 29; of python robe, 6, 24, 25, 34–35; resistance to, 42; of telescopes, 79; of tribute gifts, 205n30
classical biographies, 55, 57–58, 60, 75, 77, 190n4
classical fiction, 3, 93, 157; vernacular fiction and, 7, 38–39, 52–53, 176n8, 186n4, 188–89n18
classical language, 102, 176n8, 186n82, 199n70
clothing, 3, 214n22; interiority and, 22, 181n24; in *Plum in the Golden Vase*, 5, 12, 17–18, 30, 31, 32, 172, 177n2; pearl-sewn shirt, 62; shoes, 17, 18, 21; women's, 183n51; *Zuo zhuan* on status and, 184n63. *See also* robes
Clunas, Craig, 2, 177n2
Collected Statutes of the Ming Dynasty (Da Ming huidian), 24, 183n51
Colonna, Angelo Michele, 149, 165
Confucianism, 35, 123, 185n78, 185n80, 186n81
Confucius, 64, 133, 186n81
confusion: among boxes, 71, 73; in Baoyu's chambers, 127–30; by Baoyu's double, 133; by garden paths, 208n55; Grannie Liu's, 129, 147; by mirrors, 6, 121, 129, 132; of points of view, 170; productive, 6, 11, 129; of readers, 3, 4, 11, 115
connoisseurship, 2, 58, 89, 104

234 Index

contracts, 49–51, 53
courtesans, 12, 64, 66, 190n2; containers and, 54–56, 61–62, 65, 73, 77. *See also* Du Shiniang
Crary, Jonathan, 192n2
cups, 3, 71, 202n14

daguan, 109, 123, 143, 200n2
Da Ming huidian, 24, 183n51
Da Ming lü, 33
Daoists, 123, 125, 182n35, 207n42, 209n69
Daosheng, 148
Da xue, 35
Details of Affairs Recorded in the Ming History (*Ming shi jishi benmo*), 29
Ding Naifei, 12, 177n3
disorientation, 115, 123, 127–30, 132, 136, 139, 208n51, 210n72
Dong Fangshuo, 215n27
dongxi, 13–14, 88, 179n9
doors: false, 126, 128, 138, 151, 165–66, 211n78; in Juanqinzhai, 137–38, 165–66; mirrors on or as, 130, 132, 135–37, 143, 150–51, 210n70, 210n77; moon gates, 165–66; paintings of, 10, 154, 158, 164–66; secret, 4; in Yanghe jingshe, 162–63, 211n78; in Yonghe Temple, 137
Douglas, Mary, 34
drama, 3, 6, 24, 43, 179n12, 186n82
drinking games, 36, 186n82
Du Jun, 195n25
Du Shiniang (character), 1, 5, 7, 32, 143; box as emblem of, 54–55, 56, 58, 62–66, 70, 73, 75–77; box of (*see under* boxes); brothel madam and, 54, 57, 60; death of, 54, 63–65, 67, 73, 74; in "Faithless Lover," 56–58, 60, 65, 73–75, 190n2, 190n4; ghost of, 74–75, 87–88; name of, 58, 64, 76, 190n7; opacity of, 7, 56–61, 76, 190n4; red purse of, 59
"Du Shiniang" (story), 1, 57, 60, 72, 75, 170; central theme of, 5; fame or importance of, 7, 54, 56, 76; modern readers of, 56, 70; publication of, 7, 54; scholars on, 54, 191n15; translations of, 190n3; "Zhao Chun'er" story and, 56, 61–62
Du Zhen, 197n55
Dunhuang, 162

emperors: Chenghua, 42; Chongzhen, 32, 81, 185n76, 199n67; Europeans work for, 149–50, 203n19, 204n25, 213n7; glass given by or to, 118, 119, 203n22, 204n23, 204n26, 205n27, 205n33; Hongzhi, 28, 31, 181n25; Huizong, 26, 177n1; Jiajing, 31, 182n35, 183n39; Ming, 23–24, 28–29, 183n39; mirrors given by or to, 109, 119, 120, 203n20, 205nn27–28, 211n80; Qin, 140, 211n80; Qing, 91–92, 165; robes given by, 23–32, 181nn25–26, 182nn34–36, 183n39; Shunzhi, 199n67; Song, 177n1; Tang, 161, 206n37; telescopes given by or to, 91–92, 119, 196n41, 199n67, 204n23; Tianshun, 183n39; as viewers, 152, 164, 167–68, 169; Wanli, 67–68, 161; Xuanzong, 206n37; Yang, 127; Yongzheng, 116, 119, 120, 121, 137, 196–97n41, 202n16, 203n19, 205n27, 205n30, 205n33; Zhengde, 28. *See also* Kangxi emperor; Qianlong emperor
emptiness, 43, 65–66, 148, 164, 172

eunuchs, 25, 28–29, 31, 183n43, 184n70; in *Plum*, 19, 20–21, 26–27, 30–32, 34–35, 183n41, 184n70

Extensive Records of the Taiping Era (Taiping guang ji), 48

fabric or textiles, 19–21, 24, 26, 27, 120; embroidered panels, 127–28

fans, 38–39, 44, 71

Feng Menglong, 37, 178n5; "Faithless Lover" revised by, 55–58, 60, 65, 73–75, 190n4; "Jiang Xingge" by, 1, 62; *Stories to Caution the World* by, 54, 56, 61, 190n3; "Zhao Chun'er" by, 56, 61–62. *See also* "Du Shiniang" (story)

Festa, Lynn, 198n65

fetishization, 13, 40, 41, 187n7

fictional objects: circulation of (*see* circulation: of objects); as emblems for characters, 7, 15, 54–55, 56, 58, 62–64, 76–77, 109, 209n61; fungible (or not), 14, 41, 70; hidden value of, 7, 39, 41, 46; historical antecedents of, 3, 5, 11, 120, 143, 167, 173; inconsistent representations of, 2, 3–4, 6, 11, 32, 37, 67, 73, 76, 130, 132, 138–39, 143, 170; as literary objects, 1, 3, 143, 145, 167, 170; material histories of, 1–3, 8–10; mimetic (or not), 115, 170–71; narrative technique prompted by, 78–79; owners of, 58, 89; as signs of fictionality, 5–6, 142, 170; as textual effects, 4, 173

fictionality, 1–2, 4–6, 37, 142, 168, 170–73

food and drink, 3, 5, 12, 182n34; in *Plum in the Golden Vase*, 16, 17, 21, 177n2

Freedgood, Elaine, 4, 187n9

Fujian, 46–47, 96, 188–89n18, 199n67

furnishings, 5, 12, 127, 205n35, 211n77; Dongpo chairs, 16; Nanjing alcove bed, 14

Fuwangge, 114, 127, 165

Galilei, Galileo, 107, 193n7, 194n19

Gallagher, Catherine, 176n10

Gandharvas, 112, 200n5

Gao Lian, 71

Gao Qi, 59–60

Gao Shiqi, 118–19, 202n18, 203nn19–20

Gao Yun, 78, 79

gardens: *daguan*, 109, 143, 200n2; Gao Shiqi's, 202n18; in *Jiang Heng Qiu*, 208n54; Qianlong emperor's, 114, 127, 162, 165, 167–68, 170–71, 219n29 (*see also* Fuwangge; Juanqinzhai); southern literati, 151; in *Story of the Stone*, 109, 123, 126, 131, 135, 141, 143, 161

Gherardini, Giovanni, 116, 150, 152, 165, 203n19; altar or church paintings by, 155–56; *quadratura* introduced to China by, 145, 149

ghosts, 74–75, 87–88

gifts: Ming encyclopedias on, 181n23; in *Plum in the Golden Vase*, 19–22, 26, 180n17, 180n21; to emperors, 120; recirculated, 21–22; scholarship on, 180n21

gold: in "Du Shiniang," 56, 58, 63, 66, 67; fabric embroidered or set with, 25, 127–28, 129, 184n60; hairpins made of, 140, 141; inlay or tracing of, 19, 56, 58, 67, 68, 126, 179n12, 197n55; miser hoards, 13; purple, 66, 191n19; as tribute, 25

Gongshu Ban, 89–91, 196n36

Grannie Liu, 10, 133, 135, 136, 145, 155, 165; "bumps head" with painting,

236 *Index*

146–48, 164, 167, 168, 212n1; lost in garden, 129–30, 208n55; mirror image of, 127, 130–32, 134, 143, 146; mirror touched by, 131, 139, 148; painting touched by, 147–48
Great Learning (Da xue), 35
Great Ming Code (Da Ming lü), 33
Guangdong xinyu, 81
Guanghan Palace, 112, 200n4
Guang yi ji, 48
Guangzhou, 202n17, 204n25, 205n33, 216n28
Guixin zashi, 70, 191n22
Gu Qiyuan, 161, 215n28

hairpins, 17–18, 140, 141, 183n41
Hanan, Patrick, 178n5; on Feng Menglong, 189n2, 190n4, 191n15; on Ling Mengchu, 46; on Li Yu, 194n17, 195n26; on *Plum*, 178n7, 179n11; term *jing* translated by, 197n46; on vernacular fiction, 176n8; on Zhu Sheng, 196n39, 199n68
Han Feizi, 65
Hangzhou, 202n18; Jesuits in, 82, 194n16; lens makers in, 78, 82, 90–91, 96, 105, 107, 192n4, 193n12, 196n41; Li Yu in, 82, 194n17; python robes from, 26–27, 35; telescopes in, 196n41
Hawkes, David, 131, 146–48, 290n58, 210n72, 215n25, 216n1
Hay, Jonathan, 10
He, Yuming, 185n81
Heavenly Maiden, 158–60, 172, 173, 214n19
historical sources, 34; *Collected Statutes of the Ming Dynasty*, 24, 183n51; *Details of Affairs Recorded in the Ming History*, 29; *Extensive Records of the Taiping Era*, 48; *Great Ming Code*, 33; *Ming History*, 24, 25, 28, 29, 35, 181n25, 184n54, 184n68, 188n17; records from imperial workshops, 3, 120, 121, 211n78; *Veritable Histories of the Ming Emperors*, 24; *Veritable Records of the Xizong Reign*, 27
History of Lenses (Jingshi), 8, 95–98; on children's eyesight, 97, 198n57; discovery of, 95; gazetteer on, 97–98; illustrations in, 98, 100–101, 198n58; kinds of lenses in, 97, 100, 200n74; on telescope, 98, 100–101; language of, 102, 199n70; Li Yu's use of, 82–83, 95–96, 101–3, 105–7, 194n18, 199n70, 200n74; preface to, 82, 102, 107; Zhu Sheng on, 97
History of the Ming. See historical sources: *Ming History*
Honglou meng. See *Story of the Stone*
Hooke, Robert, 103, 198n65
Hsi-men Ch'ing. See Ximen Qing
Hsu, Hui-Lin, 79
"Huabi." See Pu Songling
Huaji, 161, 215n27
Huang Lin, 177n2
Huang, Martin, 178n6
Hui Yuan, 125
Huntington, Rania, 74

Idle Chatter in the Guest's Seat (Kezuo zhuiyu), 161
illusion: architectural, 149, 154, 164–66, 171; artistic, 115, 130, 148, 155–57, 162; Buddhist analogies or view of, 200n5, 206n40; fictional, 172; "is not illusion," 112, 115; land of, 124, 136; manipulation of, 156; material form as, 10, 125, 135, 142, 163; mirrors and,

Index 237

illusion (*continued*)
139, 142, 148; telescopes and, 8, 78; Qing notion of, 162–67; world as, 116, 142, 148, 166, 167. *See also* optical illusions

India, 119, 161, 188n17

Intorcetta, Prospero, 119

jade: belts or girdles of, 29, 32, 34, 182n35; in clear glass, 116; inlaid, 127; Jia Baoyu and, 144; misers cherish, 13; in "Du Shiniang" story, 63–65, 76; radical, 49; rhinoceros-horn, 71; substitutes for, 116; as symbol, 65, 66, 77

Jartoux, Pierre, 156

Jesuits, 82, 91, 118, 150; glassware of, 203n22, 204n23, 204n25; telescopes given by, 199n67; missions or missionaries, 79, 83, 119, 149, 193n6, 194n16, 197n55, 199n67, 204n25. *See also* Castiglione, Giuseppe; Schall von Bell, Adam

Jia Baoyu, 4–5, 9, 120, 142–44; chambers of, 123, 125–30, 132, 134, 137–39, 143, 155, 165, 170, 205n35, 208n51, 208n54; double of, 133–34, 143; dream of, 131–36, 142, 143; flowers fall on, 171–72, 216n1; mirror as emblem of, 109, 209n61; name of, 132–33, 136; riddle of, 209n61

Jiangnan, 24, 216n28

Jiang Xingge, 1, 62

Jia Rui, 123–24, 132, 135, 136

Jia Yun, 139

Jia Zheng, 125–26, 132, 133, 139, 208nn55–56, 209n61; mirror confuses, 128–29, 135, 143, 210n70; sophistication of, 129, 131, 143

Jiling, 45–46, 51, 188n17

Jingshi. See *History of Lenses*

Jingshi tongyan, 7, 54, 56, 61, 190n3

Jing Zhang, 195n24

Jin Ping Mei. See *Plum in the Golden Vase*

Jin Shengtan, 43, 188n14

Jin Weihou, 40–42, 47, 49, 52, 53, 186n4, 187n5

Jiuye ji. See Song Maocheng

Ji Yun, 120, 205n31, 214–15n22

Jones, Ann Rosalind, 179n10

Juanqinzhai, 114, 162; mirrored doors in, 137–38; paintings in, 145, 149–53, 155, 165–68, 170; *Story of the Stone* and, 127, 137, 145, 167, 212n1; theater room of, 150–53, 165, 167–68, 210–11n77

Kangxi emperor, 150, 202n18; Cao family and, 120; Europeans and, 118–19, 150, 202n17, 203n22, 204n23, 204n25; Gao Shiqi and, 118; imperial workshops of, 117–18, 162, 203n22; telescope of, 91, 196n41, 204n23

Kezuo zhuiyu, 161

Kile, S. E., 2, 193n14, 198n58

Kleutghen, Kristina, 2, 164, 193n14, 198n58, 213n7, 216n30

Ko, Dorothy, 10

Kronfeld, Chana, 191n18

Laurifice, Emmanuel, 119

Liao, Chaoyang, 36, 186n84

Li Fang, 189n23

Li Jia, 54, 57, 60, 62, 65, 67, 76; drawers opened by, 58, 63, 66; madness of, 75; shame of, 58–59, 64; travel pass of, 63, 71

Lilou, 89–91, 196n36

Lin Daiyu, 136, 142, 146, 160–61, 205n30, 215n27, 217n2

Ling Mengchu, 5, 37, 54, 71, 169, 188n14; *Chuke pai'an jingqi* by, 7, 186n1; destiny in stories of, 46; ellipses or omissions of, 7, 52–54; "ethnographic" narrator of, 49; "Man Whose Fortune" by, 5, 7, 38; prologue tale by, 39–42, 47, 51–53, 178n5, 186n1, 186–87n4, 187n4; *shi/xu* and, 43–44, 46, 47; sources used by, 7, 48, 52–53, 188–89n18
Li Ping'er, 14, 26–27, 183n41
Li Renfu, 70–71
Li Rihua, 43
lists, 15–20, 102, 177n3, 179n12, 180n13, 180n17, 205n28
literary criticism, 35, 39, 43, 49
Liu Jian, 28, 31, 181n25
Liu Jin, 28–29, 35
liuli, 212n82, 212n86
Liu Ruoyu, 29, 184n63
Liu Yuchun, 58, 75–76
Li Wai-yee, 2
Li Yu, 5, 8, 78–79, 82–83, 194n17, 195n28, 197n49, 198n67; *Carnal Prayer Mat* by, 195n21; *Casual Expressions of Idle Feeling* by, 100, 102; editions of, 82, 84, 95, 102, 105, 194n18, 196n39; ethnographic tone of, 105; *History of Lenses* used by, 8, 82–83, 95–96, 101–7, 194n18, 199n70, 200n74; narration of, 8, 85, 87, 108, 195n26; poems or lyrics by, 84, 89–91, 195n25; "Tower for the Summer Heat" by, 5, 8, 78–79, 82–84, 91, 104–5, 107–8, 195n24, 197n49; on Western scholars, 199n67; Zhu Sheng and (*see* Zhu Sheng: Li Yu and)
Lu Ban, 89–91, 196n36
Lu Ji of Shanghai, 178n4
Lu Jun, 90, 199n68
Luo Wenhua, 191n19
Lu Tao, 74–75
Lu, Tina, 188n17
Lü Zhan'en, 159

Ma Baoha, 38, 40, 46, 48–51
Madhyamaka, 164, 207n41
Mañjuśrī, 159, 216n29
"Man Whose Fortune Has Turned . . . ," 5, 7, 38
Marriage Destinies to Awaken the World (*Xingshi yinyuan zhuan*), 24
Marx, Karl, 179n10, 187n7
Mauss, Marcel, 180n21
medicine, 3, 96
meditation, 47, 125, 159, 206n39, 209n69, 210n70; spaces designed for, 10, 114, 162, 164, 171, 216n29
Mencius, 90, 123–24, 196n36, 206n38
Meng Longtan, 158
Meng Yulou, 14, 180n14
metaphorical mapping, 7, 55–56, 65–66, 67, 70, 73, 76–77, 170, 191n18
microscopes, 100, 103, 106, 198n65
Ming History (*Ming shi*), 24, 25, 28, 29, 35, 181n25, 184n54, 184n68, 188n17
Ming shi. See *Ming History*
Ming shi jishi benmo, 29
Ming shilu, 24
mingwu xue, 3, 176n5
mirrors: bronze, 8, 102, 106, 110, 111, 112, 121–24, 139, 143, 211n80; characters enter, 124, 142, 143; characters' thoughts evoked by, 134; in contemporary Beijing, 169; cosmetic, 97, 98, 100, 102–3, 106, 119; doors and, 130, 132, 135, 136, 143, 150–51; double-sided, 122–24, 134, 142; in dressing cases, 72; as

Index 239

mirrors (*continued*)
  emblems, 109, 209n61; European or Western, 121, 129, 139, 142, 143; "flowers in . . . ," 140, 142; frames of, 121, 132, 139; half-legged, 121, 122, 137, 150; incense-burning, 97, 100, 106; magic, 79, 93, 124, 132, 140, 211n80; material properties of, 109, 112, 123; as mechanism for narration, 134; plate-glass, 4, 5, 7–9, 32, 109–10, 113, 120–21, 123–25, 139, 142, 169, 170; poems about, 9, 110–16, 118, 119, 123, 139–42, 171; religious or philosophical views of, 123–25, 142, 143, 200n5, 206n39, 207n41; self-reflection prompted by, 9, 124, 143, 169, 206n37, 206n39; as sign of fictionality, 142; in *Story of the Stone*, 4, 5, 6, 8–9, 32, 109, 116, 121, 123–25, 128–32, 136, 139, 142–44; terms for, 197n46, 201n8; touched, 131–32, 139; tribute or gifts of, 119–21, 139, 203n20, 205nn27–28; windows as, 9, 111–15, 123, 142
misapprehension, 4–6, 206n37
Miscellaneous Gleanings from Guixin Street (*Guixin zashi*), 70, 191n22
misers, 13, 40, 47, 52–53, 169, 178n4, 186n4
misperception, 4, 5–6, 10–11, 117, 125, 148, 171
Mitelli, Agostino, 149, 165
Mote, Frederick, 190n10
Musillo, Marco, 213n7

Nanjing, 141, 181n27; Cao family in, 120; robes from, 27, 31; Zhen family of, 133

narration: omniscient, 8, 94, 134; of thoughts, 56–57, 60, 62, 78, 79, 84, 93, 107–8
New Account of Guangdong (*Guangdong xinyu*), 81
Nylan, Michael, 135

opacity, 38–39, 49; in "Du Shiniang" story, 7, 56–61, 67, 70
optical illusions, 10, 130, 139, 148–49, 154–57, 162–67
oranges, 44–45, 188n18

"Painted Wall" ("Huabi"). *See* Pu Songling
paintings: characters enter or leave, 158–59, 213n6, 214–15n22; lady with the clock, 145, 149, 151–52, 154–55, 167–68; misperception of, 10 (*see also* Grannie Liu); panoramic, 149, 151, 166, 170, 171 (see also *tongjing hua*); perspectival, 8, 116, 145–49, 151, 164, 167, 168; placement of, 8, 10; recession or protrusion in, 10, 149, 155–56, 160–62, 167, 214n22; space in, 149, 155; touching of (*see* touching); wall-mounted illusionistic ("affixed hanging," *tieluo*), 130; Zhang Yanyuan on, 161
Pan Jinlian, 14, 17
Park, Julie, 181n24
partitions, 126–29, 131–32, 164, 207n48
Peach Blossom Fan, The, 6, 24
pearls: curtains glittering with, 129; in Du Shiniang story, 54, 63, 65–66, 73; in *Han Feizi* anecdote ("buying the box"), 65; shirt sewn with, 62; vendor of, 1; in Wen Shi story, 38, 46, 48–49, 51, 54

Persians, 48, 189n23. *See also* Ma
    Baoha
perspectivalism, 10, 100, 149, 160, 164,
    214n22; monofocal vs. polyfocal,
    167; monocular vs. binocular, 192n4;
    in *Story of the Stone*, 145, 215n27
pirates, 80–81
Plaks, Andrew, 35, 200n2, 206n36
plate glass, 116, 119; in windows, 113–15,
    123, 201n7. *See also* mirrors:
    plate-glass
Plum in the Golden Vase, The (*Jin Ping
    Mei*), 2, 5–6, 195n24; capital in,
    13–14, 178n6, 178n8; commentaries
    on, 32, 35, 36, 180n17, 185n76;
    Confucian norms of, 35, 185n78,
    185n80, 186n81; editions or recen-
    sions of, 178n7, 179n11, 180n17,
    185n78; gifts or regifting in, 16,
    18–22, 180n21; lists in, 15–19, 36,
    177n2, 179n12, 180n13, 180n17;
    objects in, 14–15, 20–21, 26, 36, 62,
    177n2; phrase "thing that likes to
    move" in, 13–14, 88; plot of, 12–13;
    python robe in, 25–36; *Story of the
    Stone* and, 15; translation of, 179n11
poems: by Chang Jian, 210n70;
    classical, 176n8; by Daiyu, 217n2; by
    Li Yu, 84–85, 87, 90, 195n25;
    lotus-picking, 85, 87; mirrors or
    windows in, 9, 123, 125, 127, 140–42,
    171; in Platform Sutra, 125; by
    Qianlong emperor, 9, 110–18, 123,
    127, 141–42, 171; Sun Fu recites,
    59–60; Xianxian writes, 94–95;
    Ximen Qing recites, 13, 178n7; by
    Yuan Mei, 119, 140–41; by Yu Xin,
    212n83; by Zhao Sui, 29
polyfocalism, 10, 148–49, 152, 167
Prajñāpāramitā, 208n56, 210n71

protrusion, 155–56, 160–62
Purtle, Jennifer, 79, 192n4
Pu Songling, 157–60, 168, 171, 173
python robes (*mang pao*). *See* robes

Qiancheng Li, 129, 208n52, 208n55
Qianlong emperor, 120, 169; art
    commissioned by, 165, 201n9; as
    Buddhist, 10, 162, 164, 207n41,
    216n29; Fuwangge built by, 114, 127;
    glass of, 116, 201n7, 201n9,
    204nn25–26, 205n27; glass owned
    by, 204n25; inscriptions of, 201n9;
    palaces of, 10, 113, 201n7; poem by,
    9, 110–18, 123, 127, 141, 142, 171,
    200n4, 201n8; telescope used by,
    91–92; throne of, 116, 118, 201n11.
    See also gardens: Qianlong
    emperor's; Juanqinzhai
quadratura, 8, 10, 116, 138, 145, 150–52,
    154–55, 167; in Beijing churches,
    155–57; Bolognese school of, 149,
    151; Chinese viewers of, 155–57;
    recession produced by, 155–57;
    techniques derived from, 165;
    tongjing hua and, 213n7
Qu Dajun, 81
Qu Jiren, 78–79, 104, 197n49; as false
    immortal, 88, 93, 94; name of, 83,
    194–95n20; "omniscience" of,
    83–84, 86–88, 93, 102; reads with
    telescope, 92, 94–95; recognition by,
    89; telescope purchased by, 78, 88,
    91–93; as voyeur, 83, 85, 195n24

realism, 12, 177n3
recession, 155–56, 160–62
recognition trope, 83, 89
Records of Painting (*Huaji*), 161, 215n27
Reeves, Eileen, 194n15

Ricci, Matteo, 96, 97, 161
Ripa, Matteo, 150
robes, 5, 181nn25–27; black, 184–85n70; circulation of, 6, 24, 25, 34–35, 182n33; Daoist patriarchs given, 182n35; disjunction of, 35–36; dragon vs. python, 23, 28; enlivened, 33; flying-fish, 28, 30–31, 33, 34, 184n68; "flying-fish python," 31–33, 36; Grand Secretariat given, 25, 181n25, 182n34; historical sources on, 24–25, 27, 181n25, 183n51; horned-bull, 28, 31, 33, 184n68; illicit, 6, 24, 25–29, 33, 35, 183n51; imperial, 31, 33; as inalienable possessions, 25, 182–83n38; Li Ping'er's, 26–27; misperception of, 6; in *Peach Blossom Fan*, 24; in *Plum and the Golden Vase*, 25–36, 180n14; production of, 24, 25, 26–27, 109; recipients of, 25, 28, 31, 33; red or scarlet, 26, 181n25, 183n39; roundels on, 29, 31, 184n60; yellow, 31. *See also* emperors: robes given by
rock crystal, 81, 96, 98, 202n16
Rolston, David, 177n1, 188n11, 195n28
romans-à-clef, 2, 175n4
Ruan Dacheng, 24
Ruoxu, 38–39, 42, 46, 51–52. *See also* Wen Shi

salt merchants, 54, 59–60
Śāriputra, 159–60, 172
Schall von Bell, Adam, 79–80, 82, 104, 193n6; Sun Yunqiu's knowledge of, 96, 97, 98, 100, 102, 107, 198n56; 199n70; as Tang Ruowang, 79, 193n7, 200n70
Scholars, The (*Rulin waishi*), 6
shad, 16, 20–22, 181n23

Shandong, 29, 202n17
Shang Wei, 35, 137, 176n8, 186n81, 186n83, 209n66, 212n1
sheet glass, 116, 119, 204n25
shells, 5, 53, 54, 83; for divination, 47, 64; in Ling Mengchu story, 7, 38–39, 42, 46–51
Shen Congwen, 3
Shen Defu, 27–28, 183n39, 184n54
Shen Guangren, 54, 192n29
Shen Yue, 207n42
Shen Zhou, 44
shi, 43. *See also shi/xu* dyad
Shi Xiangyun, 133, 160–61, 215n27
shi/xu dyad, 39, 42–44, 47, 49, 51, 52, 66, 77, 170, 187n10, 188nn11–12, 201n10
short fiction or stories, 3, 5, 6, 178n5
Shuihu zhuan, 12, 43, 188n14
silver, 1, 47, 50, 54, 59, 61–64, 182n34; animacy of, 13–14, 39–41, 187n6; ingots, 40–42, 49, 52–53, 169, 186–87n4, 187nn5–6; value of, 44–46, 51
Sima Guang, 206n38
Simmel, Georg, 180n21
Slapping the Table in Amazement (*Chuke Pai'an jingqi*), 7, 186n1
Song Maocheng, 55–56, 60, 61, 65, 73–75, 190n2. *See also* Du Shiniang: in "Faithless Lover"
Stallybrass, Peter, 179n10, 187n7
Stories to Caution the World (*Jingshi tongyan*), 7, 54, 56, 61, 190n3
Story of the Stone (*Honglou meng*), 2, 3, 4, 5–6, 8–9; "truth becomes fiction . . ." in, 115; characters' thoughts in, 134; commentary on, 124; confiscation in, 24; criticism of, 109, 120, 127; editions of, 209n61;

242 *Index*

mirrors in (see under mirrors); objects in, 15, 120, 143–44, 205n30; sequels to, 208n54; sighs in, 148, 168; term *aotu* in (see *aotu*); title of, 141; translation of, 131, 146–48, 290n58, 210n72, 215n25, 216n1; *Western Wing* in, 171–72, 216n1. See also Grannie Liu; Jia Baoyu; Jia Rui; Jia Zheng; Zhen Baoyu

Struve, Lynn, 189n2

Stumpf, Kilian, 118, 202n17

substitution, 116, 125, 151, 202nn14–16

sumptuary laws, 17, 29–31, 33–35, 184n70

Sun Chengsheng, 95–96, 194n18, 199n70

sundials, 98

Sun Fu, 54, 57, 62–63, 65, 67, 71, 73; haunted, 75; poetry recited by, 59–60

Sun Yunqiu: background of, 96; cosmetic mirrors of, 97, 98, 100, 102–3, 106; lenses sold by, 100, 198n57; 200n74; Zhu Sheng and, 82, 96–97, 102, 105, 107, 196n39. See also *History of Lenses*; Schall von Bell, Adam: Sun Yunqiu's knowledge of

Superfluous Things (Zhangwu zhi), 71

sutras, 209n69, 212n86; Prajñāpāramitā, 208n56, 210n71; mind as mirror in, 125; Vimalakīrti, 159–60, 172

Suzhou, 50, 81; fans from, 44; gazetteers on, 82, 97–98; lens makers from, 8, 82, 96–98, 107, 193n12, 196n41; python robes from, 27; telescopes in, 196n41

Taiping guang ji, 48

telescopes: astronomical observation by, 192n7, 196–97n41; commercialization of, 105; gazetteers on, 97–98; history of, 83, 95–96, 104, 194n15, 194n19; as instruments, 84, 87, 90–95; limitations of, 83–84, 93–94; lyric on, 89–90; magical or oracular, 5, 79, 82, 84, 95, 194n15; as magic mirrors, 79, 93; as mechanisms for narration, 84, 108, 134; military use of, 91–92; monocular, 8, 78–79, 85, 88, 90, 95, 98, 107; recognition trope and, 83, 89; Schall on, 79–80, 82, 96–98, 100, 102, 104, 107, 193nn6–7, 199–200n70; selective power of, 79, 83–84, 91, 95, 102; Sun Yunqiu on, 98, 100–102, 199n70; technology of, 7–8, 78–79; term *dongxi* used for, 88; as thousand-*li* glass, 104, 105; as toys, 88, 89; as tribute items, 197–98n55, 199n67, 204n23; viewers transported by, 92, 93, 104; Western makers of, 82, 103, 104–5, 194n19, 199n67

temples, 214n22; *aotu* painting in, 161–62; in "Painted Wall" story, 157–59; *tongjing hua* in, 162–63; Yicheng, 161–62

Tian Xiaofei, 125, 179n11, 185n78, 207n42

tongjing hua, 149, 152–53, 162–68; defined, 213n7

touching: of mirror, 131, 139, 148; of paintings, 147–48, 155–57, 164

"Tower for the Summer Heat" by, 5, 8, 78–79, 82–84, 91, 104–5, 107–8, 195n24, 197n49

trompe l'oeil, 5, 7–8, 10, 126, 128, 157, 171; in Juanqinzhai, 150, 210n77; substitution of substance vs., 116; *tongjing hua* and, 164–66, 168

true/false dyad, 116, 132, 138, 151, 165, 166

Index 243

valuation, 7, 39–49, 51–52, 56, 58, 60
van Helden, Albert, 194n19
verisimilitude, 2, 9, 43, 109, 171; ellipses and, 39, 52–53; of fictional objects, 11; mirrors or reflections and, 115, 142; multiplicity and, 15; in painting, 157, 167; readers' expectation of, 170; perspectivalism and, 167; vernacular vs. classical stories and, 52
Veritable Histories of the Ming Emperors (*Ming shilu*), 24
Veritable Records of the Xizong Reign (*Ming Xizong shilu*), 27
Veritable Record of Jiankang (*Jiankang shilu*), 161
vernacular fiction, 7, 9–11, 38–39, 50, 85, 108; aesthetic of, 38, 52; classical works and, 7, 52–53, 57–58, 60, 75, 77, 176n8, 188n18, 189n2, 190n4; classical texts quoted in, 35, 36; conventions of, 52, 87, 189n25; crime stories, 189n25; defined, 176n8; historical referents of, 3, 5, 11, 49; *huaben* genre of, 38; objects in, 1–3, 62, 76, 170; verisimilitude in, 39, 52–53
Vimalakīrti, 159–60, 172
von Glahn, Richard, 187n8
voyeurism, 20, 84–87, 195n21, 195n24

Wang, Eugene Y., 206n37, 211n80
Wang Jide, 187n10
Wang Qi, 90, 196n38
Wang Shizhen, 30–31
Wang Youxue, 163–64, 216n30
Water Margin, The (*Shuihu zhuan*), 12, 43, 188n14
Wayman, Alex, 206n39, 207n41, 208n56
Weiner, Annette, 182–83n38

Wei Zhongxian, 29
wen, 39, 42, 46, 51, 52
Wen Shi: fans sold by, 38–39, 44, 47; name of, 39, 42, 44, 51; overseas trade by, 39, 40, 44–46, 188n17; shell sold by, 46–51
Wen Zhenheng, 44, 71, 100
Western Wing, The (*Xixiang ji*), 171–72, 216n1
Winnicott, D. W., 187n6
workshops, imperial, 3, 25–28, 165; boxes made in, 67; enameled porcelain tray made in, 162–63; glass made in, 116, 118–21, 202n17, 203n22, 204n25; mirrors made in, 109, 121; Ripa's description of, 150; records of, 3, 120, 121, 211n78; robes made in, 25; substitution of substances by, 116, 118, 125, 151, 202n16
Wu Hsiao-yun, 201n10
Wu Hung, 212n1
Wu Meifeng, 202n16, 211n78
Wu Song, 12

Xiaofei Tian, 185n78
Xifeng, 123–24, 205n30
Ximen Qing, 12, 88, 178n4; capital fetishized by, 13–14; clothing or robes of, 17–18, 25–27, 30–36, 184n70; food for, 16, 17, 21; friends of, 13, 18–19, 32, 180n20; furnishings or household of, 14, 16, 19, 177n1, 179n12, 180n17; gifts of, 19–22, 26, 180n17; miser ridiculed by, 13, 178n5; poem recited by, 13, 178n7; servants of, 180n20; sexual exploits of, 12–13, 178n6, 183n41, 178n6; study of, 16, 18–20, 177n2; wives of, 12, 14, 17, 21, 26–27, 180n14, 183n41

244 *Index*

Xingshi yinyuan zhuan, 24
Xiren, 135–36
Xixiang ji, 171–72, 216n1
xu, 43, 188n12. See also shi/xu dyad

Yan Shifan, 33
Yang Boda, 119, 204nn25–26, 205n33
Yanghe jingshe, 162, 211n78, 216n30
Yang Lin, 179n9
Yang Shen, 215nn27–28
Yang, Shuhui, 58, 190n7
Yang Xin, 192n4, 196n39
Yao Wenhan, 163–64, 216n30
Yao Yuanzhi, 157, 168
Ying Bojue, 13, 18–22, 32–34, 180n20, 181n23, 185n76
Yu, Anthony, 206nn39–40
Yu Xin, 212n83
Yuanjing shuo, 79–80
Yuan Mei, 119, 139–42, 212n83, 212n86
Yuanming yuan, 203n19, 204n25, 211n78
Yucui xuan, 162

Zeitlin, Judith, 2, 190n6, 214n19
Zhaijin qiyin, 179n12
Zhang Chaojin, 139, 212n83
Zhang Jingyun, 157, 160, 168
Zhang Sengyou, 161–62
Zhang Shuxian, 136–37, 205n35
Zhangwu zhi, 71
Zhang Xinzhi, 124–25, 128, 135, 136
Zhang Yanyuan, 161, 215n27
Zhang Yimin, 215n27
Zhang Zhupo, 35, 180n17
Zhan Xianxian, 83–87, 93–95, 107, 194n20
Zhao Chun'er, 56, 61–62
Zhao Sui, 29, 35
Zhejiang, 81, 139, 196n39
Zhen Baoyu, 132–34, 143
Zhou Hui, 52, 187n4
Zhou Mi, 70, 191n22
Zhou Yuanwei, 188–89n18
Zhu, 158–60, 173, 214n19
Zhuangzi, 90, 159, 200n2, 207n42; butterfly dream in, 135, 143, 209n66; mirror in, 125
Zhu Sheng, 103, 199n68; *Mustard Seed Garden Manual of Painting* by, 90, 192n4; Li Yu and, 82, 90–91, 102, 105, 107, 192n4, 196n39; as Sun Yunqiu's mentor, 82, 96–97, 102, 105, 107, 196n39

GPSR Authorized Representative: Easy Access System Europe, Mustamäe tee 50, 10621 Tallinn, Estonia, gpsr.requests@easproject.com

www.ingramcontent.com/pod-product-compliance
Lightning Source LLC
Chambersburg PA
CBHW022049290426
44109CB00014B/1031